# THE WORLD BANK AND EDUCATION

# COMPARATIVE AND INTERNATIONAL EDUCATION:
## A Diversity of Voices

Volume 14

*Scope*

*Comparative and International Education: A Diversity of Voices* aims to provide a comprehensive range of titles, making available to readers work from across the comparative and international education research community. Authors will represent as broad a range of voices as possible, from geographic, cultural and ideological standpoints. The editors are making a conscious effort to disseminate the work of newer scholars as well as that of well-established writers.

The series includes authored books and edited works focusing upon current issues and controversies in a field that is undergoing changes as profound as the geopolitical and economic forces that are reshaping our worlds.

The series aims to provide books which present new work, in which the range of methodologies associated with comparative education and inter-national education are both exemplified and opened up for debate. As the series develops, it is intended that new writers from settings and locations not frequently part of the English language discourse will find a place in the list.

# The World Bank and Education

## Critiques and Alternatives

*Edited by*

Steven J. Klees
*University of Maryland, U.S.A.*

Joel Samoff
*Stanford University, U.S.A.*

and

Nelly P. Stromquist
*University of Maryland, U.S.A.*

SENSE PUBLISHERS
ROTTERDAM / BOSTON / TAIPEI

A C.I.P. record for this book is available from the Library of Congress.

ISBN 978-94-6091-901-5 (paperback)
ISBN 978-94-6091-902-2 (hardback)
ISBN 978-94-6091-903-9 (e-book)

Published by: Sense Publishers,
P.O. Box 21858, 3001 AW Rotterdam, The Netherlands
https://www.sensepublishers.com/

*Printed on acid-free paper*

# CONTENTS

# FOREWORD

This remarkable volume brings together the most consistent and thoughtful critics of World Bank education policies and practices over the past three decades. Since the World Bank emerged as the major intergovernmental agency funding education change initiatives around the world in the mid-1980s, these scholars have systematically examined the potential of the World Bank to benefit or harm the development agendas of low- and middle-income countries. They have provided penetrating and comprehensive critiques of the evolving priorities, strategies, values, rationales, discourses, processes, and outcomes of the World Bank. They have pointed out the narrow economistic and utilitarian goals set for education, the limited and misleading input-output and cost-benefit analyses employed, the inadequate knowledge base on which decisions are made, the failure to take into account the context as well as the voices of the intended beneficiaries of proposed reforms of education systems, and the general neglect of teachers and the conditions that would enhance their work. The book is particularly timely with its focus on the *Education Strategy 2020* document issued by the World Bank in 2011. Not satisfied with criticizing missteps and missed opportunities, they also offer alternative visions of what education is and can be. The various authors provide useful suggestions as to how the World Bank, with its enormous resources and strategic position in influencing economic and education agendas, can contribute to policies that are more appropriately geared to strengthening the potential of countries to determine their own paths to poverty alleviation and to individual and societal flourishing.

Over the years, the critiques and alternatives found in the book have been presented directly to World Bank officials at international professional conferences, notably those of the Comparative and International Education Society (CIES), at think tanks, such as the Brookings Institution, and at invitational meetings at World Bank headquarters. Whatever interest the World Bank's education program officials might have in adopting the recommendations offered by progressive scholars is structurally and ideologically tempered by these considerations: the World Bank, after all, is not only a financial institution, but a key actor in determining the architecture and workings of the global political economy; the lion's share of the World Bank's funding comes from the United States, a superpower persuasively promoting the neoliberal economic agenda since the 1980s; and it exhibits the reluctance or inability of an entrenched bureaucracy to admit its errors and learn from past mistakes. Whether the Bank is responsive to the critiques and alternatives brilliantly offered by the present authors, the book is certain to influence development and education scholars, policymakers, and practitioners around the globe. The insights, lessons, and visions contained in *World Bank and Education: Critiques and Alternatives* provide ways in which decision-makers and educators can more effectively respond to external forces on their societies and take action to shape more equitable education institutions, policies, and practices that reflect their existential realities. Kudos to the editors and authors for this most significant contribution to scholarship and praxis in the realms of education and social change.

*Robert F. Arnove*
*Chancellor's Professor Emeritus of*
*Educational Leadership and Policy Studies*
*Indiana University, Bloomington, U.S.A.*

# ABBREVIATIONS

| | |
|---|---|
| AAWORD | Association of African Women for Research and Development |
| CIDA | Canadian International Development Agency |
| DANIDA | Danish International Development Agency |
| DAWN | Development Action for Women Network |
| DFID | Department for International Development (U.K.) |
| EFA | Education for All |
| EKMS | Education Knowledge Management System |
| ICAE | International Council for Adult Education |
| ICTs | Information and Communication Technologies |
| IFC | International Finance Corporation |
| IMF | International Monetary Fund |
| MDG | Millennium Development Goals |
| NGOs | Non-Governmental Organizations |
| OECD | Organization for Economic Cooperation and Development |
| PIRLS | Progress in International Reading Literacy Study |
| PREAL | Programa de Promoción de la Reforma Educativa de América Latina y el Caribe |
| PRSP | Poverty Reduction Strategy Papers |
| REPEM | Red de Educación Popular entre Mujeres |
| SABER | System Assessment and Benchmarking for Education Results |
| SAL | Structural Adjustment Lending |
| TIMMS | Trends in International Mathematics and Science Study |
| UN | United Nations |
| UN Women | UN Entity for Gender Equality and the Empowerment of Women |
| UNDP | United Nations Development Programme |
| UNESCO | United Nations Educational, Scientific and Cultural Organization |
| USAID | United States Agency for International Development |
| WEDO | Women's Environment and Development Organization |
| WHO | World Health Organization |
| WTO | World Trade Organization |

# CONTRIBUTORS

*Xavier Bonal* is special professor in Education and International Development at the University of Amsterdam and Associate Professor in Sociology at the Universitat Autònoma de Barcelona. He is the director of the Social Policy Research Group at the Department of Sociology of UAB, and a member of the Network of Experts of Social Sciences and Education of the European Commission.

*Mark Ginsburg* is a senior advisor for research, evaluation, and teacher education in the Global Education Center of the Global Learning Group at FHI 360 (formerly Academy for Education Development); a visiting professor at Columbia University and University of Maryland; and coeditor of the *Comparative Education Review*. He has published extensively on topics of policy/institutional reform, globalization, teachers' work, teacher education, and policy/practice-oriented research and evaluation.

*Anne Hickling-Hudson* is associate professor at Australia's Queensland University of Technology. Born and raised in Jamaica, she was educated at universities in the West Indies, Hong Kong, and Australia, and has been a pioneer in applying postcolonial theory to the comparative analysis of educational change and national development. She is recognized for her national and global leadership role in academic associations of education, especially as past president of both the World Council of Comparative Education Societies and the British Association of International and Comparative Education.

*Sangeeta Kamat* is associate professor in education policy studies at the University of Massachusetts at Amherst. Her publications include *Development Hegemony: NGOs and the State in India* (OUP, 2002) and several articles on globalization and education, the politics of international aid, and Hindu nationalism in the diaspora. She is presently researching the growth of private higher education in India and its regional impact.

*Steven J. Klees* is the R. W. Benjamin Professor of International and Comparative Education at the University of Maryland. His work examines the political economy of education and development with specific research interests in globalization, neoliberalism, and education; the role of aid agencies; education, human rights, and social justice; the education of disadvantaged populations; the role of class, gender, and race in reproducing and challenging educational and social inequality; and alternative approaches to education and development.

*Bjorn H. Nordtveit* is associate professor at the Center for International Education, School of Education, University of Massachusetts. He previously served for five years at the University of Hong Kong. He has six years of experience with the

World Bank (mainly in Francophone Sub-Saharan Africa) and five years with UNESCO in Laos. He has published extensively on the topics of aid effectiveness and globalization, as well as on schooling and child labor.

*Susan Robertson* is professor of Sociology of Education, Graduate School of Education, University of Bristol. She is Director of the Centre for Globalisation, Education and Societies, and founding co-editor of the journal, *Globalisation, Societies and Education*. She has published widely on the political economy of education, with a particular interest in transformations of the state and education.

*Joel Samoff* is an educator, researcher, and evaluator with a background in history, political science, and education. Since 1980 a faculty member at Stanford University, currently at the Center for African Studies, he has taught at the Universities of California, Michigan, and Zambia and in Mexico, South Africa, Sweden, Tanzania, and Zimbabwe, is the North America Editor of the *International Journal of Educational Development*, and serves on the editorial boards of the *Comparative Education Review*, the *Journal of Educational Research in Africa*, and the *Southern African Review of Education*.

*Angela de Siqueira* is associate professor in the faculty of education at the Universidade Federal Fluminense in Brazil, where she teaches and participates in research groups and extension projects. She has experience with both public and private institutions of higher education. She has presented papers at national and international academic meetings as well as taken part in debates in various public settings on issues dealing with education policies, multilateral agencies, and education finance.

*Crain Soudien* is professor and deputy vice-chancellor at the University of Cape Town. He writes in the areas of comparative education, educational reform, higher education, race, class, gender, the history of South Africa and cultural studies. He is past president of the World Council of Comparative Education Societies.

*Carol Anne Spreen* is assistant professor at the Curry School of Education at the University of Virginia. Her teaching and academic experience is in the field of comparative education and international education policy, with an emphasis on studies of school reform, education rights, curriculum planning, and instructional leadership. Her research focuses on equity, diversity, and social justice; globalization and educational policy reform; and teachers and teacher education.

*Gita Steiner-Khamsi* is professor of comparative and international education at Teachers College, Columbia University. She has published extensively on globalization and educational reform, comparative policy studies, and teacher salary reform. Her most recent books include *Policy Borrowing and Lending* (co-edited with Florian Waldow, 2012) and *South-South Cooperation in Education and Development* (co-edited with Linda Chisholm, 2009).

*Nelly P. Stromquist* is professor of international education policy in the College of Education at the University of Maryland. Her research interests focus on the dynamics among educational policies and practices, gender relations, and social change. She has written several books and numerous articles. Her most recent books include editing *The Professoriate in the Age of Globalization* and writing *Feminist Organizations and Social Transformation in Latin America.*

*Salim Vally* is senior lecturer at the Faculty of Education, University of Johannesburg and director of the Centre for Education Rights and Transformation. His academic interests include critical and liberatory pedagogies, teacher education and development, curriculum issues, qualitative forms of educational inquiry, and extensive involvement in participatory action research. He serves on the boards of various professional and non-governmental organizations and is active in various social movements and solidarity organizations.

*Antoni Verger* is a Ramón y Cajal Research Fellow at the Department of Sociology of the Universitat Autònoma de Barcelona. His main areas of expertise are global education policy and international development, focusing on the role of international organizations and transnational civil society networks and privatization/quasi-markets in education.

# INTRODUCTION

For decades, the world community has agreed that education matters. However development is defined, education is at its core. Since at least 1948 (when the Universal Declaration of Human Rights was enacted) the world has agreed that everyone has a right to education. Yet in the 21st century millions of young people and adults have no or very limited learning opportunities. Rather than liberating the human spirit and fostering individuals' and societies' development, far too often and in far too many places education systems entrench inequalities and are more concerned with inculcating obedience than with nurturing democratic participation.

Over the past three decades or more, the World Bank has sought to play a major role in education, both directly in the countries to which it lends and indirectly much more broadly. With what has become a large staff of employed and commissioned economists and educationists and an education research and communications budget that far exceeds the resources available to most universities and research institutions in less affluent countries, it has worked to situate itself as the architect, implementer, and enforcer of global education policy. In that role, sometimes it collaborates with other organizations, but more often it insists that others follow, pointing to its research to justify its authority.

The World Bank's enthusiasm for its own policy pronouncements and practical advice has not been matched by sustained progress in the implementation of education as a human right or in the achievement of quality education for all in the settings in which it is most active. Regularly, its recommendations are a problem, not a solution. Of course, the determinants of education progress are multiple and situational. Still, since the World Bank intends its education policies and strategies to be prime movers for global education, it is essential to subject them to systematic, grounded, and critical scrutiny.

This book is a broad critique of World Bank policies and, in particular, of its recently released *World Bank Education Strategy 2020. Learning for All: Investing in People's Knowledge and Skills to Promote Development* (hereafter *WBES 2020*). The World Bank periodically produces a new education sector document, some formally designated as policy, others termed strategy or review, all intended to shape education policy and practice in countries where the World Bank is active. Such documents are extremely influential as they reach policy and decision makers in countries that borrow from the World Bank. These documents reach as well a large audience of educational practitioners and other lending institutions that work closely with the World Bank, both through handsomely produced free distributions and through the World Bank's website. Unquestionably, the World Bank's education sector policies are used as a key referent in negotiations and decisions by lending countries.

Closely watched by both practitioners and academics, the World Bank's perspectives, political strategies, analyses, and proposals have regularly been challenged by scholars representing the disciplines of sociology, economics, political science, cultural studies, critical studies, and education, among others. While previous critiques of World Bank education policy have generally appeared in individual articles, this book brings together for the first time a group of some of the most widely known observers of the World Bank's education policy. All the authors in this book have engaged in rigorous comparative research in developing countries. They are also familiar with policy developments in industrialized countries and how ideas and experiences from the North are routinely channeled to less wealthy countries without first subjecting these ideas and experiences to careful assessment of what they offer and what they in fact accomplished in their original settings. Our efforts here seek to raise a group of significant voices to question and reflect upon what the World Bank recommends with claimed demonstrated positive results for educational systems in all parts of the world. We find it timely and essential to focus our collective efforts and experience (from Asia to Africa and Latin America) on examining what purports to be the most authoritative source of education policy.

The new strategy was announced in 2011 with many participatory claims. Through the work of 15 scholars, the collective response developed here seeks to examine both the surface and the underlying texture of *WBES 2020* by unpacking the arguments it presents, the evidence it brings to bear, the theories on which it builds (or fails to build), and—most of all—its education prescriptions based on its version of "knowledge." While *WBES 2020* remains a focal point of most chapters, all offer a more encompassing critique of World Bank education policy than that embodied in the current strategy. *WBES 2020* does not actually offer much in the way of a change in the prescriptions that the World Bank has been touting for over the past 30 years, during which neoliberal doctrine has dominated. Therefore, the critiques offered in this collection also have implications far beyond the World Bank as they are responses to the neoliberal global education policy recommendations that have dominated for several decades in developed and developing countries alike. We believe that this collective response is more important than ever given the ever stronger dominance of neoliberal policies in general, and, in particular, the World Bank's ascending role as an undisputed influential actor in education, often more so than UNESCO.

This book is organized in four parts: framing the issues; learning, assessment, and the role of teachers; research and policy; and reshaping the future. The chapters in each of these areas build on the contributors' research strengths and provide a deeper look and keen insight into specific educational aspects touched by World Bank policies. To do so, the chapters cover both theoretical and empirical ground, as manifested in the broad educational literature and in the World Bank's framing of issues and solutions.

## FRAMING THE ISSUES

We begin the book with an account of the process by which the World Bank claims legitimacy for its policy recommendations. In these days of increasing importance attached to democracy, invoking participation in decision-making—and, in this case, in policy formulation—should be welcomed. World Bank authors assure us that the development of the new strategy was subject to an extensive consultation process, with World Bank staff meeting with more than a thousand individuals in gatherings held around the world. Once produced, this strategy has been disseminated around the world with physical copies of the strategy distributed to people all over the world who work on educational projects. But what was the nature of the involvement and what were its consequences? The chapter by Gita Steiner-Khamsi traces in detail the four-stage process by which *WBES 2020* was developed and examines the attempt to secure global and broad stakeholder review systematically pursued by the World Bank. Although the World Bank sought external review of its proposals by holding many meetings with a large array of stakeholders, including government officials in partner countries, representatives from civil society, and business leaders, Steiner-Khamsi finds little similarity between the feedback provided to the World Bank and the final strategy it selected. She asserts that, as in previous instances, the World Bank followed a strategy of "rhetorical harmonization," a phenomenon she attributes to the self-referential system endorsed by this institution. Her chapter raises questions about the emerging international aid architecture, one in which the World Bank is assuming uncontestable leadership of its peer institutions.

In the chapter that follows, Bjorn Nordtveit engages in a meticulous examination of the discourse used by the World Bank document. Exploring the intentional use of discursive strategies—that include the selection of particular terms and their frequency, the claims made about having learned "lessons" from past experiences, being a "knowledge bank," and basing its findings exclusively on "research"—Nordveit deconstructs the architecture of a document aimed at persuading readers to accept its worldview of education and development. He also notes how the absence of certain terms and the recurrent portrayal of education as an investment and not as a human right conveys through sentimental as well as diagnostic linguistic devices what is essentially a particular ideology backing World Bank claims about the nature and role of education in society.

Sangeeta Kamat's contribution addresses the World Bank's new system approach to education policymaking, which purports to provide a more integrated comprehensive approach that will accomplish the mission of "learning for all" by 2020. The distinctive feature of the system approach according to the World Bank is the recognition that learning occurs outside formal education systems and that non-state actors, including private investors, faith-based groups, individuals, and communities are part of the education system. Kamal's analysis shows how the system approach remains faithful to neoliberalism, i.e., a market-driven approach to education policy that contradicts the stated mission of "learning for all."

Closing the first part of the book is the chapter by Steven J. Klees. Exposing the World Bank's neoliberal ideology, Klees demonstrates that this institution persists in its unshakeable endorsement of neoliberal principles despite multiple studies that show serious negative consequences attached to this approach. In this way neoliberalism functions as a de-facto ideology rather than as a sound economic approach to development and the World Bank, as a consequence, continues to ignore other productive approaches to education and development. Klees traces the World Bank's recommendations regarding learning, reading, testing, and user fees as well as its self-appointed mission as a "knowledge bank." On the basis of previous practices and empty rhetoric, the World Bank is found to be unfit to serve as a knowledge bank or even to provide evidence-based advice on critical educational issues.

## LEARNING, ASSESSMENT, AND THE ROLE OF TEACHERS

This part of the book focuses on educational issues. Here, the question of learning acquires center stage, since *WBES 2020*, after all, intends to promote the acquisition of knowledge by all. Deconstructing the learning architecture proposed by the World Bank, Angela de Siqueira initiates this section by zeroing in on a core strategy of *WBES 2020*, the one dealing with the System Assessment and Benchmarking for Education Results (SABER). This strategy, which comprises 13 policy domains, proposes a conceptual framework and diagnostic tools for each policy domain, and in doing so it offers a "one-size fits all" solution. Siqueira engages in content analysis to examine three of the policy domains (assessment, education finance and engaging the private sector, and teachers). On the basis of the recommendations for these three policies, Siqueira identifies likely negative consequences for learning and teaching, as the World Bank domain strategies are likely to bring an iron-clad standardization of objectives and functions that rejects the need to consider the social and economic context of many developing countries, installing instead an overwhelmingly Western-based model of education.

Teachers, an essential party to the process of learning, should receive a major share of the attention in the consideration of educational policies. Without them, little can be accomplished at the classroom level—the closest setting in the process of formal learning. And yet the fundamental role of teachers is often disregarded. The contribution by Mark Ginsburg focuses on teachers and examines *WBES 2020* from the perspective of what it means and advocates for these professionals. It finds that the current sector strategy gives some attention to teachers. However, they are mainly defined as human resources or human capital, requiring targeted investment. This contribution to the proposed volume critically analyzes how teachers are characterized in *WBES 2020* as well as in selected prior World Bank documents (1995 and 1999). It also presents an alternative image of teachers—as human beings—for whom opportunities to learn need to be structured into education systems so that daily life in schools builds learning communities for educators as well as students.

In recent years, quality has been receiving a great deal of discursive attention. It is frequently said that access to schooling without quality is an empty exercise, for students who do not learn have not really benefited from schooling and will likely not reap the benefits that ideally accrue to formal education. Quality is precious and one would hardly find any one who does not want schools to be of high quality. But how do you determine that the education provided is good and relevant? Whose standards and criteria are to prevail? The purpose of Crain Soudien's contribution is to interrogate the meaning of "quality" in the *WBES 2020*. Soudien argues that while the new education sector strategy repeatedly emphasizes the importance of an education that is holistic and meaningful, there is clear evidence of the difficulty in substantively realizing these qualities—"holistic" and "meaningful"—through the transnational standardized benchmarking tests the World Bank proposes. The chapter examines the degree to which tests such as TIMMS and PIRLs have been able to develop frameworks of value which are, first, sensitive to differences across boundaries and, second, able to provide educational systems across the world with the guidance that will enable them to create conditions in which learners everywhere will flourish.

Closing the second part of the book is a reflection on learning by Joel Samoff. At first glance, *WBES 2020* seems to mark significant progress: from attention to education for all to a focus on learning for all. In practice, however, there is very little research or analytic attention to the learning process. Instead, Samoff finds a learning model whose narrow focus on acquiring knowledge and skills leaves little space for learning defined as the initiative, actions, and responsibility of learners, or for developing competences like framing problems, developing concepts, and drawing inferences—all essential components of a broader understanding of learning and critical for development. That orientation is reinforced by the World Bank's uncritical adoption of a schooling model designed to educate elites. The learning model and schooling models combine with the World Bank's efforts to deprofessionalize the teaching corps, apply a technocratic management approach, and support privatization to constitute fundamental obstacles to achieving learning for all. Moreover, that combination reinforces and entrenches systematic inequalities across society.

## RESEARCH AND POLICY

The global education community regularly reiterates the importance of developing and maintaining a strong link between research and policy. Essential are theoretical frames resting on grounded research that makes explicit the connections underlying policy recommendations. Action without understanding is unlikely to be effective, and theories without empirical support are generally poor guides to action. The chapter by Verger and Bonal calls our attention to an ostensible shift in the World Bank moving from emphasis on educational access to a concern for learning. The authors find that *WBES 2020* seems more disposed to abandon its position that there is a trade-off between equity and quality and more willing to recognize that more equitable systems achieve better results. However, upon further reading of the Bank's new education strategy, Bonal and Verger find that little has been changed. There is still a very inward view of education that gives much weight to economic and technical factors while ignoring contextual issues that greatly affect education. The Bank's position in favor of standardized testing and private schooling remains, and these two strategies are held to be the key mechanisms to ensure learning and efficiency in schooling, irrespective of varying cultural and social contexts.

The second contribution in this part of the book is provided by Joel Samoff, who shows that, notwithstanding the World Bank's insistence on evidence-based policy and practice and its insistence that learning is now to be the primary focus of education support efforts, *WBES 2020* reflects very little evidence and research on the learning process. For the most part, what happens in schools and classrooms remains unaddressed, ignored in favor of attention to inputs, outputs, and the education system. At the same time, reinforced by its inclination to rely on research that it has commissioned or supported, the World Bank seeks to impose a constraining methodological orthodoxy. That orientation is especially problematic in Africa, where institutional research capacity remains limited and where education research as consulting has become commonplace. Needed is support for the sustained development of a competent, independent, and innovative research community. The World Bank finds it difficult to pursue that agenda, since doing so could well undermine its inclination to rely on its own research and challenges both its claim that it provides high quality development advisory services and its role in managing the integration of poor countries into the global political economy.

Three specific aspects are addressed in the chapters that follow: gender, human rights, and the growing attention to collaboration between the school system and other social actors. Nelly P. Stromquist centers her analysis on the gender component of *WBES 2020*. The new education strategy recognizes structural barriers to education and identifies gender as one of several forms of discrimination. Yet it fails to situate gender in a deeper theoretical framework that would enable its consideration as a core social phenomenon with multiple simultaneous causes and consequences, one of which is its "normalization" in varying cultures. The World Bank declares a commitment to redress asymmetries through education, yet its proposals do not build on gender theory nor consider the potentially adverse consequences of World Bank policies on women. Consequently, the educational strategy proposed by the World Bank continues to focus almost exclusively on increased access by girls to formal education and does not acknowledge schools as gendered institutions through which the knowledge they convey and the experience they foster tends to reproduce gender rather than challenge it.

For their part, Salim Vally and Carol Anne Spreen critique *WBES 2020*'s lack of attention to education rights and specifically the faulty assumptions promoting the role of education in "development." They argue that despite a rhetorical nod to human rights in the introduction of the sector strategy, evidence of supporting rights "to, in, and through" education are absent in *WBES2020*. Vally and Spreen examine the document's framing of "development" and show how the new sector strategy continues human capital prescriptions for the role of education that rest on the false assumption that a narrow investment in technological and skills development will lead to greater productivity and economic growth, which will in turn alleviate poverty. Vally and Spreen contrast the World Bank's human capital approach with a rights-based perspective that builds on Katarina Tomasevski's "Four As" framework for the Right to Education as well as on Amartya Sen's "capabilities" discourse and practice.

Susan Robertson focuses her critique on the World Bank's key strategy of involving the private sector in education—public-private partnerships (PPPs). Robertson holds that given widespread resistance to privatization from several sectors in the developing world, PPPs are being used to reintroduce it under another name. Her analysis probes into the World Bank's claim that the private sector is more efficient than the public sector and finds that *WBES 2020* offers little evidence to support it. What Robertson finds instead is the relentless defense of the neoliberal political ideology as an economic perspective and project, despite strong evidence about its shortcomings.

## RESHAPING THE FUTURE

Education policies can be useful instruments to guide decisions concerning the improvement and transformation of educational systems. Such instruments require great sensitivity to national contexts and objectives determined by their own citizens. It is possible to think of a global institution that could coordinate the design of suitable educational policies, but the World Bank has not demonstrated that it is the most appropriate institution for this task.

The chapter by Anne Hickling-Hudson and Steve Klees posits a Global Fund for Education as an alternative to the World Bank. They argue that the World Bank's narrow, neoliberal, ideological framework greatly restricts the choice of alternative educational policies. Building on issues raised in previous chapters and exploring others, Hickling-Hudson and Klees consider theories and evidence that support such alternatives, including: implementing the right to education; relying on different models of the connection between education and development; changing the stratified and unequal nature of schooling; eliminating the consumerist paradigm underlying education and emphasizing ecological sanity; making curriculum interdisciplinary and assessment authentic; recognizing that attention to quality means attention to equity; focusing on public schooling, not private; and realizing that "evidence-based policy" is a call for participation and debate, not a technical search for truth.

We conclude the book by integrating some of the key arguments in the various chapters into several concrete themes. There has long been widespread dissatisfaction with the role played by the World Bank in education. Our intent here is to provide a well-argued and well-researched concrete challenge to the World Bank's influential role in education policy.

# PART I

# FRAMING THE ISSUES

CHAPTER 1

GITA STEINER-KHAMSI

# FOR ALL BY ALL?

*The World Bank's Global Framework for Education*

The 2020 World Bank Education Sector Strategy *Learning for All* (*WBES 2020*, hereafter) was presented in its final form to the public in February 2011 (World Bank, 2011a). The enthusiasm of Elizabeth King, chief architect of *WBES 2020*, perhaps best captures the great expectations associated with the launch of the new strategy:

> *Let's Make It Learning for All, Not Just Schooling for All.*
> … Having spent nearly 18 months traveling the world to consult with our partners (government, civil society, NGOs, development agencies) about the best experience and evidence of what works in education and about the role of the Bank Group in the next decade, I feel somewhat like I've given birth, in this case to a global framework for education which we believe is the right one for the coming decade. (King, 2011)

Regardless of the debate on whether *WBES 2020* truly sets new accents or merely reaffirms the World Bank's technical approach to educational development,[i] the insistence on fundamental change begs for explanation. Why is it so important to the World Bank to emphasize the novelty of the approach? Strategy development is steeped in a political process in that it helps to garner support from within as well as from outside an organization to channel resources into particular activities. Applied to *WBES 2020*, the question becomes: which adversaries does it attempt to convince and which new coalitions does it intend to form? According to the World Bank, *WBES 2020* heralds a novel approach that is supported by major actors in development: donors ("development partners"), recipient governments ("clients"), and broadly defined civil societies (businesses, non-governmental organizations, people). The comprehensive stakeholder review of this latest educational strategy seems to suggest that it has been endorsed by diverse groups of stakeholders, inside and outside the World Bank, and by implication is no longer a World Bank strategy but rather should be treated as everyone's strategy. Furthermore, the ambitious claim of having "given birth" to "a global framework for education" positions the document as a strategy with global reach and with universal

*S.J. Klees et al. (eds.), The World Bank and Education, 3–20.*

solutions. In this analysis, I attempt to study the grand claim of universality reflected in the World Bank's insistence that *WBES 2020* is not only a global framework for All but, as this chapter will show, also one that has been developed by All.

Since the focus of this chapter is not so much on the content of *WBES 2020*, but rather on agency and process, the following research question arises: How and when did the transformation from a World Bank framework for education to a "global framework for education" occur? I will address this question in this chapter from a perspective that is informed by systems theory (see Luhmann, 1990; Schriewer, 1990). The World Bank is analyzed here as a *social system* with its own regulatory regime that draws its legitimacy from a clearly defined mandate, a strategy, a set of actors, and a set of beneficiaries. This particular research question reflects an interest in understanding the social system rather than criticizing individual authors that work for the World Bank.

Many concepts introduced in this chapter are informed by system theory. For example, donor logic, self-referentiality of knowledge, and functional integration of aid systems—presented in the following sections—are used to explain the ever expanding scope of conditions that the World Bank established over the years for determining the eligibility for loans or grants. For the longest time, recipient governments had to subscribe to a structural adjustment policy (reducing public expenditures and increasing revenue from private sources). Heavily criticized by many in development work, the economic straightjacket of structural adjustment was preserved but in the 1990s supplemented with a social dimension (poverty alleviation) and later on, at the turn of the new millennium, with a political requirement (good governance). Over the past decade the World Bank re-invented itself in the education sector and presented itself as a knowledge producer and knowledge manager. In this particular role as knowledge bank the World Bank now determines what works and what does not work in terms of educational development. The knowledge-based regulation of the World Bank has, in effect, generated a fourth conditionality for recipient governments: programmatic conditionality. In addition to the economic, social and political conditionalities (structural adjustment, poverty alleviation, good governance), they now have to subscribe to a particular reform package ("best practices") that was first piloted in a few countries, analyzed in impact evaluations, and then disseminated to other recipient governments.

## ON DONOR LOGIC

There has been a proliferation of studies that analyze "donor logic," investigating who has given aid to whom (and why, and how), or trying to understand more broadly the idiosyncrasies of the various aid agencies in education. Such studies demonstrate that, for example, the World Bank's rationale for lending money or giving grants is distinct from a foreign policy framework, as pursued by bilateral aid, and is also fundamentally different from the donor logic of UN agencies, philanthropies, non-governmental organizations, or, more recently, of celebrities (see Alesina & Dollar, 2000; Richey & Ponte, 2008; Silova & Steiner-Khamsi, 2008). Phillip Jones' historical accounts of multilateral aid organizations greatly advanced this line of research (Jones, 1998, 2004, 2005). He scrutinizes the donor logic of multilaterals, including the World Bank, and finds great differences, depending upon how they are funded. He points out that UNICEF relies on voluntary donations from governments, private foundations, and individuals, and therefore "its analyses of need tend to be dramatic, its projections tend to be alarmist and its solutions tend to be populist" (Jones, 1998, p. 151). In contrast, UNESCO runs on membership fees that are, unfortunately, more successfully extracted from low-income governments than they are from high-income governments. Given the global scope of UNESCO's operation, supported by minimal funding, UNESCO relies on building alliances with resourceful development agencies.[ii]

I concur with Jones' observation that the World Bank has reinvented itself at the turn of the millennium and now functions as a knowledge bank. The concept of an international knowledge bank was first discussed at the Board of Governors of the World Bank in March 1996 (see Jones, 2004 and 2005). One of the options discussed was whether the financial lending operations should be delegated to the regional development banks (Asian Development Bank, African Development Bank, etc.) while the Bank itself focused on the lending of ideas. Three years later, in 1999, the World Bank's Global Development Network (GDN) was launched at a conference in Bonn where South-South cooperation, in particular, the dissemination of "best practices" within the global South was discussed (see Stone, 2000). As a result, policy transfer would ideally occur within and among the countries that are perceived as being similar, replacing the practice of transplanting reform packages from the First to the Third World.

Although the World Bank has not decreased its role as a lender of money, it has acted increasingly, over the past decade, as a global policy advisor for national governments.[iii] Needless to state, the World Bank's use of baseline analysis, target setting, and benchmarking as policy tools to coerce national governments into adopting a particular reform package, designed and funded by the World Bank, has come under serious attack. It has been rightfully pointed out by many, including several authors in this book, that the World Bank has elevated itself into the role of the "super think tank" among the aid agencies that, based on its extensive analytical work, knows what is good for the recipient countries but also what other aid agencies should support. Its self-described role as a knowledge bank, combined with the expensive impact evaluations which, in some countries, cost more than the actual "intervention" whose effectiveness they are supposed to measure, epitomizes the "what works approach." Worse yet, by implication the super think tank also functions as a judge on what does not work and consequently does not receive external financial support even if national governments prove the contrary and request funding for reforms that they deem important for their country.[iv] For many, the World Bank has remained arrogant and big-footed, this time around not only because of the volume of money it holds but also because of the masses of data it collects as well as the multitude of technical reports it produces. Having

5

reviewed the World Bank's analytical work on teachers, I make the argument in this chapter that the international databases of the World Bank are often agenda-driven and therefore vulnerable to methodological bias and coercive recommendations.

## THE FUNCTIONAL INTEGRATION OF THREE AND MORE AID SYSTEMS

From a systems perspective, it is striking that the boundaries between the World Bank and other major development actors, in particular the United States and the United Kingdom, have become blurred. The strategies of the World Bank, DFID, and USAID have converged towards the same knowledge-based approach for delivering aid and chosen the same narrow focus on measurable student outcomes, notably on literacy and numeracy. Regardless of aid agency, there is nowadays an obsession with identifying progress indicators, a preoccupation with measuring results (including student results), and an institutional pressure to demonstrate the impact of an aid intervention. This is not surprising given the indicators of effective aid that the 2005 Paris Declaration on Aid Effectiveness established. In addition, the education sector strategies of the two largest donors[v] are remarkably similar to the World Bank's *Education Sector Strategy 2020* (World Bank, 2011a). In fact, *WBES 2020* adopted a title that was already in use in U.K. bilateral aid: *Learning for All: DFID's Education Strategy 2010-2015* (DFID, 2009). For DFID, but also for the World Bank and for USAID, skills development for youth is one of the strategic priorities (along with access and quality). The bilateral aid plan of the United States, released a few months before *WBES 2020*, also highlights student learning and skills development, and is entitled *USAID Education Strategy: Improving Lives through Learning* (USAID, 2011).

Even though the World Bank has a tendency to see itself as the representative of all bilateral donors,[vi] there are many bilateral aid agencies that share neither its focus nor its technical approach to aid. The Government of Denmark, for example, represents the largest donor in terms of per-capita spending on aid. Its aid agency (Danish International Development Agency, DANIDA) follows to the letter the 2005 Paris Declaration on Aid Effectiveness, and implements, among other features, results-based aid (DANIDA, 2010). At the same time, it pursues a human rights approach to education that does not reduce the value of education to literacy and numeracy. In the same vein, the Children and Youth Strategy of the Canadian International Development Agency (CIDA) is more holistic than *WBES 2020* and concentrates on three areas: child survival, access to quality education, and safe and secure futures for children and youth (CIDA, 2011). Similarly, Japan's Education Cooperation Policy 2011-2015 has also moved beyond narrowly defined strategic goals that coerce recipient governments into adopting donor-driven reform priorities (Ministry of Foreign Affairs of Japan, 2010). In stark contrast to the aid strategies of Denmark, Canada, and Japan—which are sufficiently broadly defined to allow for national governments to set their own agendas—the recipients of a grant or loan from the World Bank have to adopt the narrowly defined (global) framework of education that is advanced by the World Bank but also to some extent by DFID and USAID. The recipient governments have to subscribe, at least rhetorically and at the stage when international funding is secured,[vii] to the donor's focus on measurable student-outcomes, testing, impact evaluation, and a host of other priorities that match the aid strategy of the donor but not necessarily the need of their country.

There used to be distinct differences between the various aid agencies, including between the World Bank, DFID, and USAID. In fact, they thrived from being different. They were, in terms of systems theory, "environment" to each other and thereby defined themselves in terms of how they differed from one another. We have witnessed over the past few years, however, a functional integration of the various actors. These three large donors, but also others, now inhabit the same system, that is, subscribe to the same international agreements (e.g., EFA, MDG) and adhere to the same standards of aid effectiveness (e.g., Paris Declaration 2005) that regulate the aid relationship between donors and recipients.

The argument is made here that *WBES 2020* attempts to cement a new aid environment, one in which World Bank tries hard to dissolve its boundaries with other development agencies—such as bilateral aid, multilateral agencies, non-governmental organizations—in order to assume global leadership on matters of aid. Thus, the standardization of aid that we are currently witnessing is very strongly dictated by standards propelled by the World Bank and with knowledge-based regulation tools used by commercial banks and businesses: ratings/rankings, performance assessments, targets, benchmarks, and progress reporting.

There are three aspects of the new strategy that deserve closer investigation: first, the broad stakeholder review process; second, the emphasis on "what works" and, finally, the circularity or self-referentiality in its knowledge production.

## THE WORLD BANK: A HARMONIZER?

Stakeholder review is not out of the ordinary in democratic settings. This is not to say that the opinions voiced by stakeholders are considered and ultimately find entry in the published version of the strategy. In the case of the USAID education strategy, the stakeholders reviewed in fact the "wrong draft," that is, the version that they reviewed was not the one that got published. A first version of the USAID Education Strategy was carefully researched by experts brought in from outside the USAID system and the draft was circulated for feedback among internal and external stakeholders over a period of several months in 2009. At the end, the version reviewed and revised by the stakeholders was shelved. A new USAID strategy document was commissioned from scratch, completed within a short period of time, and approved within an even shorter time. The valid version was not stakeholder-reviewed.

Different from USAID, the World Bank stakeholder review process was orchestrated publicly and documents related to the strategy and to the strategy development process were posted on the web. The Consultation Plan included feedback on the overall approach and the concept note as well as on the draft strategy. The consultations were scheduled over the period February to November

7

2010 (see World Bank, 2010). The concept note was translated into Arabic, Chinese, French, Russian, Portuguese, and Spanish and feedback on the strategy material was solicited from a broad array of experts based in governments, non-governmental organizations, think tanks, and universities. The *WBES 2020* team visited over two dozen cities across the globe to solicit feedback and also presented the draft at the 2010 annual meeting of the professional association of researchers and practitioners in educational development, the Comparative and International Education Society (CIES).

The content of the *WBES 2020* is as important as the process of (1) developing, (2) reviewing, (3) approving, and (4) presenting the new strategy. The following summarizes the four phases of strategy development for *WBES 2020*.

*Development of the Strategy*

It has become customary to have experts produce background papers on lessons learned, trends observed, and issues arising in educational development. These background papers provide the "scientific rationality" (see Luhmann, 1990, and Schriewer, 1990) for the priorities proposed in the strategy. They later on serve as quasi-scientific stamp of certification when political disagreements surface. As with the Global Monitoring Reports of UNESCO but also with (the first version of) the USAID Education Strategy, the World Bank had background papers produced that synthesized evaluations and other empirical studies on aid interventions and educational reforms. An important detail here is that all the papers were produced internally reinforcing the point that I will be making later about the self-referentiality of the World Bank's analytical work.[viii]

*Review of the Strategy*

The review of the strategy was, as mentioned above, staged as a public enterprise; internal *and* external feedback was solicited. It was important to the *WBES 2020* team to point out that all products of the strategy development process—the technical approach, the concept note, and the draft strategy—were reviewed by a broad array of stakeholders including, for example, by students and parents who typically have little to say on matters related to formal education. The participation of the broad range of stakeholders in education is acknowledged in the preliminary pages of *WBES 2020*:

> The strategy team is grateful to the government officials of partner countries, global development partners, representatives of civil society organizations, students, teachers, parents, and business leaders who made valuable recommendations throughout the strategy development and drafting process. (2011a, p. vii)

The list of those that "deserve special mention" is actually shorter than one would expect, given the extensive stakeholder review. It must be assumed that some consultations were deemed politically more important than others—e.g., "a consultation dinner for representatives from Angola, Ethiopia, Kyrgyz Republic, Mozambique, Tajikistan, Vietnam and Zambia" hosted by the Government of

Russia (World Bank, 2011a, p. viii)—and therefore were listed in the acknowledgment section of the 97-page strategy document.

*Approval of the Strategy*

It is customary that authors of strategies and other texts acknowledge the feedback received from reviewers and mention that some of the proposed changes have been incorporated into the final revision. This is not the case in *WBES 2020*, probably because indeed there is little similarity between the draft strategy presented for review, the feedback given, and the final strategy that was approved. The stakeholder review process (phase 2) was sufficiently broad to enable the *WBES 2020* team to selectively adopt the feedback that best matched the World Bank's idiosyncratic priorities and aid agenda. Contrary to the publicly open review process (phase 2), the approval process (phase 3) occurred behind closed doors. As with the first phase (development of the strategy), the third phase (approval of strategy) is for individuals outside the system a black box because it was carried out internally.

*Presentation of the Final Version of the Strategy*

Outsiders were again involved in the final stage of the strategy. The document was translated into many languages, publicly launched, and widely disseminated.

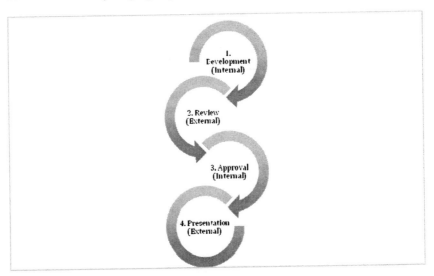

*Figure 1. The Four Phases of WBES 2020 Production*

As Figure 1 illustrates, the development (phase 1) and the approval of the strategy (phase 3) were carried out internally, that is, within the World Bank system. However, by emphasizing the inclusive approach and inviting outsiders to comment, that is, by visibly opening up the review (phase 2) of a product that was exclusively developed by World Bank staff and affiliates, the final version of the strategy (phase 4) was presented as *everyone's* strategy. The systemic shifts, internal-external-internal-external, illustrated in Figure 1 and explained in the previous paragraphs, enabled the World Bank to present its own education strategy as a product that was developed and endorsed by experts in *and* outside the World Bank system.

In policy studies, the process of consolidating various interests and agendas is called harmonization. What I have described with the four phases of *WBES 2020* is a process of *rhetorical harmonization* that enabled the World Bank to pretend that it has integrated divergent interests and agendas to the extent that their own education strategy now passes as everyone's "global framework of education."

## "WHAT WORKS": IMPACT EVALUATIONS AND PROGRAMMATIC CONDITIONALITY

It is a bad idea to have the same institution review the education sector, identify a reform package, lend the money for implementing the reform package, and evaluate its effectiveness. In the same vein, it is ill conceived to have the World Bank analyze the problem and lend money for its solution. More often than not, the solutions exist before the analysis is carried out, turning the sequence of policy formulation on its head (see Steiner-Khamsi, 2010). Rather than first defining the problem and then searching for solutions, the reality on the ground differs: the formulation of the (local) problem is aligned with the already existing externally funded (global) solution. To be fair: the same applies to other aid agencies. They tend to invent problems and create a crisis in areas for which they have solutions to offer. Similar to other aid agencies, the World Bank pursues a limited number of educational reforms that it tests in a few countries and then disseminates—with a few adaptations here and there to reduce transfer cost—across the globe, regardless of country context. It would be more accurate to consider this particular reform package a portfolio of eligible reforms for World Bank funding rather than to use a label that carries a positive connotation: transfer of "best practices." I therefore suggest that the concept "transfer of best practices" be replaced with a term that captures the economics of policy borrowing as well as the power asymmetry between recipient and donor more poignantly: "programmatic conditionality."

The point I make in this section is that impact evaluation, for the World Bank and many other aid agencies the preferred mode for justifying their aid portfolio, has become a means for imposing programmatic conditionality on recipient governments. At closer examination, programmatic conditionality is, in effect, similar to the earlier, highly unpopular structural adjustment reforms that the World Bank and IMF imposed on recipients of grants and loans. Many of the pilot projects that nowadays make it into the World Bank portfolio of fundable projects aim at reducing public expenditures in education (by means of privatization, rationalization, etc.), increasing revenue for the national education budget (from tuition, fees, etc.), and by reducing inefficiencies and wastage.

If it were not for the high cost associated with impact evaluations, one could simply criticize the World Bank for encouraging economists with doctoral degrees to carry out educational research. In teacher policy research, for example, the World Bank is enamored with impact evaluations that show that underpaid contract teachers produce better student outcomes than regular teachers who are not accountable, do not fear losing their jobs, and therefore either do not show up regularly in school, or if they show up, do not teach, or if they teach, do not teach effectively (see Bruns et al., 2011; Duflo et al., 2010). This complex causal chain of explanations is often simplified and reduced in the end to two variables only: low payment of teachers and job insecurity—both, according to the economists cited in World Bank publications, considered highly desirable for education systems that attempt to improve teacher effectiveness. Whether the contract teachers were members of the same community, perhaps spoke the same language as the students they instruct, or were more highly motivated because they were early-career teachers in a system that is, for a variety of reasons, demotivating for teachers, are all issues that educational researchers have examined in great detail. Alternative explanations are simply "noise" for a research agenda that attempts to scientifically prove that cutting public expenditures is not only necessary from a financial perspective but also, as impact evaluations supposedly demonstrate with "hard fact," better for student learning.

Impact evaluations should also be criticized for being far too expensive for what they are able to offer in terms of explanations. A good case in point is the impact evaluation of the READ (Rural Education And Development) project in rural Mongolia, funded by the World Bank. READ provided children's books to classrooms (40 books per grade level) in rural primary schools. The impact evaluation sought to assess two questions: first, do books make a difference for improving literacy skills of students and, second, does the preparation of teachers for integrating children books into their teaching matter? As with all quasi-experimental designs, the impact evaluation worked with large, representative samples. The design of the impact evaluation study is presented in Table 1.

The same standardized student achievement test was administered to primary school students and used as a tool to assess the effectiveness of the two interventions: (1) books only and (2) books with training. Even though the design of the study was methodologically solid, the research questions were for policy experts and practitioners banal. For the project staff in Mongolia, a formative project evaluation with recommendations on how to improve the implementation of the project was of much greater utility than the comprehensive impact evaluation with its quasi-experimental design. Furthermore, the research questions pursued in the impact evaluation were irrelevant for decision-makers in the Mongolian education sector. They had no doubt whatsoever that both children's books and teacher training are much needed and they found it unethical to withhold books and training from rural schools in fifteen provinces (control group) only to

Table 1. Design of the Impact Evaluation of the READ Project in Mongolia

| "Semi-Treatment" Group: Two Provinces | All primary classrooms in rural schools (in two provinces) receive 40 children books per grade |
|---|---|
| "Full-Treatment" Group: Three 3 Provinces | All primary classrooms in rural schools (in three provinces) receive 40 children books PLUS all teachers in these schools receive training on how to integrate children books into their teaching |
| "No Treatment Group" [Control Group]: 15 Provinces | None of the primary classrooms in rural schools (in 15 provinces) receive children books and none of the teachers receive a training |

see whether the two interventions really have had an impact on students' literacy skills. Finally, the decision-makers resented at the time that such a great amount of money was spent on the impact evaluation, and in particular on international consultants conducting the study, rather than on distributing books and training to more schools and provinces in Mongolia.

There was no doubt in anyone's mind that the READ project filled an important gap in rural schools: provision of books and training. There was a great sense of gratitude towards this World Bank grant that enabled a revitalization of schools in rural Mongolia. But whom did the impact evaluation serve? As mentioned above, it was not meant to serve Mongolian decision-makers, but rather it was commissioned for the funder itself, more precisely for the knowledge bank of the World Bank. The World Bank evaluates its own projects and selects a few projects as "best practices" which it subsequently disseminates to other countries in the world. As mentioned above, what some scholars call the "scientific method" in educational research (quasi-experimental design) or "evidence-based policy planning" serves international organizations to package existing projects, brand them as "best practices" or a "global framework of education," and transfer them—as part of the programmatic conditionality of a loan or grant—to developing countries.

## WORLD BANK KNOWLEDGE: A SELF-REFERENTIAL SYSTEM

Over the past few years, I observed a growing interest of the donor community in issues related to teacher salaries, management, and deployment. Each of the funders is interested for different reasons in the topic, interprets the findings differently, and draws different conclusions from one and the same study. The World Bank, for example, is interested in this research area because 80 or 90 percent of national education budgets are allocated for salaries. UNICEF, in turn, is concerned with how to supply qualified teachers to schools that are marginalized in terms of location or in other regards and has, against this backdrop, launched the Teachers for the Marginalized Initiative.

In the same vein, each agency uses the findings from the various studies differently. A few comments on the idiosyncrasies of agency-funded educational policy research in developing countries might be in order here. The following presents examples of World Bank-funded policy research in the area of teacher salaries, management, and deployment in which I participated as researcher: one in Tajikistan (see Steiner-Khamsi, 2007) and another one in Mongolia (World Bank, 2006). There is a disjuncture between the type of teacher reform studies that the World Bank funds in-country and how it represents them in the headquarters. As I will demonstrate in the following, the analytical work in-country (exemplified by studies in Tajikistan and Mongolia) is less agenda-driven than its international database (exemplified by SABER-Teachers) in Washington.

The study in Tajikistan explored the structure and composition of the teacher salary which teachers and government officials found fragmented and non-transparent. Teachers in Tajikistan as well as in other post-Soviet countries are paid a very low base salary (based on a weekly teaching load or, in Russian, referred to as *stavka)* and a series of salary supplements for teaching additional hours, for grading student notebooks, for serving as homeroom teachers, for managing a resource room or laboratory, etc. International agency after international agency have provided in Tajikistan, but also in other countries of the region, wrong advice and coerced the government into ill-informed reform priorities because they failed to understand the huge difference in teacher salary and work conditions in countries with a weekly workload system (used in Europe and North America) as opposed to the weekly teaching load system (used in the post-Soviet region). However, the important study on the "*stavka* system" (teaching load system in post-Soviet countries) was poorly timed. It was completed at a time when the Government of Tajikistan had just passed a comprehensive teacher salary reform by consolidating several salary supplements into the base salary and thereby lifting the teacher salary. Understandably, the Government of Tajikistan was not prepared to publish yet another report that proposed a revision of the salary structure, a better utilization of teachers, greater weekly statutory teaching load, and a much higher base salary for teachers. The ambitious World Bank study on the *stavka* system was exclusively read by World Bank staff and government officials but remained unpublished and underutilized.[ix]

The opposite occurred with the World Bank-funded study in Mongolia. The Public Expenditure Tracking Survey in Mongolia (PETS Mongolia) included a large component on teacher salaries (World Bank, 2006). The timing for the study could not have been better: Mongolia experienced rapid economic growth, triggered by a booming mining industry, and the Government of Mongolia was therefore receptive to the recommendations of lifting the teacher salary, adapting a weekly workload system and thereby replacing the previous teaching load system, as well as making the salary structure more transparent and less vulnerable to deductions that were regularly and arbitrarily made by school principals.

13

In both countries with a socialist past, Tajikistan and Mongolia, accountability was not an issue, but the low payment and morale and the big shortage of teachers in rural areas represented major concerns. In fact, in both countries—but also in several other former socialist countries examined in the UNICEF CEECIS Study on Teachers (UNICEF CEECIS, 2011)—teachers are heavily controlled and their salaries or salary supplements are deducted if they do not show up in school, come late, do not grade the notebooks of students, damage school equipment, and are constantly humiliated in many different ways by school principals and education managers. PETS Mongolia addressed how teachers in Mongolia lacked support at all levels of the education system and also demonstrated the huge inequality of teacher salaries in rural and urban schools. PETS Mongolia, funded by the World Bank, was without exaggeration one of the most influential policy analyses in Mongolia that had a major positive impact on the country's educational system. Many commentators in Mongolia attributed the 2007 teacher salary reform to the findings presented in the PETS Mongolia study. As the most recent UNICEF Mongolia Study on Teachers (UNICEF Mongolia, 2011) demonstrates, teacher salaries almost quadrupled, teacher shortage in rural schools disappeared, enrollment in pre-service teacher education doubled and, most importantly, teachers are nowadays able to make a living from their salary and do not have to rely on additional sources from teaching excessively, farming, selling products in the market or on the streets, or from privately tutoring students after class. Naturally, the economic boom in the country made the implementation of the proposed changes possible. Nevertheless, the World Bank-funded PETS Mongolia study laid a foundation to garner political support for a major salary increase that was long overdue in Mongolia.

There is a gap that yawns between World Bank-funded analytical work carried out in various countries and its global representation by World Bank Headquarters. Therefore, the flattering comments on the two World Bank-funded studies—the study on the *stavka* system in Tajikistan and PETS Mongolia—need to be put in perspective and compared with the global knowledge bank on teacher policies, SABER-Teachers, that the World Bank Headquarters is currently setting up. World Bank Headquarters seems to have the mandate of coming up with a global policy framework for all kinds of reform areas, including for teacher reforms. Such a mandate is in itself problematic. In the area of teacher reforms, SABER-Teachers (System Assessment and Benchmarking for Education Results) documents "teacher policies for public schools in developed and developing countries in order to inform policy choices and promote policy dialogue, globally" (World Bank, 2011b). SABER-Teachers pursues eight policy goals:

– Setting clear expectations for teachers
– Attracting the best into teaching
– Preparing teachers with useful training and experience
– Matching teachers' skills with students' needs
– Leading teachers with strong principals
– Monitoring teaching and learning
– Supporting teachers to improve instruction

– Motivating teachers to perform

As the eight policy goals listed above illustrate, the emphasis of SABER-Teachers is on teacher accountability. Both the language and the policy goals used in SABER-Teachers clearly depict a negative image of teachers. It is an image that does not do justice to many regions and countries in the world, including, for example, Eastern Europe, Caucasus, Central Asia, and Mongolia, where teachers are micro-managed, controlled, and sanctioned. The language and concepts reflected in the policy framework of SABER-Teachers should be read as an invitation to decision-makers to come up with reforms that police and sanction the masses of underperforming teachers and provide material incentives to a small group of teachers who perform well. Without any doubt, the programmatic conditionality of the World Bank in the area of teacher policies is teacher accountability. This particular policy orientation is presented in detail in the World Bank publication *Making Schools Work. New Evidence on Accountability Reforms* (see Bruns et al., 2011, chapter 4). Judging from the list of "best practices" presented in the publication, the portfolio of eligible projects for World Bank funding are contract tenure reforms, pay-for-performance reforms, and other types of accountability reforms that, if implemented globally, make a profession that already suffers from universal shortage and low prestige even less attractive.

What bothers in publications of the World Bank, such as in *Making Schools Work* (Bruns et al., 2011), is the ambiguous case selection. As explained above, PETS Mongolia was an influential study in Mongolia and had a major positive impact on educational development in Mongolia. Yet, PETS Mongolia and numerous other World Bank-funded studies that paint a positive picture of teachers and contradict the larger agenda of teacher accountability are not presented in World Bank publications. Given the geographical scope of World Bank operations, one needs to be alerted if only a few countries are presented. One must assume that all the excluded case studies apparently did not fit the World Bank canon of teacher accountability reforms. Public Expenditure Tracking Surveys, for example, were conducted in dozens of countries but it is always the same handful of countries that are mentioned in World Bank publications; typically countries where major leakages and massive teacher absenteeism occur.

Methodologically speaking, the sample selection in World Bank reporting is seriously flawed. The bias has to do with the broader agenda of establishing a scientific rationality for teacher accountability reforms. The agenda-driven analytical work of the World Bank may lead to wrong conclusions and inappropriate policy recommendations that match the available project portfolio of the World Bank rather than the situation analysis that was carried out in-country.

The tendency to blend out any evidence from cases that do not fit the larger agenda is also reflected in the constant switch between internal and external agencies during the *WBES 2020* production process. In terms of system theory, the World Bank is a good case in point to illustrate the workings of the World Bank's knowledge bank as a self-referential system. It only absorbs knowledge that perpetuates its own system logic. At the expense of being perhaps too polemic but for the sake of clarity, the point on self-referential systems may be summarized as follows: The *WBES 2020* as well as other World Bank publications reflect the tendency of the World Bank to talk with everyone, speak on behalf of many, and listen only to their own. The self-referentiality of knowledge production is also reflected in the SABER-Teachers project:

> *Why did the World Bank embark on SABER-Teachers?*
> When client countries ask World Bank front-line staff how top-performing countries tackle different issues related to teacher policies (e.g., teacher training, incentives or accountability), project leaders have to respond to such requests on a case-by-case basis—*either by using Bank publications and databases or taking the initiative* to find out more about policies in top-performing education systems. (World Bank, 2011b; italics inserted by author)

As the excerpt from the SABER-Teachers portal website indicates, the World Bank is its own frame of scientific reference, that is, "Bank publications and databases" are the only source of information worth considering. Academics rightfully wonder whether there would be any harm to pick up a book or read articles in refereed academic journals on issues related to teacher policy. Research on teachers is not a rare commodity and others already took the "initiative" to study the topic in great detail. It is striking that the only quasi-external source of authority for World Bank publications are databases or student achievement studies (TIMSS, PISA, PIRLS, etc.) published by OECD or IEA.

## *WBES 2020*: A FUNDRAISER FOR PILOT PROJECTS

Many multilateral, bilateral, and non-governmental organizations concentrate their efforts on funding pilot projects and hope that their projects are eventually funded from sources other than their own. They expect that the recipient government, upon successful completion of the externally funded pilot will scale up the project with funding from the education budget or from other external financial sources.

UNICEF Kyrgyzstan commissioned a donor involvement analysis that yielded interesting results with regard to the preferred aid modality of donors (UNICEF Kyrgyzstan, 2008). The study found that, with the exception of textbook publishing and standards reform, not one single donor-funded project was carried out nationwide. All donor-funded projects, including the multi-million dollar loans and grants by the World Bank, Asian Development Bank, and USAID were designed as pilot projects, concentrated in a particular geographic region of the country and targeting a relatively small number of institutions or individuals.

In several other countries of Central Asia, the Caucasus, and Mongolia, the role of funding incubator projects or pilot projects with innovative practices is typically reserved for NGOs, UNICEF, and UNESCO, which, despite their influence on the government, have to operate with limited funds. It is typical of these organizations to pilot innovative practices in the expectation that the government or larger donors carry on with institutionalizing or funding their incubator projects. In the Kyrgyz Republic, in contrast, the two development banks favor the same aid modality that typically smaller organizations with limited funding pursue. ADB, the World Bank, and later on, also the EFA Fast-Track Initiative merely funded pilot projects for a limited time period with little attention given to how their projects will be scaled up nationwide.[x] Small and large aid agencies alike are prey to the illusion that the government will eventually scale-up their pilot project and finance them from the national education budget. For example, the World Bank and the Open Society Institute in the Central Asia region both had the same unrealistic expectation with regard to the sustainability of their projects.

The cost factor, in particular for projects of large bilateral and multilateral donors is not to be underestimated. The pilot projects are, for a variety of reasons, too expensive to be replicated and scaled-up. There are also capacity costs associated with pilot projects that weaken the institutional capacity of an education sector. The management of these short-lived pilot projects, each funded by a different donor, absorbs the capacity and the time of government officials to administer their own educational system. Donor coordination alone is unlikely to solve the problem. Impact evaluations, in turn, are part of the problem rather than the solution in that they make the pilot projects exponentially more expensive than they already are.

What is almost entirely lacking in the discussion of results-based aid is a longitudinal analysis of externally funded reforms: what is left of these reforms five, ten, or fifteen years later? Given the preferred aid modality of the World Bank—funding one's own idea of "good education" overseas and presenting it as a global framework of education—there are few lessons to be learned from the past because most externally funded projects are terminated shortly after the funding dries up. The inability of the World Bank to independently reflect on its work, however, curtails institutional learning at the Bank. Given the preferred aid modality of the World Bank as well as that of other donor agencies—funding their own "best practices" in the form of expensive and short-lived pilot projects—one wonders whether the policies which are compiled under the cover of *WBES 2020* represent anything more than expensive, and in the case of the World Bank well-studied, pilot projects that very few countries, if any, have scaled up nationwide.

As mentioned in the introduction, *WBES 2020* was released in early 2011. It is too early to fully understand the impact of the comprehensive stakeholder review on World Bank operations. I end this chapter with an invitation to examine the following provocative question in five years from now: Was *WBES 2020*, in the end, nothing more than a compilation of pilot projects for which the World Bank sought additional funding so that recipient governments had the means to scale them up nationwide? These additional funds for pilot projects—framed as "best practices"—were meant to be mobilized from within the World Bank but also from other donors. Would such an outlook on a possible scenario explain the attempt of the World Bank to present its pilot projects as everyone's and nobody's "global framework of education"?

## NOTES

[i] The World Bank approach has been polarized by supporters and opponents to an extent that makes it difficult to nowadays summarize it without making any value judgments. Formulated positively, the World Bank stance on educational development may be summarized as an approach that focuses on results, measurement, and knowledge in an endeavor to increase effectiveness and at the same time reduce cost in the education sector. With the same forcefulness, however, the World Bank has been criticized for working behind a "façade of precision" (focus on results, measurement, knowledge) to ultimately carry out its broader economic agenda.

[ii] Jones' point on donor logic is well taken even if one may find his depiction of UNICEF as too harsh.

[iii] OECD has a similar role for governments in developed countries. There is a need to analyze the close relation between OECD and the World Bank that has evolved over the past few years.

[iv] A case in point is the long decade of neglect in rural education in Mongolia (1991-2003) that reduced the enrollment and increased the dropout of children (especially boys) from nomadic herder families. The Ministry of Education of Mongolia periodically requested external financial assistance for improving the infrastructure of schools in rural areas, many of which had boarding facilities for children from herder families. However, there simply were no international "best practices" or impact evaluations available to the Asian Development Bank (biggest donor in Mongolia) or the World Bank (mostly constrained to analytical work in Mongolia) to justify—vis-à-vis their own constituents in the banks—their involvement in rehabilitating the boarding school systems and the preservation of small multi-grade village schools that secured access for a population that, at the time, was not only nomadic but also widely dispersed (see Steiner-Khamsi & Stolpe, 2006).

[v] The five largest bilateral donors in terms of volume are the United States, United Kingdom, France, Germany, and Japan (see Aid Statistics 2010 compiled by OECD DAC).

[vi] Similarly, the EFA Fast Track Initiative was renamed in 2011 to Global Partnership for Education. The secretariat of EFA FTI remains based at the World Bank.

[vii] Once funding has been secured, recipient governments sometimes undermine the project objectives either by disengaging from project implementation (and delegating implementation to an externally funded Program Implementation Unit) or by refusing to scale up externally funded projects—most of them pilot projects—with their own funds from the national education budget. Several studies have dealt with the economics of policy borrowing (see Steiner-Khamsi, 2010; Steiner-Khamsi & Stolpe, 2006) and analyzed the financial reasons for the "global speak" of recipient governments.

[viii] The authors of the *WBES 2020* background papers are listed in the Acknowledgement section of *WBES 2020* (p. vi f.). Without any exception, the authors of these background papers are all World Bank staff.

[ix] The analysis of the *stavka* system in Tajikistan, funded by the World Bank, was the first study that compared the features of the weekly teaching load system (Russian: *stavka*) with the weekly workload system. It did not have an immediate impact on educational reform in Tajikistan for the reasons mentioned above, but the categorization of teacher salary systems was subsequently used for the preparation of a GMR background paper (Steiner-Khamsi et al., 2008) as well as for ten different UNICEF studies on teachers in the CEECIS region, Eastern and Southern Africa region, and Mongolia (see, in particular, UNICEF CEECIS, 2011, and UNICEF Mongolia, 2011).

[x] The World Bank's Rural School Project, for example, initially chose the two provinces Talas and Issyk-kul as two "pilot" provinces. Teaching methods, teacher training, teaching material, and other innovative practices that were piloted in these two pilot provinces were supposed to be disseminated to the other provinces of the country. The initial scaling-up plan for nationwide teacher training, for example, had already been dropped during the second year of the project because the pilot turned out to be more expensive and therefore non-replicable.

# REFERENCES

Alesina, A. & Dollar, D. (2000). Who gives foreign aid to whom and why? *Journal of Economic Growth, 5*(1), 33-63.

Bruns, B., Filmer, D., & Patrinos, A. H. (2011). *Making schools work. New evidence on accountability reforms.* Washington, DC: World Bank.

CIDA. (2011). *Securing the future of children and youth. CIDA's children and youth strategy.* Ottawa: Canadian International Development Agency.

DANIDA. (2010). *Freedom from poverty—Freedom to change. Strategy for Denmark's development cooperation.* Copenhagen: Danish International Development Agency.

DFID. (2009). *Learning for all: DFID's education strategy 2010-2015.* London: U.K. Department for International Development.

Duflo, E., Hanna, R., & Ryan, S. (2010). Incentives work: Getting teachers to come to school. Unpublished manuscript, Abdul LatifJameel Poverty Action Lab (JPAL). Cambridge, MA: Massachusetts Institute of Technology.

Jones, P.W. (1998). Globalisation and internationalism: Democratic prospects for world education. *Comparative Education, 34*(2), 143-155.

Jones, P. W. (2004). Taking the credit: Financing and policy linkages in the education portfolio of the World Bank. In G. Steiner-Khamsi (Ed.), *The global politics of educational borrowing and lending* (pp. 188-200). New York: Teachers College Press.

Jones, P. W. with D. Coleman (2005). *The United Nations and education. Multilateralism, development and globalization.* London and New York: RoutledgeFalmer.

King, Elizabeth (2011). *Education in 2020? Interview.* Washington, D.C.: Human Development Network, World Bank.

Luhmann, N. (1990). *Essays on self-reference.* New York: Columbia University Press.

Ministry of Foreign Affairs of Japan. (2010). *Japan's Education Cooperation Policy 2011-2015 is entitled Education for Human Security: Building Human Capacity, Nations and World Peace Through Educational Development.* Tokyo: MOFA.

Richey, L. A. & Ponte, A. (2008). Better (Red)TM than dead? Celebrities, consumption and international aid. *Third World Quarterly, 29*(4), 711-729.

Silova, I. & Steiner-Khamsi, G. (Eds). (2008). *How NGOs react. Globalization and education reform in the Caucasus, Central Asia and Mongolia.* Bloomfield, CT: Kumarian/Stylus.

Schriewer, J. (1990). The method of comparison and the need for externalization: Methodological criteria and sociological concepts. In J. Schriewer (Ed.), *Theories and methods in comparative education* (pp. 3-52). Bern: Lang.

Steiner-Khamsi, G. (2007). *The Stavka system in Tajikistan. Background, challenges, and recommendations for teacher salary reform.* Dushanbe: Ministry of Education, Education Modernization Project (funded by World Bank).

Steiner-Khamsi, G. (2010). The politics and economics of comparison. *Comparative Education Review, 54*(3), 323-342.

Steiner-Khamsi, G., Harris-van Keuren, C. with I. Silova & K. Chachkhiani (2008). Decentralization and recentralization reforms: Their impact on teacher salaries in the Caucasus, Central Asia, and Mongolia. Background Paper Prepared for the EFA Global Monitoring Report 2009. Paris: UNESCO EFA GMR.

Steiner-Khamsi, G. & Stolpe, I. (2006). *Educational import in Mongolia: Local encounters with global forces.* New York: Palgrave Macmillan.

Stone, D. (Ed.). (2000). *Banking on knowledge: The genesis of the Global Development Network.* London: Routledge.

UNICEF CEECIS. (2011). *Teachers: A Regional Study on Recruitment, Development and Salaries of Teachers in the CEECIS Region.* Geneva: UNICEF CEECIS.

UNICEF Mongolia. (2011). *UNICEF Mongolia Study on Teachers.* Authors: G. Seiner-Khamsi & B. Batjargal with O. Sarantsetseg and Kh. Munkhtsetseg. Ulaanbaatar: UNICEF Mongolia.

USAID. (2011). *Education: Opportunity through learning. USAID Education Strategy.* Washington, D.C.: USAID.

World Bank. (2006). *Public financing of education. Equity and efficiency implications.* Washington, D.C.: World Bank.

World Bank. (2010). *2020 Education Strategy. The World Bank Group's Education Sector Strategy 2020 Consultation Plan.* Washington, D.C.: World Bank.

World Bank. (2011a). *Learning for all. Investing in people's knowledge and skills to promote development. Education Sector Strategy 2020.* Washington, D.C.: World Bank.

World Bank. (2011b). *SABER-Teachers.* Brief on SABER. Teachers. Human Development Network. Washington, D.C.: World Bank.

*Gita Steiner-Khamsi*
*Teachers College*
*Columbia University, U.S.A.*

CHAPTER 2

BJORN H. NORDTVEIT

# WORLD BANK POETRY

*How the Education Strategy 2020 Imagines the World*

> Baa baa black sheep; have you any wool?
> Yes sir, yes sir, three bags full;
> One for the master; one for the dame
> And one for the little boy; who lives down the lane.

This well-known nursery rhyme had a different ending line until the middle of the eighteenth century, when the more palatable "one for the little boy who lives down the lane" substituted "none for the little boy who cries in the lane." The text in all probability refers to a royal tax of six shillings imposed on wool in 1275, representing one-third of the wool income that henceforth needed to be paid to "the master" (the king). The remaining two thirds would be claimed by "the dame," the church or monasteries. Nothing remains for the shepherd, the little boy who cries in the lane. Hence, "rather than being a gentle song about sharing things out fairly, it's a bitter reflection on how unfair things have always been for working folks throughout history" (Jack, 2008, p. 11). For four hundred years this text thus represented a critique of inequitable economic distribution practices, until it merged into mainstream child poetry. It is reflecting reality, but also shaping it in the form of creating a "discourse," an understanding about reality. The poignancy of the earlier imaginary has been replaced, by changing only a few letters, into a sweet little rhyme depicting a just and uncomplicated world.

Why does it matter and to whom does it matter how the World Bank imagines the world? As in the nursery rhyme above, inattention to inequality and injustice in text may produce or reinforce inequality and injustice in the real world. In this way, certain texts—or dominant discourses—create reality. It is my belief that the World Bank's texts represent such dominant discourse because they contribute to shape people's lives. A few seemingly trivial words from the World Bank can convince politicians to adopt policies with far-reaching consequences.

Since the antiquity, people have tried to understand how discourse constructs the world. As shown by Aristotle, the "fields of logic, rhetoric, and dialectics are all about arguments" (Walton, 2007, p. 7), but each of these fields approaches

*S.J. Klees et al. (eds.), The World Bank and Education, 21–32.*

argumentation in a different way. Here, I try to demonstrate how discourse can impel people to adopt certain ideologies or courses of action that may not, in fact, represent the best way of proceeding. In this vein, fallacy theory can show that a notion that "seems to be good in a certain way ... isn't in fact good in that way" (Woods, 2004, p. xx). This chapter seeks to demonstrate ways of constructing and planning a world that apparently seems to be good, but that may lead to other consequences than those intended. In particular, it seeks to reveal how the World Bank is imagining the world—and how it is at the same time creating the world in its image. The main research question of this chapter is to define how the *World Bank Education Strategy 2020* re-invents education and in which direction the strategy may influence national education policies.[1]

World Bank texts can be read as poetry—it is language that has evocative and suggestive qualities in addition to its apparent meaning. *Poetry* derivates from the Greek, meaning "a making" or "a creation"; hence, it is not neutral but creates reality. I seek to establish, through critical discourse analysis, how the World Bank strategy is creating a worldview. The analysis attempts to explore patterns within the strategy document—seeking to identify possible social consequences of how reality is being described. Using the allegory of "Baa, baa, black sheep," the study questions whether the World Bank world is where the little boy or girl gets his or her dues, or whether he or she remains crying in the lane. In its role as the world's largest external financier of education, the World Bank, with its strategy, becomes an international reference that will exert a great deal of pressure on individual countries and the development of their education systems in the years to come.

World Bank poetry is thus both text and a *discourse*, understood as constitutive of the social, encompassing not only language but also social phenomena (Laclau & Mouffe, 2001). Hence, the Education Strategy is not seen as an abstract document, but also as situated practice that is dynamic, flexible, and changing. The clash of various discursive practices may result in adaptation and transformation. World Bank poetry is often argumentative, in which the term "argument" is used as a "position that is reasoned out" (Wilson, 1986, p. 3). Other times, it is assertive, where claims are put forward without providing supporting reasons.

The text of the document (whether argumentative or assertive) is used to create a reality of the world—and of education—that is translated into implementation strategies; and into educational philosophies, aims and values. Norman Fairclough (2003) argues that discourse analysis focuses on interpretation of texts, on these texts' relation with social practice, and on the way they are made and disseminated in the world: "I see discourse analysis as oscillating between a focus on specific texts and a focus on what I call the 'order of discourse,' the relatively durable social structuring of language which is itself an element of the relatively durable structuring and networking of social practices" (p. 3). Terry Locke, drawing on Fairclough, segregates text analysis into four different categories: vocabulary (analysis of individual words), grammar; cohesion (argumentation), and text structure (Locke, 2004). The next sections of this chapter are dealing with the strategy's appearance and structure, as well as its vocabulary and cohesion (including argumentation and assertions), since these categories arguably reveal parts of the ideology that is underpinning the strategy.

TEXT STRUCTURE

The structure and vocabulary of the World Bank's education strategy are tools of persuasion. This in itself is not surprising or off-putting in any way—"in almost every kind of situation—language seems to have persuasive effects, whether calculated and intentional or not" (Toolan, 2011, p. 15). As far as the strategy goes, the persuasion is intentional; the World Bank would of course like us to adhere to its views. Hence, the title and internal architecture of the strategy are of interest, insomuch as they are windows into the document.

As for the title, the reference to the year 2020 (and not a range of years such as 2011-2020; or the MDG target date of 2015) gives a first impression of a vision that is reaching beyond the immediate future; it is felt like science fiction, with resonance to titles such as *2020 Vision* by Poul Anderson et al.(1980), or even to Arthur C. Clarke's various *Odyssey* books (*2001, 2010, 2061*...). The cover picture of the strategy document emphasizes this feeling: it is depicting the world shown from afar, with various symbols (mathematical, monetary, musical...) covering the continents—almost like carpets of magic. The continents themselves are seemingly reinvented, and the perspective is quasi-eliminating certain countries and drawing the viewers' regard towards Africa.

The subtitle of the strategy creates a sense of inclusion, and at the same time of great abstraction: *Learning for All: Investing in People's Knowledge and Skills to Promote Development*. The strategy concerns us all; the World Bank, presumably, is willing to invest in people to promote development. Little boys and girls are not left crying in the lane, neither are illiterate moms and dads. The vagueness of the vocabulary should be noted: what does the sentence "investing in people's knowledge and skills" mean? Who are these people? Which knowledge and skills? The subsequent text clarifies that "people" are "not just the most privileged or gifted," but also "girls, people with disabilities, and ethnolinguistic minorities" (pp. 4-5). The juxtaposition of these three "problem" categories and their opposition to the "privileged" and "gifted" are in itself interesting. As for the references to "Knowledge and Skills," the strategy indicates, "recent research shows that the level of skills in a workforce—as measured by ... PISA and TIMSS—predicts economic growth rates far better than do average schooling levels" (p. 25). The focus therefore goes beyond school retention and is related to the actual learning taking place at school and elsewhere. The references to skills are also pointing to the need of better "linkages between education systems and labor markets" (p. 44). The type of development referred to, here and elsewhere, is largely economic.

It should be underlined that terms commonly related to education, such as schools, teachers, or curriculum, are curiously absent from the title. It is as if the World Bank is creating knowledge and skills in a vacuum, through "investment." Later, this omission of references to schools and teachers is explained. The World Bank is operating with an "expanded" definition of education, which "includes the full range of learning opportunities available in a country, whether they are provided or financed by the public or private sector (including religious, nonprofit, and for-profit organizations)" (p. 5). The definition makes it clear that the World Bank seeks to continue previous practices of operating outside state-run school systems, drawing on a range of private entities for the implementation of various educational activities: "This more inclusive concept of the education system allows the Bank Group and its partner countries to seize opportunities and address barriers that lie outside the bounds of the system as it is traditionally defined" (p. 5). The first elements of the World Bank's views, then, are already present in the title, albeit in a hidden way–and are subsequently unpacked in the strategy's executive summary and in the main text: the strategy promotes skills that fit the labor markets, and the private sector should be a main implementation partner of the "service" of education.

The body of the document, laid out in the "Contents" list, is divided into four parts: first, the rationale for the strategy is given in the first section; then the second lays out the strategy; the third backs it up by providing an overview of the World Bank's "lessons" in education; and the forth section is providing the implementation arrangements. This logic composition is centered on the strategy. The structure, thus, is another example of persuasive argumentation: the World Bank is repeatedly trying to convince the reader that its policies are well founded. Detailed examples of this can be seen in the "lessons" section. For example, regarding the topic of economics of education, the World Bank indicates that it "has published more journal articles than 14 top universities—only Harvard University comes close" (p. 53). Hence, it is presenting itself as a direct competitor to the best universities; it is a "knowledge bank;" "a generator of new knowledge and a synthesizer of existing knowledge" (p. 53). This is a version of an *argumentum ad populum* in which the World Bank "appeal[s] to popular opinions and feelings to accept a conclusion or a course of action" (Walton, 2004, p. 15). This can be seen as a fallacy of irrelevance: the argument implies that the World Bank's publishing record is guaranteeing the soundness of its policies. The external debates, for example of public vs. private provision of education, and a clear positioning of the World Bank's stance in this debate, are omitted.

Other persuasive strategies, including evocative and sentimental ones, are employed from the very beginning of the document, when the World Bank is referring to human rights and the current state of the world (unemployment and global economic downturn) to justify its policies. The "disappointing" results of former schooling are related to lack of quality, making youth leave school and enter the workforce "without the knowledge, skills, or competencies necessary to adapt to a competitive and increasingly globalized economy" (p. 17). The needs of this global economy is one main rationale for the new education strategy, the others being rapid urbanization, the existence of a "youth bulge," and the emergence of new middle-income countries. A medical model of early childhood is presented to provide further evidence of the soundness and necessity of the strategy, and in particular, the need for early childhood education (see for example box 3 on pp. 27 and 28). It should be noted that the World Bank's text mixes educational arguments (e.g., early childhood education) and implementation arguments, such as the need for private provision of education. The relevance of this reasoning can be questioned.

All along the strategy document, marginal annotations are providing persuasive "snapshots" from the main text. Some are playing on the emotions of the reader, such as "Learning for All means ensuring that all students, not just the most privileged, acquire the knowledge and skills they need to live happy, productive lives" (p. 4). The reference to happiness is repeated in the strategy's first sentence which also contains a certain intertextuality with Adam Smith's *Wealth of Nations* (1904); we learn that "people are the real wealth of nations" and that education leads to "healthier, happier and more productive lives" (p. 11). Other annotations use rhetorical devises such as anaphora (repeating a word at the beginnings of each sentence, to add emphasis): "Invest early. Invest smartly. Invest for all" (p. 9). The casual reader, when browsing through the document, will get a first sense of the content through the information in these annotations. For the thorough reader, the marginal annotations will recapitulate essential tenets of the text, using a simple vocabulary, thus helping to assimilate the message. The general cohesion and architecture of the text, then, aim at bringing the reader to an understanding of the World Bank's position with regards to education, and persuade him or her to take up the same position. Presenting itself as a "learning bank" at par with universities such as Harvard, the World Bank's education strategy seeks to convince the reader about its strategies—its vision of the future—for 2020 and beyond.

## VOCABULARY AND COHESION

An analysis of the frequency of terms employed in the document further demonstrates how the World Bank is creating meaning.[ii] Not surprisingly, the top terms employed are related to key terminology of the sector, such as (in order of frequency) *education, World Bank, countries, development* and *strategy*. Then some terms emerge that are more surprising: *System* (with its inflexed variants systems, systemic) is used 320 times; *skill* is used 196 times (against 170 for *knowledge*), underlining the strategy's emphasis on employment and skills development. Likewise, *income* (used 128 times) is found much more frequently than other indicators of impact of education, such as *health* (43 times), *nutrition* (14 times), *equality* (21 times), *agriculture* (14 times), *literacy* (8 times), and *empower* (6 times). This use of vocabulary reveals what is most important for the World Bank, which is also found in the title of the strategy: improved skills for economic development.

As for the quality of education provided, it is noteworthy that the term *assessment* is used 123 times, *quality* 111 times, *improve* 147 times, *performance* 96 times, *results* 91 times, and *accountable* 50 times. The term *corruption* is used only 5 times–at the same level as *decentralization*. In terms of implementation, the terms *economic* (exact word match) is used 94 times, *finance* 52 times, and *private* is used 81 times. The term *state* (exact word match[iii]), as opposed to *nonstate*, is found 4 times; *public* (exact word match) is found 26 times, and *government* (exact word match—to avoid confusion with *governance*) is found 38 times. It is noteworthy that the term *private*, most often referring to private implementation and/or partnerships with private entities, is employed more frequently than the term *teacher*, which is used 66 times, or *curriculum/curricula* which is found only 9 times. For the World Bank, the quality of education is connected to improvements in assessment, governance and accountability—as well as the use of private provision for implementation of certain educational services. Teacher training and curriculum development, while underlined as important facets of the education strategy, are not given much space in the text. The strategy, however, does not dismiss these areas: it subordinates them to the system approach. Hence, education is presented as a technical management and governance issue, rather than a pedagogic process.

As for the education provided, the term *primary* is found 52 times, *secondary* 47 times, *tertiary* 37 times, *vocational* 17 times, *nonformal* 10 times, and *TVET* (technical and vocational education and training) 8 times (all these terms are exact word matches). As for the learners, the term *student* is employed (109 times), as well as *child/children* (91 times), *youth* (35 times), *girls* (38 times), *vulnerable* (4 times; exact word match), *disability* (11 times), *boys* (9 times), and *adolescent* (7 times). Likewise, for other stakeholders, the term *people* is used 100 times, *population/s* is used 49 times (exact word match), followed by *poor/er/est* (47 times), *community/ies* 30 (exact word match), *family* (20 times), and *parent* (15 times). *Marginalized* which appeared 5 times in the draft version of the strategy, only appears once in the final version: "improving education quality is a pro-poor objective, because quality is typically worse in the schools serving poorer and more marginalized communities" (p. 51). Again, the terminology is revealing: it is assumed that general improvements in education quality will trickle-down to schools in marginalized communities.

As evidenced by the vocabulary, the strategy emphasizes primary and secondary education, followed by tertiary. Nonformal education, including adult literacy training, which often is seen as key to skills development, is getting less space. There is an apparent contradiction, in that the title of the strategy insists so much on skills and employment for all people, including the poorest and most marginalized, whereas the strategy does not seem to reflect this in its vocabulary: for example, adult literacy training seems to be conspicuously absent from the strategy. A figure depicting the share of World Bank's lending in education (p. 49) confirms this contradiction. In the period covering 2006-10, adult literacy received 0.7 percent of the World Bank's educational funding; vocational training received 5.3 percent and pre-primary 3.3 percent. In the period from 1991-1995, literacy received 0.8 percent, vocational training 13.4 percent, and pre-primary 2.1 percent. The trend therefore seems to diminish the focus on literacy, non-formal adult education, and on vocational training. Nothing indicates that this new strategy will entail a fundamental shift in the World Bank's budgeting priorities.

A closer look at the cohesion (argumentation) of the text strengthens and nuances earlier findings: using a technical and business language, the World Bank is proposing two core directions—reform of education at country level, and building a "global knowledge base ... to guide [education] reforms" (p. 1). These reforms will focus on the inclusion of various private groups as providers of educational services, and at the same time increase accountability and effectiveness of the existing school system through school-based management, greater autonomy, and "effective assessment systems" (p. 33). Hence, even the references to education as a human right in the second sentence of the strategy document is used as a devise to introduce the terminology of smart investment: "Access to education, which is a basic human right enshrined in the Universal Declaration of Human Rights and the United Nations Convention on the Rights of the Child *is also a strategic development investment* [my emphasis]" (p. 1). Again the combination of different types of arguments (human rights *and* strategic investment) is used as a device to convince the reader about the World Bank's seriousness and to frame the analysis of education as a business investment from the beginning of the strategy. The angle of analysis, then, is not related to human rights, but to strategic development investments and, in particular, processes of implementation, or "service delivery."

This system approach, with emphasis on reform and accountability is deemed to be relevant everywhere. The World Bank world is divided into fragile states, and low- and middle-income countries. Different approaches could be followed for different categories: "Client groupings based on economic and educational development, overlaid on geographical location, can lead to clearer, more strategic priorities and assistance [than the prior geographic focus]" (p. 56). However, looking closer at the three groups, their differentiation (in terms of strategies) becomes less clear: "Countries in all three groups share many common challenges ... that are best addressed through a set of cross-cutting priorities ... such as increasing the efficiency and effectiveness of resource use, improving transparency and accountability in education systems, and promoting investments in high-quality learning opportunities" (p. 55). These crosscutting themes are not further explained. The investment and system approach—and presumably also the focus on the private sector, therefore seem to be universal strategies for the World Bank. Adaptation based on economic and educational development, as well as geographical location, is related to communication methods rather than to different strategies: "differentiating countries by both level of economic development and institutional capacity helps organize knowledge exchange and policy debate, staff assignments and training, as well as the identification and design of programs" (p. 55). These methods are not further described.

At the global level, this effort will be matched by establishing "system tools" for "assessments and benchmarking" (p. 7). The tools will also, presumably, strengthen the World Bank's own role as a "learning bank" and as a center of data and knowledge. A large part of the strategy is related to these system tools, much more than issues such as teacher education and curriculum development, which are hardly mentioned at all. The vocabulary and cohesion of the text thus mirror the text structure: the overall arguments are related to sound investments, private provision of a service, and system tools that, it is presumed, lead to better quality of education. These strategies are presented as a result of World Bank expertise and as a natural evolution of past strategies. Alternatives and debates are therefore irrelevant.

CRITIQUE

In critical discourse analysis, it is generally assumed that "facts can never be isolated from the domain of values or removed from some form of ideological inscription" (Locke, 2004, p. 25). Therefore, it is believed that the way the World Bank organizes data is in itself revealing of a certain ideology. A number of fundamental principles can be extrapolated from the World Bank strategy. As in the newer version of "Baa baa black sheep," these principles are not stated; they are taken for granted—they are a part of a pre-analytic imagining of the world. They are thus essential parts of World Bank poetry:

> The world is *just*.
> The world is on *the right track*.
> People are *good*.

These principles can be deducted from the strategy's non-problematic description of the state of the world. It is assumed (not stated) that people make informed, rational choices, and that they are mostly honest and efficient, or at least, that efficiency can be controlled for.

The notion of education as a human right is not emphasized. As the Global Campaign For Education, a network bringing together major NGOs and Teachers Unions in over 120 countries, noted in their response to a draft version of the World Bank Strategy (January 17, 2011, p. 2), "the strategy lacks recognition of education as a human right, a public good and a responsibility to citizens that the state has assumed." Likewise, the terms *justice* and *injustice* are not found in the strategy document. The World Bank strategy for education does not consider issues of wealth distribution, power relations, or the possible role of education as a tool to propagate disparities and to continue patterns of injustice.

The lack of references to human rights and justice does not mean that the World Bank ignores problems related to disparities and inequality. The draft version of the strategy was clearer in its disclosure of how it will address "disparities and disadvantages suffered by marginalized populations" (draft version, p. 56). These problems will be fixed by "going beyond the educational services delivered by the public sector," using for example "civil society organizations" and also establishing a "multisectoral development approach" (draft version, p. 57). Lack of education and disparity will therefore be addressed by the use of non-governmental suppliers to reach the marginalized population, as well as the provsion of additional health services and roads.

The strategy thereby seems to indicate that despite formerly insufficient provision of service, the world and the World Bank are now on the right track: lessons generated from former World Bank strategies show the way forward, and quality education and skills development, together with the provision of other needed services, will further improve the world. Such "right track" includes various levels of partnerships with the private sector, which are characterized as "good" as long as there is some level of regulation. The Global Campaign for Education, in its aforementioned reply to the strategy, noted that, "the strategy focuses too heavily on private sector and market-based approaches to education, and on education as an instrument to serve the job market" (p. 2). The reason for bypassing the government and using the private sector (including civil society organizations) is based on an "argument from consequence" in which "an argument ... draws on casual reasoning [and] ... projects a consequence that will likely follow as a result of some action or policy" and in which "the crucial factors to consider are the likelihood that the consequences will be caused by what is proposed" (Tindale, 2007, p. 183). The problem, of course, is that the World Bank rarely analyzes the consequences of privatization (or of other policies), in part because their strategy is based on prior practices (the "learning bank") as well as on "two phases of internal and external consultations [and] technical work on specialized themes carried out by staff across Bank units" (p. 17). The pre-analytic understanding of the World Bank is based on certain axioms (the need for constant and global economic growth, the primacy of the market, focus on processes rather than on pedagogy) and slight modifications from past strategies rather than the questioning of the *status quo* and the search for new directions.

Likewise, the strategy lacks engagement with pedagogical issues, such as teacher training and curriculum, or references to the hidden curriculum. Terms like rape or bullying are absent; and the possibilities of schools that are functioning as recruiting grounds for child soldiers or terrorists are not considered. Education is unproblematic and overwhelmingly positive, as long as its quality is measurable and assessed systematically. Teacher training and curriculum development are subordinated to system development, and referred to *en passant*; e.g., "The centerpiece of the learning strategy is learning for all. This goal is to be attained not only through more investments in inputs (e.g., more trained teachers or university professors, a better curriculum, more learning materials), but also *through greater attention to institutional changes in the education system* [my emphasis]" (p. 46). It continues:

> The new strategy emphasizes the importance of aligning governance arrangements, financing, incentives, accountability mechanisms, and management tools with national educational goals. It explicitly recognizes that the term "educational institutions" applies not only to formal public schools and universities, but also to learning opportunities offered by organizations outside of the government sector and formal education institutions. (p. 46)

The strategy mainly focuses on these systemic changes, rarely mentioning problems such as low-quality teachers, teachers supplementing their income through private tutoring (and thereby exasperating inequality), lack of materials, or curricula without any relevance to the local needs. Hence, education is reduced to an investment in a service and a set of logistic issues:

29

The strategy presents education as a management and governance process, promoting an overly technical and narrow view of management which fails to emphasize participation by civil society, teachers, parents and other direct stakeholders in such processes. The strategy lacks detail on the pedagogic process that is education and assumes that governance reform will automatically translate into positive outcomes at the school level. (Global Campaign For Education, 2011, p. 2)

The strategy repeatedly finds that "private entities are providing education to even the poorest communities, especially in areas that governments do not reach" and that "governments typically have to provide appropriate regulation and oversight to ensure the quality and relevance of privately provided services, as well as access for disadvantaged students" (p. 35). The draft version noted "private entities are important providers of education services to even the poorest communities" as long as "governments recognize their importance and provide appropriate regulation and oversight of private providers to ensure the efficiency and coherence of their education services" (draft version, p. 20). Private tutoring (also known as "shadow education"; see Bray, 2007), a worldwide phenomenon that is currently skewing the education systems towards enhanced provision for the rich, is not seen as a problem but rather as a solution. As noted in a marginal annotation, "a system approach can broaden the potential agenda for action in education policy, enabling governments to take advantage of a greater number of service providers and delivery channels" (p. 34).

The strategy is noteworthy for what it omits as much as for what it states. Education, and more specifically, the learning of skills is the solution to a number of societal ills: "Youth who drop out of school early are vulnerable to unemployment, poverty, teen marriage, pregnancy, and delinquency" (p. 26). Unfortunately, recent events in North Africa have shown that youth who have attended tertiary schooling also are vulnerable to unemployment and extreme poverty, and in some cases to desperation leading to self-immolation or other, more violent forms of resistance. The strategy addresses the problem of lack of connection between education and work—yet does not seem capable of proposing more inventive solutions than "recognizing employers as key stakeholders" (p. 44).

The document, in a nutshell, represents a coherent strategy of privatization and system approaches, which, it is believed, will lead to better teacher training and improved curricula. The World Bank presents itself as an unquestionable authority on education, which brings the public and private sectors into equilibrium and harmony, as "providers" of educational "services."

To sum up, the *World Education Strategy 2020* is a text that uses arguments and assertions inherent to World Bank ideology to convince its readers. It is a policy document, a World Bank vision for the future worldwide delivery of education. It in many ways remains poetry that is essentially positive and upbeat, imagining a happy world of 2020. In its way, it resembles the new version of "Baa baa black sheep," because it is hiding unfairness and injustice in a vocabulary of public-private *partnerships* (used 40 times) and *cooperation* (used 6 times; exact word match). These choices of words, constructs, and topics are not simply inconsequential preferences but rather a selection of priorities with significant direct and indirect consequences. The inattention to inequality and human rights in the strategy will produce or reinforce injustice in the real world through further privatization of education "services." The text is a dominant discourse and creates and shapes the reality for people's lives and for their relationship with local schools. And, although the poorest and the marginalized are included in the discourse as target groups (and as a focus of privatized education)—and healthcare, roads, and schools are planned for—one still must wonder whether, when the master and the dame have taken their dues, anything remains for the little boys and girls who stand crying in the lane.

## NOTES

i   Two versions of the Education Strategy have been considered for this chapter. NVivo word frequency analysis and quotations that refer to page numbers alone, concern the final version of the strategy, the PDF file dated April 12, 2011 and available on the World Bank's web site. Quotations referring to *draft version*, draw on the version discussed at the Board of Directors on April 12, 2011, which has a useful Annex 2, "Frequently Asked Questions on the World Bank Group's Education Strategy 2020." This annex is not present in the final version of the strategy (although both documents refer to the same date of April 12, 2011).

ii   The analysis of word frequency has been done through queries run in NVivo 9 (information analysis software from QSR International), displaying the thousand most frequently used terms in the sector strategy. Two basic queries have been used here; the first (and most frequently used in this chapter) counts all inflected variants of the word, using NVivo 9's stemmed word frequency function. In this mode, for example, the term *school* will be counted together with schools and schooling. Likewise, he term *assessment* will be counted together with *assess, assessed, assessing*, and *assessments*. In general, I found this to be the most logical way to proceed. In a few cases, indicated in the text as *exact word match*, I have used a query for the exact match of the term (see also note 3 below).

iii   To avoid confusion between the noun *state* and the verb *to state*, and/or the United *States*, it was necessary to run an exact word match analysis of this term, which still presented problems when it came up with 10 hits, many of which needed to be eliminated because of confusion between "the state of education," "fragile state," and what interested me, namely *state* (public) versus *private* implementation of educational services (which came up four times).

## REFERENCES

Anderson, P., Ellison, H., Niven, L., Vogt, A. E., Spinrad, N. & Bova. B. (1980). *2020 Vision*. New York: Avon Science Fiction.

Bray, M. (2007). *The shadow education system: Private tutoring and its implications for planners*. Paris: UNESCO International Institute for Educational Planning

Clarke, A.C. (2000). *2001: A Space Odyssey*. New York: ROC.

Fairclough, N. (2003). *Analysing discourse: Textual analysis for social research*. London: Routledge.

Global Campaign for Education (GCE). (2011, January 17). *Response to the World Bank Sector Strategy*. www.ifiwatchnet.org

Jack, A. (2008). *Pop goes the weasel: The secret meanings of nursery rhymes*. London: Penguin Books.

Laclau E. & Mouffe, C. (2001). *Hegemony and socialist strategy: Towards a radical democratic politics* (2nd edition). London: Verso.

Locke, T. (2004). *Critical discourse analysis* (Continuum Research Methods). New York: Continuum International Publishing Group.

Smith, Adam (1904 [1789]). *An inquiry into the nature and causes of the wealth of nations.* London: Methuen & Co.

Tindale, C. W. (2007). *Fallacies and argument appraisal.* Cambridge: Cambridge University Press.

Toolan, M. (2011). How does literary language move us? On being 'immersed' and emotionally engaged by literary narratives. In B.P. Ibáñez, M. Muñoz, & M. Conejero (Eds.), *Con/texts of persuasion.* Problemata Literaria 69. Kassel: Edition Reichenberger.

Walton, D. (2004). *Relevance in argumentation.* New Jersey: Erlbaum.

Walton, D. (2007). *Media argumentation: Dialectic, persuasion, and rhetoric.* Cambridge: Cambridge University Press.

Wilson, B. A. (1986). *The anatomy of argument.* Lanham, MD: University Press of America.

World Bank Group. (2011). *Education Strategy 2020: Learning for all: Investing in people's knowledge and skills to promote development.* Washington DC: World Bank Group. www.worldbank.org/educationstrategy2020

World Bank Group. (2011). *World Bank Education Strategy 2020.* Discussed at the Board of Directors on April 12, 2011. Draft version.
http://www.gse.upenn.edu/pdf/iaeln/world_bank_ed_strategy_2011.pdf

Woods, J. (2004). *The death of argument: Fallacies in agent-based reasoning.* Applied Logic Series, Vol. 32. Dordrecht: Kluwer Academic Publishers.

*Bjorn Harald Nordtveit*
*School of Education, Center for International Education*
*University of Massachusetts at Amhurst, U.S.A.*

CHAPTER 3

SANGEETA KAMAT

# THE POVERTY OF THEORY

*The World Bank's System Approach to Education Policy*

## INTRODUCTION

In the early decades of the World Bank's ambitious mission of crafting a "World Without Poverty," aid to education was accorded low priority among its extensive loan packages and policy formulations aimed at developing nations. Development scholars lamented the World Bank's benign neglect of education, especially given its directive role in establishing development priorities that were followed by other multilateral and bilateral agencies. The World Bank's focus for much of the 1960s and 1970s was on large infrastructure projects such as hydroelectric dams, modernizing agricultural production and in the social sectors on reducing maternal mortality, infant mortality and promoting family planning for population control. From the mid-1980s onwards education came into prominence in the World Bank's development agenda, and today it is the largest donor of education aid to developing nations (Mundy, 1998; Bonal, 2002). Rather than cause for celebration, the Bank's record in the education sector over the last three decades has caused much consternation and anguish among those struggling to build a democratic and equitable education system in developing nations.

Three decades of World Bank policy in the education sector have been marked by remarkable shifts and turnarounds, with the latest change in direction evident in its newly launched report *Learning for All, World Bank Education Strategy 2020* (hereafter, *WBES 2020*). One significant turnaround by the Bank has been on higher education. For nearly two decades as part of its structural adjustment conditionalities in exchange for loans the Bank would insist that countries divest from higher education and focus exclusively on primary education arguing that rates of return were much higher in primary education and that higher education benefited elites the most and accrued largely individual benefits and low social returns. With expanding demand for higher education in developing countries and the growth of a global information technology economy, the Bank's emphasis on only primary education has become untenable. The Bank has done a volte face, unexpectedly waking up to the importance of indirect benefits of higher education to society to justify investment in this sector. After four decades of de-emphasizing higher education, the Bank's position is that a reputable and thriving national

*S.J. Klees et al. (eds.), The World Bank and Education,* 33–47.

higher education system is absolutely essential for developing countries to be viable and competitive in the global knowledge economy (Post et al., 2004).

In *WBES 2020*, the Bank has moved to a expansive all-inclusive position on education that does not pit one segment of education against another but concedes that attention and investment is necessary at all levels of education and that education as a whole is integral to achieving the most fundamental development goals. These dramatic swings and variations in the World Bank's education policy over three decades are presented as based on 'hard data' and an exercise in evidence based policy-making. However, Mundy's research shows that the World Bank faces a growing "legitimacy deficit" that has made this powerful institution more responsive to pressures from its client states (2002). Notwithstanding the World Bank's evolving perspective on education that now appears more closely aligned with its client states and leading international agencies in education such as UNESCO, a sustained examination of the World Bank's changing policy directives reveal that a predetermined logic of neoliberal economics underlies each new policy shift. In other words, the World Bank's new position appears more inclusive, valuing education for itself and in the interests of developing countries but as I attempt to demonstrate in this paper, the rhetoric masks the true implications of the World Bank's new strategy that is oriented toward maintaining the present day unequal and exploitative world economy.

In the following section, I critically examine the neoliberal economic doctrine that permeates all sectors of World Bank policy making and casts its long shadow on education. As a consequence, even when the World Bank states in grandiose terms that there is no better tool than education to "unleash the potential of the human mind" (World Bank, 2011, p. 6) and that equitable education is an essential part of achieving the Millenium Development Goals (World Bank, 2011, p. 6), its policy recommendations replicate an economistic and instrumentalist approach to education. *WBES2020* is a compelling illustration of how even as the strategy is couched in democratic egalitarian terms as "learning for all," the neoliberal orientation operates as the basic framework of the strategy and informs key policy recommendations that negate this ethical ideal. Moreover, the "system approach" that the World Bank proposes as offering a comprehensive framework to guide education reform has echoes of Parsonian systems theory embodying the same fatal flaws of Parson's theory of social action, a theory that eschews historical, cultural and political-economic analysis. Similar to Parsonian systems theory, it outlines a pragmatic set of strategies but does not offer a principled direction or ethical reasoning on the raison d'etre of education for a rapidly transforming global society and economy.

## NEOLIBERALISM AND THE EDUCATION SECTOR— THE WORLD BANK'S LEGACY

The post cold war context and the breakup of the Soviet Union provided the ideal conditions for discrediting development economics that derives from Keynesian economics and the idea of the welfare state to make way for the ascendancy of neoliberal economics characterized by a strong anti-state and pro-market approach to growth and development. Known as the Washington Consensus, a phrase popular in the early 1990s to describe the consensus among Washington based think tanks, lobbyists, U.S. administration and the World Bank and the IMF (notable here is that both agencies are regarded as part of Washington's inner circle and less as international agencies), neoliberal economics was first implemented in South American and Caribbean countries at the behest of the U.S. government, and soon after in several African nations. The World Bank and the IMF became leading global agents of neoliberal economics by enforcing a regime of policies and conditions on developing countries known as the structural adjustment program (SAP) that required countries to liberalize trade barriers, eliminate subsidies, dismantle public services, privatize, deregulate, and promote markets as extensively as possible while "shrinking" the state. In exchange for loans, recipient countries were forced adhere to SAP policies and conditionalities. Any deviation from structural adjustment program threatened suspension of further loans and aid not only from the World Bank but from other bilateral agencies and commercial banks as well.

Several scholars have documented the disastrous results of structural adjustment on education in Latin American and African nations in the 1980s where SAPs were aggressively implemented (Samoff, 1994; Reimers, 1994). Before the implementation of World Bank reforms and conditionalities in 1986, Tanzania's primary school enrolment rates were almost a hundred percent, but within a few years of the structural reforms on the public sector including primary education, enrolment rates dropped sharply. Almost half of the country's children missed out on their legal right to primary school enrolment due to World Bank reforms. As per the structural adjustment program, the Tanzanian government could no longer subsidize primary education and had to charge tuition and other fees to downsize state expenditure and encourage private expenditure. The rationale provided by the World Bank was that since most families in Tanzania send their children to school it proves that there is demand even among poor families. This demand should be successfully tapped to earn revenue for debt payments rather than be subsidized by the state. The gains that Tanzania had made in universal primary education in the early postcolonial period were lost entirely due to the World Bank's flawed economic reasoning. It is plainly evident who stood to gain the most from the World Bank's expert advice on the removal of subsidies to primary education, the World Bank's shareholders, all powerful rich countries of the Western world. For two decades since, Tanzania spent a third of its budget for debt repayments, four times what it spent on primary education. Tanzania's experience with World Bank reforms and conditionalities is by no means unique and is common among all the countries of Latin America and sub-Saharan Africa.

Primary education was thus one of the early victims of the World Bank's neoliberal policies, but so also was higher education. Higher education was seen as unreasonably subsidized by governments of developing nations. To justify public divestment from higher education, the World Bank once again used a spurious economic argument of rates of return to argue that higher education benefits have lower rates of return to the economy and that returns are really to individual income hence it is good economic sense for individuals to pay. Higher education's vital role for national development in postcolonial societies and the need for state investment in this sector, albeit widely acknowledged, was minimized by the World Bank. Internal to the World Bank there was strong opposition to this reform but it prevailed nevertheless (see Heyneman, 2003). These instances illustrate how the World Bank is directed by neoliberal orthodoxy and not sound social science reasoning or empirical evidence as it claims. It also indicates that it suited the World Bank to have a public image as a development bank that represents the interests of its debtors (i.e., developing nations) but it consistently acted as a commercial bank, prioritizing the interests of its shareholders (in this case, developed countries) (Pereira, 1995).

The severe hardships caused by the World Bank's structural adjustment program have instigated food riots and protests against visiting World Bank officials in many developing countries (Patel, 2008). Modest social and economic gains made by developing countries in the early postcolonial period were lost and poverty and inequality have worsened. The spectacular failure of its policies and the backlash in developing countries was a wakeup call for the World Bank and led to minor modifications in the neoliberal orthodoxy. The World Bank conceded that the state has an important role in achieving development goals and that markets and the state are not necessarily antagonistic to each another but are mutual partners in economic growth. The current position of the World Bank is that building state capacity for effective governance is as important as expanding private sector growth. It is important to note here however that market-led growth remains the guiding logic for World Bank policies with the state as facilitator of the process. The *WBES 2020* reflects this renovated Washington Consensus, and once endorsed by the World Bank it has become the operative framework for the field of international development and aid policy in general.

## THE WORLD BANK IN THE NEW GLOBAL ENVIRONMENT

An analysis of the *WBES 2020* shows that while the World Bank remains faithful to neoliberal economic doctrine, in other words, firmly pro-market and pro-privatization and rejects the principles of a welfare state, the new education strategy reflects an amended policy that takes into account a significantly altered global economic landscape. Post-war development policy presumed a division of the world into developed and underdeveloped economies with the latter serving primarily as sources of cheap raw material and unskilled labor. Today, this global economic arrangement, though still largely prevalent, has been partially destabilized with new centers of economic growth emerging in Asia and Latin America, while China and India, two of the world's most populous countries represent two of the world's strongest economies with high growth rates. The stability of the post-war, post-communist world in which the U.S. reigned as the global hegemon has come unhinged to a significant degree. Juxtaposed with the emergence of new regional powers located in the erstwhile "Third world," the economic slowdown and soaring sovereign debt to GDP ratio in advanced countries of the West, and particularly the United States has resulted in an unpredictable and precarious situation for global investment, and for growth and employment trends. Add to this the imploding economies of European nations and the volatility of global capital flows that neither states nor global institutions such as the World Bank, the IMF and the WTO are able to restrain, and we are indeed dealing with a new economic environment that global policy actors have yet to come to grips with.

The reorganization of the world economy or for that matter the 2008 financial crisis in Europe and the U.S. were not anticipated by the World Bank despite its scores of experts and masses of data that presume to foretell world development trends. The recalibration of development strategy in education and other sectors is the World Bank's attempt to come to terms with the new global reality, but as I argue in this essay, in ways that uphold the interests of its shareholder economies and their capitalist classes. Enumerated in greater detail in its *New World, New World Bank Group: (I) Post-Crisis Directions*, a background document released in April 2010, the report on *Post-Crisis Directions* marks the financial crisis of 2008 as a turning point that has led the World Bank to reassess its current priorities and also call for a change in its own mode of operations if it is to be relevant as a leader in shaping world development policy. The report is unusually frank in its opening, conceding that while there have been some development gains the optimism of the last two decades have been ill-founded. Beginning in the 1990s, the information technology sector generated unexpected windfalls in terms of investments and profits, new markets and skill sets, and a greater flow of ideas and information across borders that seemed to finally announce the passing of the cold war era into a new global order where technological innovations of the free world would lead us toward development and progress. The optimism of this period was short lived. The authors identify the Wall Street crisis of 2008 and its international impact as reasons for the new pessimism stating that, "Events of the last two years have changed this outlook with progress stalled or reversed and millions pushed back into poverty" (2010, p. 8). In other parts of the report, worrying trends in global poverty and inequality are highlighted as elements of an impending crisis. Given that the World Bank has always maintained an optimistic outlook regardless of very bleak circumstances for developing and debtor nations, admitting to an imminent crisis on a world scale is highly unusual for the World Bank and not something to be taken lightly. The *Post-Crisis Directions* report reveals yet again the World Bank's bias toward its primary shareholders. It recognizes a crisis only when the Euro-American economies are at peril. No alarm bells were rung in the aftermath of the Mexican peso crash and bailout in 1994, or the East Asian economic crisis in 1997, or the Argentine financial collapse in 2001-2002.

The World Bank presents *WBES 2020* as its response to the financial crisis of 2008 and advocates a "system approach" as a viable strategy to move the world in a "post-crisis direction," primarily by "creating opportunities for growth" and "targeting the poor and vulnerable" (p. 7). One can only read with incredulity the World Bank's claim that a more comprehensive approach to education planning is required that accords importance to the social (e.g., health services), the economic (work skills), the role of technology (mobile telephony), infrastructure (roads) and political will in achieving the millennium development goal of Education for All. To those working in the field of development, the relevance of these factors is hardly revelatory and did not need a Euro-American financial collapse as a wake-up call. Equally incredible is the notion that a system's approach is about considering all societal actors as stakeholders in delivering educational services, be it the private sector, the state, or community and religious ("faith-based") initiatives. The image evoked here is if only everyone were to put shoulder to wheel, we would achieve education for all in no time at all. In its unproblematic clubbing together of all actors and institutions as part of the universal education mandate, the World Bank would have us believe that the world comprises of unmarked generic agents with a shared interest in universal education without separate and conflicting interests and positions on the matter.

The World Bank shies away from the fundamental question that drives the new strategy: how exactly does the new approach move the world in a post-crisis direction? If the World Bank were sincere about adopting a system's analysis to avert a repeat of the 2008 crisis, it would begin by asking: What are the roots of the crisis of 2008? What does the crisis reveal about the nature of the world economy? Is the direction of the world economy compatible with sustainable livelihood opportunities, balanced growth, good governance, and community empowerment (the World Bank's stated development mission)? How does the new education strategy avert another economic crisis? There is a deafening silence on these questions, on concretely identifying how the new education strategy will redress elements of the crisis.

If one were to set aside *WBES2020* for a moment, logically one would expect to find an explanation of the 2008 economic crisis in the *Post-Crisis Directions* report, but here too you will be disappointed. The report begins with an exaggerated proclamation that the "[T]he most acute phase of the global crisis is now behind us" (2010, p. 1) and goes on to elaborate on the strategy for recovery which reiterates the World Bank's programs of the neoliberal period: greater private sector participation, effective national governance, better international coordination with the World Bank as the master coordinator, and individual incentives for social programs such as conditional cash transfers. How these policies will help overcome or mitigate the crisis caused by "jobless" recovery, or "corporate/financial institutional failures," or "asset price bubbles" or excessive "sovereign debt," identified by the World Bank as the challenges to global recovery (2010, p. 3) is left to our imagination. Tackling this question in a forthright manner would mean examining the fundamentals of the world economic system, its laws and politics that result in periodic crisis, in other words, we need a systems analysis that critiques the system rather than a "system approach" that simply holds it together, however provisionally.

What I have so far outlined is the failed promise of the World Bank's system's approach. Following Foucault's suggestion, the more important task is to examine not what *WBES 2020* does not achieve, but to ask what are its true consequences?

In this section, I focus on the policy proposals in *WBES* to show that they achieve little by way of mitigating global inequality and instead the current package of reforms propel us further into a more unequal world and into deeper social and economic crisis. I explain how the renovations in the World Bank's education strategy represent an effort to contain the global economic crisis and secure the future of the capitalist classes.

The World Bank's new motto "learning for all" while rhetorically implies inclusiveness actually institutionalizes inequality through its key recommendations. Primary among these is the way in which the motto "learning for all" is operationalized in the new strategy. The World Bank adopts the rather clichéd observation that learning occurs in different contexts, inside and outside schools, and in formal and non-formal ways and translates it into a new policy orientation wherein even those who may never have access to formal education would be accounted for as meeting EFA (Education for All) targets. This reformulation effectively permits governments and international institutions to minimize the salience of quality formal education for economic and social mobility in the current economic context and places different forms and contexts of formal instruction and even non-formal learning on par with formal education. In the current economic context where degrees and formal qualifications of all varieties, dubious and otherwise, have become even more essential to survival in a competitive world economy, those who are excluded from formal education will be excluded from worthwhile opportunities in the current economy.

The EFA mission endorsed in the MDG goals is to expand access to quality formal education in order to achieve democratic and equitable development. In abandoning this commitment, the World Bank's current policy will further widen the gap between those that benefit from quality formal education and the millions who will never be able to access the job opportunities and rewards that naturally seem to follow such an education.

A second part of the World Bank's strategy of achieving EFA by any means necessary is related to the provision of education. The new policy determines that anyone investing in some form of schooling and instruction should be considered legitimate stakeholders in the EFA mission, along with states and elected governments. Faith-based initiatives and private entrepreneurs in the education sector are welcomed as valuable partners in the new strategy to help achieve the EFA mission. To concede ground to private actors, whether faith based non-profit initiatives or profit oriented investors is to forfeit education as a human right (a value commitment the strategy paper mentions in passing). As we already know, the growth of private education does not result simply in greater access as the World Bank claims but also leads to highly stratified education markets, intensifies competition for access in which large swathes of young people are poorly served or not at all, and allows investors to reap profits from the desperation of poor and middle class families. In absolving states from being the primary providers of education, and encouraging the growth of private providers the World Bank institutionalizes inequality by guaranteeing unequal access and uneven quality of education.

While the World Bank's support for for-profit private providers is deeply problematic, it is not surprising at all and is consistent with neoliberal ideology. However what is quite astounding is the World Bank's endorsement of faith-based groups in education. Though not limited to the South Asian subcontinent, the growth of schools sponsored by religious groups has led to a serious political and cultural crisis and conflict in the region. It has not only significantly eroded secular and democratic culture in these countries and led to an assault on gender and sexuality rights but the spread of religious based schools has also provided the basis for an extended war on terror in the region (Gupta, 2010; Nisar, 2010). The consequences of US funding of fundamentalist Islamic schools in Pakistan and Afghanistan, a legacy of cold war politics continue to reverberate around the world perpetuating endless war and conflict in the region and outside. There is sufficient scholarship that disproves the World Bank's expectation that the influence of conservative religious groups can be curtailed by greater monitoring of these groups by states and funding agencies. Recent studies on Pakistan, Indonesia and Britain show that policy that endorses faith based initiatives ultimately strengthens the hands of reactionary community "leaders" and weakens secular democratic ideals and marginalizes feminist and minority struggles (WAF-SBS, 2007; Zia, 2009a, 2009b; Nisar, 2010).

The efforts of progressive democratic minded citizens in these countries that have been strenuously engaged in pressuring their governments to scale back their support for religion-based schools have had little success. Governments in these countries as elsewhere find it more convenient to pander to the religious right that albeit represent a minority of the population but are extremely powerful and militant. Further, these groups often do not depend upon state funds or development aid to run schools and hence can easily disregard the regulations of state and international agencies. The World Bank's endorsement of faith-based initiatives will only embolden the religious right whose political influence in South Asia and Africa has been growing in the last two decades. These are serious concerns that are shared by citizens in recipient and donor countries, yet are wholly ignored in the World Bank's strategy document. Ten years after September 11th and the relentless war on terror and terrorist warfare that continues to devastate whole societies it is scandalous and highly irresponsible of the World Bank to blithely promote faith based groups in education all in the name of achieving EFA targets.

My review of *WBES 2020* shows that key policy prescriptions in the new strategy significantly contradict the World Bank's own stated intentions of "education for all" for economic and sustainable development. The strategy may have a positive impact on EFA targets, especially when the basic conception of education has been reformulated to include anything remotely identifiable as learning, but it is also designed to exacerbate existing inequities and dilute the idea of education as a universal human right. When read as part of the logic of neoliberalism however the strategy makes sense. The basic assumption of neoliberalism is that free markets, privatization, and deregulation are the drivers of economic growth from which progress and prosperity naturally follow. Neoliberal doctrine supports the creation of markets in sectors where they do not exist (such as education, health and the environment) and limiting the state to security and monitoring functions that guarantee an enabling environment for markets. Without explicit reference to neoliberalism of course, *WBES 2020* outlines precisely such a strategy. Redefining education to mean learning of diverse kinds in diverse sites is a technique of deregulation; it will be impossible to have consistent and uniform benchmarks and criteria to determine quality education at national and global levels. Further, in keeping with the disciplinary strategies of neoliberalism, the World Bank's plan to enforce standards for performance assessments of teachers and learners shifts risk onto learners and their families who "choose" the education that suits them. The input side is deregulated and left to the free will of the state and its citizens, while outputs will be assessed against universal standards set by global actors. And we are expected to believe that this makes for a level playing field for all countries and their citizens! Second, the strategy of opening education to private providers of all manners, including for faith based and for-profit groups is intended to multiply markets in education and greatly expand the private sector in education, which undermines the importance of public education as the basis for equitable education and a democratic polity.

In the new strategy, the World Bank's advice is that states focus on establishing the right incentive structures, accountability mechanisms, and operational standards for an efficient and results oriented education system. The reformulation of the role of the state from primary provider of school and university education to an entity whose main function is to regulate and monitor the sector in ways that allow entrepreneurial activity to flourish is also characteristic of neoliberal economics. Neoliberalism as the economic theory that serves as the framework for the strategy paper finds no mention in *WBES 2020* (or other documents of the World Bank). There is an effort however to rationalize World Bank policy as based on a sound theoretical framework in its repeated references to a "systems" approach. In the following section, I discuss the World Bank's system approach and show how it does not contain even the rudiments of a system approach.

## THE RELEVANCE OF A DIALECTICAL APPROACH

The assumption in the World Bank's analysis is that if all societies followed the same prescriptions of export-led growth, private sector growth and an efficient results oriented government then the same outcomes are guaranteed, i.e., stable economic growth. The analytical model assumes that the development of countries follows a linear progression and with the correct mix of technical fixes all countries will exhibit the virtues of liberal capitalism, good governance, and civic democracy. This is an outdated theory of development that has been extensively critiqued and history continues to confound these assumptions. A historical analysis of global capitalism shows that each country has its own trajectory of development and therefore the same reforms and inputs will produce differential and uneven outcomes in each context. The path dependency of particular countries is also intimately connected to their political and economic relations with other societies, relations that are shaped by history and geopolitics. Finally, national economies and particular regions and classes within nation-states are linked in highly disparate ways to the globalized and financialized economy that produce highly uneven and contradictory trends within the same region for different social groups, which begs the question of what one means by *national* development in the present historical conjuncture.

While the World Bank acknowledges that the global situation is significantly altered and requires new thinking and new strategies, it continues to assume a generalized model of development for all countries. The transformations in the world economy itself are underplayed and underestimated in terms of their implications. For one, the financial crisis of 2008 is presented as episodic and its structural determinants and long term impacts are not examined. Second, recent developments in Latin America where left-leaning governments have been elected, the crisis in U.S. and European economies, and the influence of emerging economies of India and China portend a historic reorganization of the world economy with significant political and economic implications. Methodological nationalism however continues to inform the World Bank's analysis of the global economic crisis. Interdependencies and disjunctures between economies, regions, and sectors are not examined and instead it continues to adopt a hermetic view of societies. Nation-states are assumed to be homogeneous entities whose economies can be categorized quite simply as high-income, middle-income, or as low-income countries. In the World Bank's view, the distinctive feature about the new reality is that a few low-income countries have now advanced into the middle-income bracket. Really not much else has changed! Should we infer from this that if we just continue to follow the World Bank's development wisdom, in another fifty years perhaps another few poor countries will move into the middle-income bracket and so on until all countries are at the same level? The World Bank of course is not foolish enough to make such predictions, given the climate crisis, urgent ecological issues and uncertain world economy but it's the "trickle down" theory all over again that we are implicitly asked to repose faith in.

To understand the nature of the current global economic crisis, we have to turn to Marx and Marxist scholars who have elaborated the most systematic theory of capitalism to show how crisis is an unavoidable and recurrent feature of capitalism (Marx, 1990; Polanyi, 1944; Galbraith, 1954; Keynes, 1973). Contemporary scholars have found Marxian economics to be instructive in understanding the roots of the recent global financial crisis whose origins are traced to the 1970s (Harvey, 2005; Hoogvelt, 2010). Marxian analysis of capitalism also explains the rise of certain national economies and the decline of other erstwhile powerful economies. To briefly restate the observations of Marxist scholars on economic trends from the 1970s is that consumption in old core economies was saturated and this negatively impacted capital accumulation and led to a decline in the rate of profit. The search for new markets and new production systems that would accelerate the rate of profit resulted in the globalization of production (global assembly line that reduced costs significantly), the financialization of capital (speculative capital markets disconnected from the actual production of goods and services), and the globalization of finance (deregulated free flows of capital across national borders in search of untapped resources and markets). Neoliberal doctrine provided the ideological justification for these economic policies that emphasized the positive aspects of "self-regulating" markets and capital. Once again Marxian dialectics comes to our rescue to show that the "solution" to the problem of capital accumulation creates additional new problems that have far reaching and deep structural consequences. The increased social polarization, stark levels of uneven development within and between countries, the volatile nature of capital flows that have sunk entire national economies, the endemic disequilibrium between deficit and capital country accounts, increased exploitation that has created a global elite of super rich and rising numbers of working poor and an intensified ecological crisis are some of the direct consequences of the globalization and financialization of capital.

The search for new ways to increase profitability and accumulation lead the capitalist classes to adopt transnational labor strategies (e.g. outsourcing) through which new classes ascend in other countries that are structurally positioned to benefit from the capital flows and new labor markets. The rise of the Indian and Chinese economies are a result of these dynamics of capitalism and not due to "trickle down" theory of development nor is it the success story of capitalism as neoliberal gurus would have us believe. Rather the rising economic powers of India and China represent the uneven development of world capitalism, where certain groups and classes within these countries are able to make good of the new forms of capital mobility and become more closely aligned with the Euro-American capitalist classes, that in turn unleash new dynamics and contradictions that are yet to be fully realized. The *Post-Crisis* report and *WBES 2020* recognizes this new reality but lacking a Marxist analysis of these world historical changes the experts are unable to identify the contradictions that are emergent or acknowledge the impossibility of equitable development within this economic model.

The World Bank's *Post-Crisis* background paper while it admits to crisis (and hastily concludes we are over it) is completely silent on the historical trajectory of this crisis and how the rules of capitalism itself engender crisis, each one different and more intense than the next. The report evades analyzing the roots of the crisis and jumps straightaway into providing remedies to reign in the crisis. So much for the World Bank's scholarly repute! It is no surprise therefore that in laying out the challenges of the new economy and the need for "rethinking development after the global crisis" (World Bank, 2010, p. 4), the World Bank's proposals in the *Post-Crisis* discussion paper and *WBES 2020* are wholly inadequate to reigning in the structural and systemic crisis of global capitalism. The proposals offered are to extend the reach of markets, strengthen exports, expand private sector activity, and improve links between education and labor markets. In other words, there is no new paradigm of development on offer but rather it is business as usual.

How do we improve links between education and labor markets in ways that will contribute to meaningful and secure employment in a world economy driven by jobless economic growth (a concern identified in the World Bank's *Post-Crisis* background paper under the title "Risks to the Global Recovery") is the conundrum we are faced with, but these connections find no place in *WBES 2020*. In what sectors and what kinds of jobs will be available in a global economy in which speculative trade and primitive accumulation yield the maximum profits and therefore drive investment? What are the projected growth areas in the global economy that will yield decent living wage employment for youth who represent the majority of the population in developing and emerging economies? The report is silent on these germane issues even as all the evidence shows that maximum profits in the global economy accrue not from manufacturing and industrial production but from speculative trade and from investment in natural resources such as minerals, rare metals, land and water. Moreover, an overwhelming number of jobs in the present economy are unskilled and low paid often in hazardous conditions. Given this is the reality of the global capitalist economy, how should we consider the purpose of education in such a context? To approach these questions with some degree of seriousness the World Bank would need to abandon its sacrosanct commitment to the neoliberal model of economic development and concede that markets, competition and profits are not harmonious with sustainable development, meaningful work and equitable societies.

In the face of jobless growth, high rates of unemployment, and a global recession, the best hope the World Bank holds out for young people is to become "skilled and agile" workers (2011, p. 6). According to *WBES 2020*, individual and national competitiveness is best ensured by education systems that train for such a highly skilled and agile workforce. The use of the term "agile" is never quite explained in the strategy paper. Within neoliberal discourse however it serves as a code word for an ideal kind of worker—one who does not aspire to stable secure employment at any stage of her career and is psychologically well prepared to bear the uncertainty and risks of an unpredictable economic environment. The desirable worker in the crisis-ridden economy is one who constantly seeks to "retool" and acquire new skills for a changing job market and remains highly motivated in the face of uncertainty and job loss. Further, the ideal worker in the global economy is not attached to place but is mobile and flexible to work any place at any time. The capitalist economy is reified as natural, inevitable, and unassailable, and the demand is for workers to adapt to the vagaries of capitalism as well as possible. The primary objective of education then is to prepare workers, in terms of skills and their value orientation to correspond to the conditions of a high- risk uncertain economy. Lifelong learning, another democratic slogan similar to "learning for all," takes on new meaning in this context.

The central feature of a systems (or systemic) approach is dialectical analysis that is completely absent in the World Bank's strategy paper and its numerous other reports including the World Development Reports. Dialectical analysis, a fundamental analytical tool of Marxist theory, considers an idea or action in its totality, that is, in its connections to other social relations to develop an understanding of the structural and ideational conditions that are necessary to realize the idea or action. Following a dialectical approach, the elementary question the strategy document should have posed would be as follows: Is "learning for all" an idea that is congruent with the existing economic and social relations? What are the social relations that correspond with an education that supports "learning for all"? What changes in social relations would be necessary to bring about such a correspondence? "Learning for all" after all implies a democratic, egalitarian and socially just approach to education and affirms education as an inalienable human right. In the World Bank's strategy document, there is no effort to examine the congruence (or lack thereof) between education as a human right and economic and social relations that make for its conditions of possibility. Rather as we have seen, the World Bank's view is that the capitalist economy is an immutable and permanent reality and education policy must simply adapt to the logic and requirements of this economy even if it means insecurity and vulnerability for a vast majority. The World Bank's non-dialectical approach is consistent with its writings in other sectors as well. For instance, in the World Development Report on *Agriculture for Development* (2008), the World Bank's policy is one of moving surplus rural populations out of agriculture into service and low wage urban segments of the economy to make agriculture more efficient. In her thought-provoking essay "Make Live or Let Die," Tania Li (2009) highlights the WDR report for its callousness in ignoring that the transition out of agriculture would entail dispossession, hunger, hopelessness and death. Second, the report assumes that changes in agricultural production and labor migration can be effectively managed within the national economy even as it admits that food production and consumption is subject to the vagaries of the global economy.

It may come as a surprise to the World Bank that "learning for all" was proposed several decades ago by anti-colonial leaders as befitting the ethical framework of postcolonial nations (Gandhi, 1953, in Brown, 2008; Nyrere, 1967). Mahatma Gandhi wrote extensively about the need for a new education model as part of forging a vision for postcolonial India. He wrote about the importance of de-schooling society, and on considering non-formal and community based forms of teaching and learning as a vital and dynamic part of India's postcolonial education policy (also see Illich, 1971). Gandhi's radical critique of schooling was dialectically linked to a critique of the hegemony of market economies and the degradation of education as a market good. Gandhi quite clearly understood that in a modern capitalist economy in which the market is hegemonic, education will become an extension of the market economy and acquire value only as a marketable commodity. In such a scenario, non-school based forms of pedagogy will have little purchase and those engaged in community based education or informal learning will be marginalized and have neither voice nor value in society. The writings of Gandhi and many other scholar-activists validate quasi-formal and non-formal modes of pedagogy, knowledge, and expertise such as artisan networks or the socio-cultural and ecological practices of communities in ways that are dialectically linked to a vision of a new economy and a new society. Given that economy and education cannot be delinked from one another, the hegemony of market economies will inevitably privilege only those forms of education that have market value while rendering other forms of teaching and learning, and different kinds of knowledge irrelevant and impossible to sustain.

These writings that propose a new educational vision explicitly recognize the connection between education and the economy and emphasize that a transformation of one requires a transformation of the other. *WBES 2020* affirms the first part of the argument, but stops short of extending the logic to conclude the second part, that is, a new education strategy requires a new economic strategy; there is simply no other way. The World Bank's proposal to legitimize different modes and sites of learning does not involve a critique of the hyper-commodified global capitalist economy. Nor do they say how non-school based forms of learning will be valued in such an economy, both materially and symbolically. As discussed earlier, the World Bank's position on the economy is quite the obverse and simply proposes to fit "learning for all" within the existing unequal economy thereby deepening inequalities. Without a dialectical critique of the capitalist economy and how it systematically precludes the valuation of diverse forms and modes of learning, the goal of "learning for all" distorts the principles of an equal and democratic education that it claims. Ironically it is the dialectical approach that leads us to anticipate that the World Bank's "learning for all" strategy will exacerbate economic instability, deepen ethnic and religious divisions, and fuel political conflict among groups and nation-states.

## REFERENCES

Bonal, X. (2002). *Plus ça change ....* The World Bank Global Education Policy and the Post-Washington Consensus. *International Studies in Sociology of Education, 12*(1), 3-18.

Brown, J. M. (Ed.). (2008). *Mahatma Gandhi: The essential writings.* Oxford: Oxford University Press.

Galbraith, J. K. (1954). *The Great Crash 1929.* Harmondsworth: Penguin.

Gupta, R. (2010, April 19). The religious lobby and women's rights. *Open Democracy,* April. http://www.opendemocracy.net

Harvey, D. (2005). *Brief history of neoliberalism.* New York: Oxford University Press.

Heyneman, S. (2003) The history and problems in the making of education policy at the World Bank 1960–2000. *International Journal of Educational Development, 23,* 315-337.

Hoogvelt, A. (2010). Globalization, crisis and the political economy of the international monetary (dis)order. *Globalizations, 7*(1-2), 51-66.

Illich, I. (1971). *Deschooling society.* New York: Harper and Row.

Keynes, J. M. (1973 [1936]). *The general theory of employment, interest, and money.* London: Macmillan.

Li, T. M. (2009). Make live or let die: Rural dispossession and the protection of surplus populations. *Antipode: Journal of Radical Geography, 41*(1), 66-93.

Marx, K. (1990 [1867]). *Capital. Vol. 1.* London: Penguin Books.

Mundy, K. (1998). Educational multi-lateralism and world (dis)order, *Comparative Education Review, 42,* 448-478.

Mundy, K. (2002). Retrospect and prospect: Education in a reforming World Bank. *International Journal of Educational Development, 22,* 483-508.

Nisar, M. A. (2010) Education, religion and the creation of subject: Different educational systems of Pakistan. *Pakistaniaat: A Journal of Pakistan Studies, 2*(1): 46-61.

Nyrere, J. K. 1982 [1967]. Education for self-reliance and freedom and socialism. Published in *Education for liberation and development: The Tanzanian experience.* Paris: UNESCO.

Patel, R. (2008). *Stuffed and starved: The hidden battle for the world food system.* New York: Harper Collins.

Pereira, L. C. (1995). Development economics and the World Bank's identity crisis. *Review of International Political Economy*, 2(2), 211-247.

Polanyi, K. (1944). *The great transformation. The political and economic origins of our times.* New York: Farrar and Rinehart.

Post, D., Clipper, L., Enkhbaatar, D., Manning, A., Riley, T., & Zaman, H. (2004). World Bank okays public interest in higher education. *Higher Education, 48*(2), 213-229.

Reimers, F. (1994). Education and structural adjustment in Latin America and sub-Saharan Africa. *International Journal of Educational Development, 14(2)*, 119-129.

Samoff, J. (Ed.) (1994). *Coping with crisis: Austerity, adjustment and human resources.* UNESCO: Paris.

WAF-SBS. (2007, January). *Joint statement by the WAF-SBS Commission on Integration and Cohesion.* Women Against Fundamentalism and Southall Black Sisters.

World Bank. (2008). *World Development report. Agriculture for development.* Washington, D.C.: World Bank.

World Bank. (2010). *New world, new World Bank Group: (I) Post-crisis directions.* Washington D.C.: Development Committee (Joint Ministerial Committee of the Boards of Governors of the Bank and the Fund).

World Bank. (2011). *Learning for II: Investing in people's knowledge and skills to promote development*, World Bank Group Education Strategy 2020. Washington D.C.: The World Bank.

Zia, A. S. (2009a). The reinvention of feminism in Pakistan. In F. Azim, N. Menon, & D. M. Siddiqi (Eds.), *Feminist review, Issue 91, South Asian feminisms: Negotiating new terrains.* London: Palgrave Macmillan.

Zia, A.S. (2009b). Faith-based politics, enlightened moderation and the Pakistani women's movement. *Journal of International Women's Studies, 11*(1): 225-245.

*Sangeeta Kamat*
*School of Education*
*University of Massachusetts at Amherst, U.S.A.*

## CHAPTER 4

STEVEN J. KLEES

# WORLD BANK AND EDUCATION

*Ideological Premises and Ideological Conclusions*[i]

## INTRODUCTION

The World Bank prides itself on being evidence- and research-based, but it is not. Its premises and conclusions are based on ideology, not evidence. The World Bank selects and interprets the research that fits with its ideology. In this sense, it resembles right wing ideological think tank institutions like the Cato Institute or the Heritage Foundation in the U.S. However, it differs in two important ways. First, everyone realizes Cato and Heritage are partisan. The World Bank, on the other hand, makes a pretense of objectivity and inclusiveness. Second, Cato and Heritage are private institutions with limited influence. The World Bank is a public institution, financed by taxes, which gives grants, loans, and advice around the world, yielding a vast global influence.

The World Bank is a monopoly.[ii] There is no other institution like it. It is not too strong to argue that the World Bank is the architect of what has become a truly global education policy (Klees, 2002, 2008a; King, 2007). UNESCO used to have a more dominant role, but withdrawal of the U.S. and U.K. contributions for a number of years forced it to play a much more minor role, and the World Bank became the true director of the Education for All (EFA) processes and more (Mundy, 2002; Jones, 2007). While the World Bank pretends everyone—countries, bilaterals, multilaterals, civil society, and more—is in partnership with it, it is the World Bank which takes the lead on education policy. With its periodic strategy reports and a virtual juggernaut of research done internal to the World Bank or financed by it, it decides on the global directions for education policy, backed by grant and loan money that ensures countries follow those directions.

The ideology that dominates the World Bank is neoliberal. I find it useful to divide the world of political economy into three broad paradigms: neoliberal, liberal, and progressive. Neoliberalism, which predominates today, focuses on market solutions, criticizing the efficiency and equity of government interventions. A liberal perspective offers greater recognition of the inefficiencies and inequities of markets and puts more faith in government. A progressive perspective, focuses on the reproductive nature of both the market and the state under current world system structures like capitalism, patriarchy, and racism, and puts greater reliance on transformation from below through more participatory forms of democracy and collective action. It should be noted that these paradigms, rather than being

*S.J. Klees et al. (eds.), The World Bank and Education, 49–65.*

mutually exclusive, do overlap to some extent, and there are significant variations within each. However, the differences between them are very important for public policy. Most particular to the subject here is that the World Bank ignores or critiques research that does not support its ideological commitment to neoliberalism.

In this chapter, I examine some of the ideological premises and conclusions that serve as the basis for World Bank policy towards education. I will focus some attention on the new 2020 Strategy Report (hereafter *WBES 2020*; World Bank, 2011b), but this Report is part and parcel of more than 30 years of the World Bank's neoliberal strategy papers, research, policy, and practice. There is little new in *WBES 2020*; antecedents can be found in the World Bank's strategy papers (1995, 1999, 2005), as well as further back. Neoliberalism rose to global dominance in the 1980s as part of the consequences of political shifts to the right embodied in politicians like Ronald Reagan, Margaret Thatcher, and Helmut Kohl. While I will not specifically focus on the history of the World Bank's stance on education policy, one can see a sharp transformation from its liberal perspective in the 1960s and 1970s to an increasingly strident neoliberal perspective since the early 1980s (Klees, 2002; Jones, 2007).

The new strategy report was initiated with much fanfare. The World Bank is especially proud of its consultation phase where dozens of meetings were held around the world with over 1000 participants from over 100 countries. In the spirit of cooperation, I helped organize a meeting with progressive World Bank critics. But the result of all this consultation did nothing to modify a thoroughly neoliberal view of education policy. While other views were obviously heard, none of them were listened to, none made it to *WBES 2020*. I do believe that World Bank staff are well-intentioned, just hopelessly biased.

*WBES 2020* and past World Bank policy have been an educational disaster, harmful to children around the world, as discussed below. There are many, many people around the world who agree with me (e.g., the authors in this book), but one will not find any of their views expressed in World Bank reports. Instead, we get the narrow, ideological premises and conclusions that the World Bank brings to education policy, as exemplified below.

## THE RIGHT TO EDUCATION

For the World Bank, education is not a right. *WBES 2020* (p. 1) says the opposite: "Access to education ... is a basic human right ...." But that is it. It is hardly mentioned again. The sentence does not even consider the key issue of quality. And most importantly, the right to education is not used in any way as a basis for World Bank strategy. The one sentence reflects either ignorance or duplicity— ignorance because anyone with any knowledge of what education as a right means understands that it fundamentally changes one's approach to education policy. Instead of the World Bank's instrumentalist, human capital approach using rates of return to establish investment trade-offs, a human rights approach does not consider trade-offs as legitimate. Access and quality are a child's right, and education must be provided to fulfill that right. For example, a child has a right to a qualified teacher; providing a barely trained contract teacher, as the World Bank has advocated, is not a legitimate substitute and violates a child's right to education (Tomasevski, 2003; Klees & Thapliyal, 2007; Right to Education Project, 2011).

The World Bank has reluctantly added a sentence or two to its reports over the years offering grudging support for the idea of the right to education while other private and public international agencies (e.g., ActionAid, UNESCO, UNICEF) have transformed their entire programming to make rights central. For UNICEF (2011), its "ultimate aim … is the realization of the rights of children"; the right to education "guides our work in all sectors." For UNESCO (2011b), its "constitutional mission" is the "right to education." On the other hand, the World Bank has not even been able to take a strong stand against user fees, which directly violate the right to education by limiting access. In its neoliberal zeal, the World Bank was actually the architect of expanded user fees in the 1980s—even for primary education. In the 1990s, it backed off a little, but it has not campaigned for the elimination of all school fees as have UNESCO, UNICEF, ActionAid, and many others (Klees, 2008a).

Most fundamentally, the World Bank is a bank and does not know what to do with a rights-based argument. Everything to the World Bank is instrumental in terms of how it affects economic growth. And a basic problem for the World Bank is that a rights-based approach does not stop at the right to education. What about a right to health? To food? To shelter? To a sustainable livelihood? To development itself? Such a perspective on development contradicts the economic logic of a bank and calls for more government intervention than a neoliberal can tolerate. It is no wonder the World Bank refuses to be serious about human rights.

## EDUCATION AND DEVELOPMENT

Development for the World Bank mainly refers to economic growth, and the approach taken follows neoliberal ideology. The ethnocentrically named Washington Consensus still prevails—cut and privatize government and deregulate and liberalize the private sector. This was and is a consensus only for neoliberals— liberal and progressive political economists see very different policies as necessary (Cornia et al., 1987; MacEwan, 1999; Reich, 2007; Reinert, 2007). Even neoliberal economists had to admit that the Washington Consensus-inspired structural adjustment policies (SAPs) followed by the World Bank, the IMF, and others in the 1980s and 1990s had devastating effects on poverty and inequality (Dollar & Pritchett, 1998). Liberal and neoliberal economists in the 1990s talked of searching for a modified approach to development, a post-Washington Consensus (Stiglitz, 2003). Very little has come of this. Current rhetoric about partnership and participation offers some different directions in theory, but in practice little has changed (Cornwall & Eade, 2010). The most visible change is the Poverty Reduction Strategy Paper (PRSP) process that now anchors the World Bank and the IMF's work in developing countries, but, at the end of the day, the called-for participation by civil society is mostly a sham, and the results look an awful lot like SAPs (Djikstra, 2005). What development means and how best to achieve it is widely contested (Yates, 2003; Stiglitz, 2003; Alperovitz, 2004; Hahnel, 2005; Reinert, 2007; Rodrik, 2007), yet what we get from the World Bank is not a fair look at the evidence and debate but a continued commitment to a particular development ideology (World Bank, 2004).

Within this neoliberal view of development, education is extolled. *WBES 2020* (p. 11) begins: "People are the real wealth of nations ... and education enables them to live healthier, happier, and more productive lives." Earlier World Bank reports sometimes made it sound like education was some sort of miracle cure: "All agree that the single most important key to development and poverty alleviation is education" (World Bank, 1999, p. iii). But this is far from agreed upon. A significant question is, given the decades of intense attention to education worldwide, why do development, poverty, and inequality continue to be so problematic? This comes as no surprise to liberals and progressives who have seen three decades of neglect of the public policies needed to change this state of affairs. In fact, the market fundamentalism promoted and practiced by neoliberals so constrains government action that one of the only things government is allowed to do is education (and even here privatization is pushed—see below). It is no wonder that neoliberals must expect a miracle out of education, because other than relying on the "miracle" of the market, education is about all they have.

The World Bank has been very pleased with a spate of studies that support the argument that education contributes to GNP. Such empirical studies have been controversial since their inception (Blaug, 1970). The World Bank especially likes the newer versions, which argue that it is less the quantity of schooling and more the quality of schooling, as measured by test scores, that result in GNP growth (World Bank, 2011b, pp. 12 and 25; Hanushek & Woessmann, 2008). However, there are many problems with these studies. Test scores are a very inadequate measure of school quality. Our ability to model the many causes of GNP variation and growth is minimal. To get their results, Hanushek and Woessmann (2008) control for only two of the literally dozens of variables that they could have included, and these two variables reflected neoliberal development ideology (openness to trade and security of property rights). There's an old saw in economics: "If you torture the data long enough, nature will confess." And to top it off, the research was funded by the World Bank.

## TESTING FOR ALL

The stated theme of *WBES 2020* is "Learning for All." Unfortunately, in practice, the real theme is a much narrower "Testing for All." In many ways, the new Strategy is an exported version of the failed U.S. strategy, No Child Left Behind, which offered narrow and extensive testing but little to improve schools (Au, 2009; Darling-Hammond, 2010; Ravitch, 2010). Under the new strategy, all countries will be pushed to test their students in reading and math.[iii] Now, of course, reading and math are important, but the tests used only offer partial and inadequate measures of reading and math and neglect the many other outcomes that we want to achieve through schools. The World Bank briefly recognizes this and mentions that other outcomes are important, like critical thinking, problem-solving, and teamwork and says it will develop broader outcome measures (World Bank, 2011b, p. 26). However, this same claim was made in their 2005 Education Sector Update (World Bank, 2005), and nothing has been done. Moreover, we need schools to foster many outcomes: critical and higher order thinking, problem-solving, creativity, curiosity, civic-mindedness, solidarity, self-discipline, self-efficacy, compassion, empathy, courage, conscientization, resilience, leadership, humility, peace, and more (Bracey, 2009). It is simply irrational and inefficient to base education policy on a partial measure of two outcomes when we want and need education to do so much more.

No Child Left Behind has shown that in a narrow testing regime, what is not tested gets de-emphasized or eliminated from the curriculum (Au, 2009; Bracey, 2009; King & Zucker, 2005; Ravitch, 2010). Children in the U.S. get much less history, social science, art, music, physical education, and play than they used to get. And language, math, and science education becomes distorted towards the test. Johnson et al. (2007, p. 61) argue that high-stakes testing has "led to shallowness or superficiality in student thinking that inhibits their ability to think deeply about complex content material." On top of this, there is no credible evidence that 10 years of this regime in the U.S. has actually improved test scores or narrowed inequalities (Au, 2009; Darling-Hammond, 2010; Institute of Education Sciences, 2009; Neal & Schanzenbach, 2010). There has been a notable increase in student and teacher anxiety and dissatisfaction (Ravitch, 2010), and the whole approach follows Freire's banking metaphor, with the job of education being to deposit knowledge in students' heads.

It is interesting to note that Finland, which has been held up as an international exemplar due to its consistently high ranking on international achievement tests (World Bank, 2011b, p. 19) follows a completely different educational path from what the World Bank usually recommends: there are no standardized tests in Finland, and grades are not even given until 5th grade; the curriculum is broad and balanced; students do not start school until age 7 and have 2 years fewer instructional hours than in the U.S.; a cooperative learning model is used, not a competitive one; teaching is a very attractive profession, well-paid with 50 percent fewer instructional hours than in the U.S.; private schools are prohibited; teachers control curriculum implementation and their own professional evaluation; and teacher unions are true educational partners (Darling-Hammond, 2010; Sahlberg, 2011; Valijarvi, 2004). The World Bank's "Learning for All" strategy is simply another expression of its neoliberal ideology, ignoring the logic and evidence of alternative educational approaches (see Hudson & Klees, this volume, for a discussion of alternative approaches).

## ADDITIONAL RESOURCES FOR EDUCATION

For the World Bank, more resources for education are not that important. In most of its reports, there is only somewhere between a sentence and a paragraph

53

concerned with resources, and most of those read something like "more resources are important, *but* the key issue is how to use existing resources better." After briefly saying that, the World Bank devotes the rest of each report to telling countries how it thinks existing resources should be used (World Bank, 1995, 1999, 2005). *WBES 2020* is no exception. In a rather bizarre paragraph (p. 15), it poses a debate over how to improve education between three positions (this is really the only policy debate posed in the whole report). The first position, which they effectively dismiss, is that more resources are needed to supply education "inputs." The second position "places less emphasis on the quantity of resources allocated to an educational system and more emphasis on the system's ability to transform those resources into learning outcomes." However, the World Bank seems doubtful that government is capable of doing this and seems to prefer their third position of restructuring education to increase school autonomy and competition. This is all pure neoliberal ideology talking. The World Bank's long-term position on resources has been simply irresponsible.

Of course, spending wisely is important, but more money is desperately needed. We have almost 70 million children of primary school age out of school (UNESCO, 2011a). They need teachers, classrooms, and learning materials. Universal primary education and other EFA goals are estimated to require an additional $16 billion per year (UNESCO, 2010). The Fast Track Initiative (FTI), promised and touted by former World Bank president James Wolfensohn as ensuring that countries could achieve EFA goals, has, until recently, only been supplying about $300 million per year. And the $16 billion per year is a considerable underestimate. For one thing, given the opportunity costs of sending children to primary school and the still prevalent fees, many families need scholarships to have their children attend school. Moreover, we need much more resources as we have many more millions of students in primary schools receiving a very low quality education who need more and better educated teachers, improved facilities, and better learning materials. Then there is the huge secondary school coverage deficit and decades of cutting back on higher education. Within a neoliberal ideology of cutting government, these resource needs are not taken seriously. I attended a recent meeting with FTI staff who actually argued that we should reduce the $16 billion estimate to something more "reasonable," not because it was incorrect but because we are not going to be able to get donors to contribute with the bar set so high.[iv] This is embarrassing. Although FTI has been separating itself from the World Bank, it is still part and parcel of the same neoliberal reasoning. Having taken responsibility for global education improvement, it is simply irresponsible of the World Bank to continually dismiss the dire need for vast additional resources and to pretend that problems can be solved cheaply by tinkering with education's governance structure.

## THE KNOWLEDGE BANK

Since, from the perspective of neoliberal ideology, resources are not that important, what is? A major answer for the World Bank is knowledge, and the

World Bank has spent many years trying to position itself as the "Knowledge Bank." Its earlier strategy report (World Bank, 1999, p. 42) emphasized the importance of the World Bank's Education Knowledge Management System, which "creates, captures, distills, and disseminates relevant development knowledge on education. Its main goals are to document the corporate memory and to include the best development knowledge." *WBES 2020* spends a lot of time on the need for the World Bank to build "a global knowledge base powerful enough to guide" educational reform (p. 1) and its "aspirations to be both a generator of new knowledge and a synthesizer of existing knowledge" (p. 53). *WBES 2020* alludes to the World Bank's latest initiative in this area, SABER, System Assessment and Benchmarking for Education Results, and makes major promises:

> This program will make it possible for stakeholders to obtain simple, objective, up-to-date snapshots of how their system is functioning, how well it is performing, and what concretely the system can do to achieve measurably better results. (p. 61)

SABER will do this by "benchmark[ing] education policies according to evidence-based global standards and best practices" (pp. 59-60).

The problems with this metaphor and practice are numerous and have been criticized previously (Stromquist & Samoff, 2000; Samoff and Stromquist, 2001). The idea of knowledge management was borrowed directly from the U.S. corporate sector, as have previous fads like Total Quality Management, strategic planning, quality assurance, performance budgeting, and current ones like benchmarking. The World Bank has tried to back off from the Orwellian specter of knowledge management, sometimes reframing the idea as "knowledge sharing" (Klees, 2002). But the "creates, captures, and distills" image connotes much more the idea of control than sharing. The World Bank wants to be a clearing-house for "best practice knowledge" from everywhere—its own and that of all its partners (World Bank, 1999, p. 42). Yet, the World Bank has long been critiqued as almost completely focused on its own research or that of its consultants. (What better way to provide "evidence" for their own ideological commitments?) Some years back, when it felt especially stung by this self-referential critique, the World Bank actually hired the U.S. Comparative and International Education Society to add 400 references to the World Bank's database so it would look like they had a broader vision.

In *WBES 2020*, the World Bank devotes some space to lauding its own contribution to the "global knowledge base" (p. 52). It talks of producing some 500 journal articles and another 500 books, book chapters, and working papers. It compares its publication record in the economics of education favorably with top universities—"only Harvard University comes close." (This should be no surprise since the World Bank has many economists of education focused on doing research.) I found most interesting that between 2001 and 2010 the education sector at the World Bank spent $49 million dollars on research and produced "about 280 pieces of research and other analytical work" (p. 52). If you do the math, that is costing about $175,000 per piece of research! In terms of productivity this is not very impressive, but it does indicate the incredible amount of resources lined up behind a juggernaut of neoliberal ideology in education (Broad, 2006).

The idea of a central repository of "best practice" is frightening. The World Bank as that repository is more frightening still. This could never be done in the North. Imagine if, in the U.S., Cato or Heritage said it was or wanted to be the central clearinghouse for distilling all ideas about educational or economic best practice. They would be laughed at. Given the diversity of views, for example, in think tanks and universities, no one would even consider having some such central knowledge manager or broker. Since the World Bank pretends we are all partners, all in this together, and ignores conflict and debate, the idea is that it does not matter by whom or for whom this knowledge is generated. We can pool our knowledge and let the best ideas win out in the "free marketplace of ideas." This is never true in the real world where knowledge is contested, and power governs the outcome of that contestation (Klees, 2002).

There is no "Knowledge Bank," only an "Opinion Bank," and, worse still, an opinion bank with monopoly power. This Monopoly Opinion Bank (I cannot resist—it should be known as The MOB) may not be the only source of knowledge in education in developing countries, but it is the predominant producer and arbiter of what counts as knowledge. If there were applicable anti-trust legislation, The MOB's research enterprise would be broken up. The MOB's defense is that they try to incorporate all knowledge from all their partners, including countries, other aid agencies, NGOs, other civil society organizations, indigenous people, the poor of the world, etc. This is neither possible nor sensible nor true in a world where knowledge is contested within and among all these groups. The MOB distills and disseminates the knowledge it wants to promulgate.

## UNDERSTANDING EDUCATION

Despite all this talk of knowledge and more than 50 years working in the area, education remains a black box to the World Bank. Little attention is paid to what happens in classrooms. Instead, World Bank ideology makes unwarranted assumptions: that teachers are the biggest problem with education, generally being ignorant and/or unmotivated; that teacher's unions work to subvert educational reform; that better governance is the key to reform; that teacher training has little payoff; that class size does not matter; that competition is more important than cooperation; and that privatization can increase efficiency and equity. The antipathy towards teachers and teacher unions is so strong that they have been portrayed as rioting in the streets (World Bank, 2004) or sleeping on the job (actually on the cover of Patrinos et al., 2009). Neoliberal principal-agent theory is used to argue that government generally does not pay attention to the public interest; therefore, government must be constrained or eliminated (World Bank, 2004).[v] The purpose and nature of education gets short shrift. The theories, practices, and even names of noted educators like Dewey, Freire, Montessori, and Vygotsky are curiously absent from decades of World Bank documents about education.

It could be argued that perhaps it is best that the World Bank does not focus on the core of education because then education would be subjected to even more neoliberal ideological premises and conclusions. Unfortunately, however, the World Bank has recently been venturing inside the classroom as a result of its attention to neuroscience. *WBES 2020* mentions the need to heed the "science of brain development" (p. 4). While *WBES 2020* does not elaborate much, the World Bank has been very active in examining this literature and in designing and implementing programs based on their interpretation of it. Helen Abadzi, one of the few psychologists at the World Bank, has become something of a guru to the World Bank, USAID, and others in the international arena looking at what neuroscience offers education policy, especially in reading (Abadzi, 2006, 2010).[vi] Her work is well known for concluding that neuroscience research implies that primary, if not exclusive, attention should be paid to reading fluency, and, most specifically, young children need to reach a level of reading 60 words/minute. There are dozens of reading interventions and assessments around the world based on these premises, many financed by the World Bank and USAID.

However, these conclusions are debatable. Recent literature reviewing neuroscience implications for reading does not find reading fluency to be more important than other dimensions of reading, such as comprehension, vocabulary, phonological awareness, and decoding (Stahl, 2004, p. 208; also see Howard-Jones, 2010; Hruby & Goswami, 2011; McCardle & Chhabra, 2004; Sousa, 2010; Wagner, forthcoming). And none of these studies offers a numerical target for fluency. In fact, most of these reviews are very cautious in suggesting that present neuroscience research has useful implications for education practice:

> I believe that expectations for neuroscience-based, easy-to-follow recipes for classroom practice are unrealistic.... The neuroscience studies reviewed in this chapter have not provided a recipe for practice or a prescription for a certain curriculum. (Coch, 2010, pp. 139 and 153)

> We believe that *much* more research on decoding processes in typically developing children is needed before profound implications [of neuroscience] for instruction can be expected. (Hruby & Goswami, 2011, p. 156, emphasis added)

Abadzi (2006) is much less cautious. She says:

> What is the minimum amount of educational inputs that will teach basic skills to the majority of students in low-income countries rather than merely the gifted? Answers to this seemingly impossible question may be deduced from some branches of "hard" science. (p. 8)

Abadzi (2006) goes even further and uses her interpretation of neuroscience findings to examine policy issues like class size, constructivism, and teacher training. I do not wish to argue here whether Abadzi is right or wrong on these issues. I only wish to show that these uses of neuroscience, like all of the World Bank's understandings of education, are debatable—and significant debate, with widespread participation of stakeholders, is absent from the World Bank (Turner, 2011).[vii]

## PRIVATIZATION

As mentioned above, for the most part, the World Bank has paid little attention to what happens in the classroom, leaving education as a black box. What attention has been paid is to governance. And, most particularly, we have seen more than three decades of a continually increasing effort to promote the privatization of education by a global neoliberal political economy in general and by the World Bank most particularly. By privatization I mean efforts to diminish public control and finance of education, thus including user fees, charters, vouchers, and other supports of private schooling (Klees, 2008a). Early on in this neoliberal era, the push towards privatization was much more tentative than now, often requiring elaborate rationales and appeals to supposed common sense and evidence (World Bank, 1995, 2004). Today, it is simply taken for granted. For the World Bank, there is no longer any question of "whether" privatization; the questions are "when" and "how." *WBES 2020* (pp. 34-35) argues that the "nonstate sector" is an integral part of offering "education services," serving "even the poorest communities," often subsidized or contracted by government.[viii] The World Bank, and others, often use the term "partnership" as a way of avoiding the negative ethos of privatization. Partnership is a misleading term in a world of vastly unequal power.

Neoliberals argue that privatization in education has generally had positive effects (Patrinos et al., 2009) while progressive critics argue that it generally has not (Education International, 2009). Most of the research in this area has been done by those who share a neoliberal perspective, so it is not surprising that results favoring privatization dominate. However, even that favorable research does not show very impressive results, and the results themselves have major problems of validity (Klees, 2010b; Center on Education Policy, 2011).

Privatization is based on ideology, not evidence. Some years ago, I attended a meeting at the World Bank soliciting comments on a health sector-oriented World Development Report. The World Bank presenter pointed out how, in many poor countries, poor people chose to be treated at private health clinics for a fee instead of going to free public clinics. This was touted as evidence of the success and value of privatization. To the contrary, I pointed out that this is simply evidence of the success of 30 years of neoliberal ideology in which public clinics had been systematically decimated, ending up without doctors, nurses, or medicine. The same has happened in education. Privatization is supposed to help meet the growing education gap resulting from years of attack on the public sector, but all it does is replace an attempt to develop good public policy with the vagaries of charity or the single-mindedness of profit-making. It boggles the imagination how we have let neoliberal ideology run so rampant that we accept "low cost private schools for the poor" as good educational policy. What kind of world is it where we consider it legitimate to charge the poorest people in the world for basic education?

## A SYSTEM APPROACH

One of the most problematic parts of *WBES 2020* is the framework the World Bank proposes to bring to its analysis of educational policy and reform. The report spends a *lot* of time talking how everything the World Bank will do in developing countries should be based on a "system approach." There is a lot of abstract talk of the "stages" of a system approach (p. 40), its need to be cross-sectoral (p. 45), or how it approaches reform (p. 52). Yet the approach is never defined or supported. In a World Bank that is obsessed by evidence, there is no evidence offered that a system approach is productive. Yet it is touted as globally applicable, one-size-fits-all yet again.

While not defined, as described, the World Bank's system approach is a resuscitated form of systems analysis that was popular in the 1960s and 1970s. Systems analysis took a simplistic view of a linear and mechanical connection between inputs, processes, and outputs (with perhaps a feedback loop included). However, it was strongly critiqued from its inception and is generally considered outmoded today. It is worth quoting an early major critic at length:

> Supposed to solve social problems, [systems analysis] has merely served to redefine them in a way amenable to ... technical treatment. Carried to logical extremes [as the World Bank does], emphasis on quantification could so limit and bias perspectives as either to distort and violate the essential nature of social problems by forcing them into a tractable ... state or to institutionalize and legitimize neglect of ... their vital parts .... As an instrument of policy-making, techniques of systems analysis have encouraged emphasis on the wrong questions and provided answers the more dangerous for having been achieved through a "scientific" or "rational" means. The ultimate result is a systematic foreclosing of promising avenues towards possible improvement and reform. Contrary to being an instrument of innovation, systems analysis encourages systematic neglect of facets and variables which could be crucial in both their generation and amelioration. (Hoos, 1972, pp. 241-242)

The World Bank's related promotion of what it has been calling Results-Based Finance (RBF) and SABER are carrying policy analysis to narrow and extreme limits. They ignore the many and repeated failures of similar efforts in the past: Program-Planning-Based-Budgeting Systems, Management by Objectives, Zero-Based Budgeting, Performance Budgeting, Performance Contracting, and Output-Based Aid—all of which relied on a narrow, mechanical, engineering version of systems analysis that inefficiently focused on narrow outcome measures and were incapable of relating cost and input measures even to the narrow outcomes chosen (Klees, 2008a).[ix]

## EVIDENCE-BASED POLICY

Part of the reason that a mechanical systems approach cannot work is that the evidence which is used to inform it and on which it depends is limited, debatable, and ideological. Partly, this is an institutional issue as ideologues group together and develop powerful institutional bases like the World Bank. But part of the problem is that our quantitative research methods are always and necessarily susceptible to researcher biases that make fair and "objective" research impossible.

I focus here on regression analysis, the set of statistical techniques (OLS, 2SLS, HLM, probit, logit, path analysis, etc.) for uncovering the causal impact of one variable on another. While some might see this as technical and esoteric, regression analysis is the dominant methodology for studying educational and social policy and practice, and it is important that all researchers and practitioners recognize its fundamental flaws. It is widely recognized that the main problem in the use of these techniques is misspecification. Proper model specification requires three conditions: that *all* variables that affect the dependent variable be included in the model; that all these variables be measured correctly; and that the mathematical relation between independent and dependent variables be correctly specified. These stringent conditions never can hold in practice and so every literature becomes a debate over who has the better specification (Klees, 2008b).

For example, the privatization debate centers around what are called educational production functions (EPFs) or input-output functions, where the dependent variable most studied is student test score, and the type of school (public, private, voucher, charter, etc.) a student attends is the independent variable of primary interest. But there are literally dozens of other school and home variables that affect test score and need to be controlled for in the equation. Moreover, our ideas for how to measure most of these variables are very imprecise (e.g., SES or school climate) and their mathematical interrelationship is unknown, leaving most researchers to use an obviously incorrect linear model. Given the almost infinite varieties of model specification available, it is little wonder that the school choice debates come down to proponents using specifications that result in a positive impact of privatization and opponents using models that show the opposite. The almost complete indeterminacy of proper model specification is not restricted to EPFs but affects the study of most, if not all, dependent variables of interest such as, earnings, voting behavior, GNP, or even agricultural production.

Some quantitative researchers, recognizing these problems, point to a "gold standard" for research methodology, namely randomization and experimental controls. But this is no gold standard for research for at least two reasons. First, experiments in areas of educational and social importance are difficult and even unethical as experimentation with people's lives is problematic, especially over the long term. Second, in practice, experimental methods are at least as flawed as any other. Educational and social experiments are never able to achieve randomization for many practical reasons (e.g., sample attrition). Therefore, they need to use the same regression analysis techniques used by survey researchers to control covariates. Thus, experimental research also turns into an issue of specification and differences in what variables are controlled for, and how they are controlled allow different researchers to come to opposite conclusions (Klees, 2008b).

I believe that this type of quantitative methodology is a dead end, no better than alchemy and phrenology, and someday people will look back in wonder at how so many intelligent people could convince themselves otherwise. This is not a problem that better modeling and data can fix. But I should say that I do not see the essence of the problem as quantification. Quantifying social phenomena clearly has its limits and, at best, yields approximations. But cross-tabulations and correlations are useful to suggest interrelationships. As is well known, however, any associations found may be spurious and have a myriad of alternative explanations. The problem is that the causal relations underlying such associations are so complex that the mechanical process of regression analysis has no hope of unpacking them. If we are interested in looking at quantitative data, I am afraid we are stuck with arguing from cross-tabulations and correlations. This is a dismal prospect for most quantitative researchers who have spent years becoming virtuosos at data analysis and see the implications of my argument as essentially abandoning the research enterprise. However, there are many alternative research methodologies which depart from qualitative and critical perspectives (Klees, 2008b; Mertens, 2010). While these alternatives have their own problems and will not yield the "objective truth" to feed naive visions of evidence-based policy, they can offer findings that illuminate and inform our policy debates.

## CONCLUSIONS

The World Bank is not evil; as I said before, the people who work there are well intentioned. Yet, if one sees the world as I do, as structured to yield poverty, inequality, and oppression through capitalist, patriarchal, racist, and other structures, the World Bank becomes a major player in their reproduction through its neoliberal ideology and resultant policies. Its ideology is so pervasive that even some of its own staff (and the IMF's) have referred to the internal "thought police" that force ideological conformity (Broad, 2006). Its ideology is so pervasive that when I did a report for the World Bank on education in Nicaragua in 1990, they tried to get me to change my conclusions. After the U.S. embargo and U.S.-backed Contra War, Nicaraguan education was in such dire straits that more resources were desperately needed from primary education to the university. However, the World Bank was only interested in charging user fees and privatizing. When I refused to go along, they simply had a more amenable analyst re-do the study. The same thing happened to a colleague studying development policies in Southern Africa. I am sure this is a common occurrence. World Bank ideology brooks no opposition.

The best evidence for that is the almost complete lack of debate in World Bank reports.[x] In a meeting about a World Development Report, I asked one of the World Bank authors why it contained no debate. The answer I got was that debate would be too confusing. This should be considered shocking, embarrassing, and completely unacceptable. In a world where truth and best practice is in the eye of the beholder and all positions can marshal supporting evidence, all we have is debate. Key policy institutions, like the World Bank, should build their legitimacy around broad, deep, and sustained participation of different stakeholders, especially those with the least power, and around processes that bring to the table the array of positions on any particular issue (Hudson & Klees, this volume). The World Bank has not and probably cannot do this.

To conclude, the World Bank is too one-sided and one-dimensional to be improved. Relying on the World Bank for education policy is not in the interests of the world's children. The World Bank needs to stop giving education advice. It probably should be replaced entirely (Klees, 2010a). At the very least, a bank has no business being the architect of global education policy.

## NOTES

[i] I would like to thank Anda Adams, Sarah Beardmore, Susanne Clawson, D. Brent Edwards, Mark Ginsburg, Wendi Ralaingita, Joel Samoff, Nelly Stromquist, and Justin W. van Fleet for comments on a draft of this paper. An earlier version of this chapter also appears in C. Collins and A. Wiseman (Eds.), *Education strategy in the developing world: A conversation about the World Bank's education policy revision.* Emerald Publishing Group, 2012.

[ii] For many low-income countries, the World Bank is one of the few available sources of external financing for social investments, financing almost 20 percent of all development programs in International Development Association (IDA) countries. Even for countries with higher credit ratings and which are eligible for loans from other sources, the World Bank's concessional loan rates make it an important source of external financing. With over $15 billion in concessional financing for development in low-income countries available annually, the World Bank is therefore able to play a unique role at country-level negotiating with ministries of finance on national development strategies and policies (World Bank, 2011b). The result is that the World Bank has a monopoly position in determining the educational and other social policies that accompany its loans and grants.

[iii] There is an increasing push to give standardized tests to all students in a country. If testing is desired, there are many reasons to prefer a small sampling of students. Some facets of performance can be assessed without the monetary costs and educational dysfunctions of a census.

[iv] Actually, estimates for meeting EFA goals and needed secondary school improvements have been estimated at $25 billion (UNESCO, 2010), and this underestimates the need for quality improvements and ignores the need for scholarships.

[v] Principal-agent theory argues, for example, that when a principal (e.g., a citizen) has an agent (e.g., government) to work for him or her, the agent may be motivated by self-interest or captured by other private interests and not work in the principal's interest. If principal-agent theory were true, it might explain how the World Bank, itself a dreaded government monopoly, has been so captured by private interests and pays so little attention to the public interest.

[vi] Abadzi's (2006) book is one of the few World Bank publications that does pay a little attention to noted educators like Montessori and Vygotsky.

[vii] Over the years, some World Bank colleagues have told me that I don't know how much internal debate there is, but others say that substantive debate is minimal. The proof is in the pudding, and World Bank reports and policies are uniformly neoliberal. If there is any significant debate, one side always wins.

[viii] A cross-country study by Woessmann (2009) is cited to argue that not only are private schools better than public schools, but that they are even better if they are publicly financed! This is an

economist's neoliberal dream result but, unfortunately for them, the methodology is completely invalid (Klees, 2010b).

[ix] Systems analysis was, in many ways, superseded early on by systems theory, a collection of approaches that were more organic, holistic, and qualitative (Bateson, 1972; Laszlo, 1996).

[x] Liberal or progressive economists in the World Bank who have been vocal have left the World Bank or been marginalized. It is not only the World Bank that has been shaped strongly by neoliberal economists but universities, think tanks, bilateral aid agencies, and governments as well. It is telling that even in the liberal Obama administration, despite the serious current economic crisis, critical voices get excluded. Paul Krugman and Joseph Stiglitz, both Nobel Prize-winning economists, have not been part of White House efforts because "an entire economics perspective... a progressive-economist wing" has been excluded from policymaking (Krugman, 2009).

## REFERENCES

Abadzi, H. (2006). *Efficient learning for the poor: Insights from the frontier of cognitive neuroscience.* Washington, D.C.: World Bank.

Abadzi, H. (2010). Reading fluency measurements is FTI EFA partner countries: Outcomes and improvement prospects, FTI EFA Working Paper Series, World Bank, Washington, D.C.: World Bank.

Alperovitz, G. (2004). *America beyond capitalism: Reclaiming our wealth, our liberty, and our democracy.* New York: John Wiley.

Au, W. (2009). *Unequal by design: High-stakes testing and the standardization of inequality.* New York: Routledge.

Bateson, M.C. (1972). *Our own metaphor.* New York: Knopf.

Blaug, M. (1970.) *An introduction to the economics of education.* London: Penguin.

Bracey, G.W. (2009). *Education hell: Rhetoric vs. reality. Transforming the fire consuming America's schools.* Alexandria, VA: Educational Research Service.

Broad, R. (2006, August). Research, knowledge, and the art of 'paradigm maintenance': the World Bank's development economics vice-presidency. *Review of International Political Economy, 13*(3), 387-419.

Center on Education Policy. (2011). Keeping informed about school vouchers: A review of major developments and research. Washington, D.C.: Center on Education Policy

Cornia, G., Jolly, R., & Stewart, F. (1987). *Adjustment with a human face.* Oxford: Clarendon Press.

Coch, D. (2010). Constructing a reading brain. In. D. Sousa (Ed.), *Mind, brain, and education: Neuroscience implications for the classroom.* Bloomington, IN: Solution Tree Press.

Cornwall, A. & Eade, D. (2010). *Deconstructing development discourse: Buzzwords and fuzzwords.* Oxfam GB: Practical Action Publishing.

Darling-Hammond, L. (2010). *The flat world and education: How America's commitment to equity will determine our future.* New York: Teachers College Press.

Dijkstra, G. (2005). The PRSP approach and the illusion of improved aid effectiveness: Lessons from Bolivia, Honduras, and Nicaragua, *Development Policy Review, 23*(4), 443-64.

Dollar, D. & Pritchett, L. (1998). *Assessing aid: What works, what doesn't and why.* Washington, D.C.: World Bank, Oxford.

Education International. (2009). *Public private partnerships in education.* Brussels: Education International.

Hahnel, R. (2005). *Economic justice and democracy: From competition to cooperation.* New York: Routledge.

Hanushek, E. & Woessmann, L. (2008). The role of cognitive skills in economic development. *Journal of Economic Literature, 46*(3), 607-668.

Hoos, I. (1972). *Systems analysis in public policy: A critique.* Los Angeles: University of California Press.

Howard-Jones, P. (2010). *Introducing neuroeducational research: Neuroscience, education, and the brain from contexts to practice.* New York: Routledge.

Hruby, G. & Goswami, U. (2011). Neuroscience and reading: A review for reading education researchers. *Reading Research Quarterly, 46*(2), 156-172

Institute of Education Sciences. (2009). *Achievement gap: How black and white students in public schools perform in Mathematics and Reading on the National Assessment of Educational Progress.* Washington, D.C.: National Center for Education Statistics.

Johnson, D., Johnson, B., Farenga, S., & Ness, D. (2007). *Stop high-stakes testing: An appeal to America's conscience.* Lanham, MD: Rowman & Littlefield.

Jones, P. (2007). *World Bank financing of education: Lending, learning, and development,* 2nd ed. New York: Routledge.

King, K. & Zucker, S. (2005). *Curriculum narrowing, Policy report.* New York: Pearson Education, Inc.

King, K. (2007). Multilateral agencies in the construction of the global agenda on education. *Comparative Education, 43*(3), 377-91.

Klees, S. (2002). World Bank education policy: New rhetoric, old ideology. *International Journal of Educational Development, 22,* 451-474.

Klees, S. (2008a). A quarter century of neoliberal thinking in education: Misleading analyses and failed policies. *Globalisation, Societies and Education, 6*(4), 311-348.

Klees, S. (2008b). Reflections on theory, method, and practice in comparative and international education. *Comparative Education Review, 52*(3), 301-328.

Klees, S. (2010a). Aid, Development and Education. *Current Issues in Comparative Education, 13*(1), 7-27.

Klees, S. (2010b). Review of *School choice international: Exploring public-private partnerships* by Rajashri Chakrabarti and Paul Peterson. *Globalization, Societies, and Education, 8*(1), 159-166.

Klees, S. & Thapliyal, N. 2007. The right to education: The work of Katarina Tomasevski. *Comparative Education Review, 51*(4), 497-510.

Krugman, P. (2009). http://www.huffingtonpost.com/2009/07/19/krugman-white-house-exclu_n_240032.html

Laszlo, E. (1996). *The systems view of the world: A holistic vision for our time.* Cresskill, NJ: Hampton.

MacEwan, A. (1999). *Neo-liberalism or democracy? Economic strategy, markets, and alternatives for the 21st century.* New York: Zed.

McCardle, P. & Chhabra, V. (2004). *The voice of evidence in reading research.* Baltimore, MD: Paul Brookes Publishing.

Mertens, D. (2010). *Research methods in education and psychology: Integrating diversity with quantitative and qualitative approaches.* 3rd ed.. Thousand Oaks, CA: Sage.

Mundy, K. (2002). Retrospect and prospect: Education in a reforming World Bank. *International Journal of Educational Development, 22,* 483-508.

Neal, D. & Schanzenbach, D. (2010). Left behind by design: Proficiency counts and test-based accountability. *Review of Economics and Statistics, 92*(2), 263-283.

Patrinos, H., Barrera-Osorio, F., & Guaqueta, J. (2009). *The role and impact of public-private partnerships in education.* Washington, DC: World Bank.

Ravitch, D. (2010). *The death and life of the great American school system: How testing and choice are undermining education.* New York: Basic.

Reich, R. (2007). *Supercapitalism: The transformation of business, democracy, and everyday life.* New York: Vintage.

Reinert, E. (2007). *How rich countries got rich ... and why poor countries stay poor.* London: Constable and Robinson.

Right to Education Project. (2011). http://www.right-to-education.org/

Rodrik, D. (2007). *One economics, many recipes: Globalization, institutions, and economic growth.* Princeton, NJ: Princeton University Press.

Sahlberg, P. (2011). *Finnish lessons: What can the world learn from educational change in Finland.* NY: Teachers College Press.

Samoff, J. & Stromquist, N. (2001). Managing knowledge and storing wisdom? New forms of foreign aid? *Development and Change, 32*(4), 631-656.

Stahl, S. (2004). What do we know about fluency? Findings of the National Reading Panel. In P. McCardle, Peggy, & V. Chhabra (Eds.), *The voice of evidence in reading research.* Baltimore, MD: Paul Brookes Publishing.

Stiglitz, J. (2003). *Globalization and its discontents.* New York: W.W. Norton.

Stromquist, N. & Samoff, J. (2000). Knowledge management systems: On the promise and actual forms of information technologies, *Compare, 30*(3), 323-332.

Sousa, D. (Ed.). (2010). *Mind, brain, and education: Neuroscience implications for the classroom.* Bloomington, IN: Solution Tree Press.

Tomasevski, K. (2003). *Education denied: Costs and remedies.* London: Zed Books.

Turner, D.A. 2011. A manifesto for a dialogue between neuroscience and education, Paper presented at the annual meeting of the Comparative and International Education Society, Montreal, May 1-5, 2011.

UNESCO. (2010). *Global Monitoring Report: Reaching the marginalized.* Paris: UNESCO

UNESCO. (2011a). *Global Monitoring Report: The hidden crisis: Armed conflict and education.* Paris: UNESCO.

UNESCO. (2011b). http://www.unesco.org/new/en/education/themes/leading-the-international-agenda/right-to- education/

UNICEF. (2011). http://www.unicefusa.org/work/education/

Valijarvi, J. (2004). The system and how does it work: Some curricular and pedagogical characteristics of the Finnish comprehensive school. *Education Journal, 32*(1), 31-55.

Wagner, D. A. (forthcoming). *Smaller, quicker, cheaper: Improving learning assessments for developing countries.* Paris: IIEP.

Woessmann, L. (2009). Public-private partnerships and student achievement. In R. Chakrabarti & P. Peterson (Eds.), *School choice international: Exploring public-private partnerships.* Cambridge, MA: MIT.

World Bank. (1995). *Priorities and strategies for education.* Washington, D.C.: World Bank.

World Bank. (1999). *Education sector strategy.* Washington, D.C.: The World Bank. Human Development Network.

World Bank. (2004). *World Development Report 2004: Making services work for poor people.* Washington, D.C.: World Bank.

World Bank (2005). *Education sector strategy update.* Washington D.C.: World Bank.

World Bank. (2011a). *Addition to IDA resources: Sixteenth replenishment.* IDA16: Delivering development results. Washington, D.C.: World Bank.

World Bank. (2011b). *Learning for all: Investing in people's knowledge and skills to promote development. World Bank Group Education Sector Strategy 2020.* Washington, D.C.: World Bank

Yates, M.D. (2003). *Naming the system: Inequality and work in the global economy.* New York: Monthly Review Press.

*Steven J. Klees*
*College of Education*
*University of Maryland, U.S.A.*

# PART II

# LEARNING, ASSESSMENT, AND THE ROLE OF TEACHERS

## CHAPTER 5

ANGELA C. DE SIQUEIRA

# THE 2020 WORLD BANK EDUCATION STRATEGY: NOTHING NEW, OR THE SAME OLD GOSPEL

## INTRODUCTION

The objective of this paper is to identify whether there is any substantial change in the most recent World Bank report on education entitled: "Learning for all: Investing in people's knowledge and skills to promote development" (2011a; *WBES 2020* hereafter) regarding the Bank's rationale and directions, including actions and expected outcomes in the area of education. The *WBES 2020* title words must be examined and the meanings of knowledge, learning for all, and the kind of development at which the Bank aims clearly unveiled. In this chapter, I compare the "new" document with previous education reports, as well as shed some light the World Bank's new System Assessment and Benchmarking for Education Results (SABER), which is one of the key programs attempting to implement or enforce *WBES 2020*.

I argue that the World Bank reaffirms the same old gospels as it continues to: (a) point to education as a panacea to solve all the problems of the world (economic, environmental, developmental, nutritional, local and regional conflicts or wars, etc.); (b) support a reductionist view of education limited to useful skills or supposedly positive outcomes, thus devaluing the experience of less educated people, that is, the poor, throughout the world; (c) use a recurrent ahistorical and decontextualized perspective, weakening or dismissing countries' relevant earlier experiences and contexts, as well as previous World Bank recommendations and their consequences; (d) provide evidence based overwhelmingly on the Bank's own studies and on research undertaken by a stable of authors who work for/with the World Bank though they may be located at other institutions; and (e) reinforce a strong market-driven bias.

The analysis and recommendations in *WBES 2020* disempower students, teachers, and communities with negative consequences for learning. Simultaneously, the Bank's analysis and recommendations reinforce a businesslike approach to education, within the context of a financial crisis associated with low or decreasing possibilities of profiting from traditional areas of capital investment (banking, industry, transportation, etc.), in which education is seen as a very interesting commodity for private providers, or, more precisely, as a chief venture for capital investments and profits.

*S.J. Klees et al. (eds.), The World Bank and Education,* 69–81.

## THE WORLD BANK'S RATIONALE FOR THE IMPORTANCE OF EDUCATION

Similar to World Bank's previous Education Sector Strategies enacted, for example, in 1995, 1999, and 2005, *WBES 2020* presents education as a panacea to solve several problems:

> Education enables (people) to live healthier, happier and more productive lives. (p. 1)

> [E]ducation enhances people's ability to make informed decisions, sustain a livelihood, adopt new technologies, be better parents, cope with shocks, and be responsible citizens and effective stewards of the natural environment … Growth, development and poverty reduction depend on knowledge and skills that people acquire. (p. 1)

Some questions should be raised: Can anyone say that better educated people are happier than less educated people? Where do we find, for instance, higher suicide rates? It seems that it is not among the less educated people. Who are the people enduring continuous shocks (lack of food, potable water, sewage facilities, jobs, hunger, diseases, medicine and health care, decent pay, peace—with no international resources, wars, etc.) and at the same time able to cope with these tremendous disrupting situations? Are these the less or the better educated people? Who is the more responsible and effective steward of the natural environment? It is not the better educated ones—those who have been defending and practicing environmental depletion with huge plantations, cattle farming, industrial fisheries, mining activities, nuclear power plants, polluting factories, bigger garbage production, and lavish consumption. Local and indigenous people, generally "less educated," often protect the natural environment because it is the environment that permits their survival, and it is not uncommon that these local people—while preserving their ancient land, knowledge, ways of doing, thinking, and dealing with nature—continue to be frightened, banished, or even killed openly or by mandate by the better educated and the rich.

In *WBES 2020*, the Bank continues and reinforces a perspective of blaming persons or countries for their own supposed failure or success. Regarding individuals, the Bank also presents a reductionist perspective of education and learning, as an individual must become skilled to increase his or her individual productivity, as though production were not a collective process, and aims solely at the adaptation of new technologies rather than at their creation, as workers need "skills that determine his or her productivity and ability to *adapt* to new technologies and opportunities" (p.12, emphasis added).

Concerning countries, all problems that they are facing are dealt with as a lack of "right learning; right skills," due to bad management, absence of knowledge, or will to implement results-driven education reforms. This way of thinking can be noticed in the following quotations:

> Countries with low levels of education remain in a trap of technological stagnation, low growth and low demand for education. (p. 2)

> The very high unemployment rate of youth in the Arab World has been attributed to the poor link between education and employment market needs. (p. 47)

Surely this is a very easy and non-conflictive way to explain worldwide disparities in economic growth as well as the unemployment problem in the Arab World. But, is this reasoning acceptable? For example, how can one explain anything in the latter region without discussing the two international petroleum wars, the territorial conflicts (for water, land, and passage to the sea), religious disputes, cultural values regarding the role of man and woman in society, the international influence on the region supporting or tolerating for many years dictatorships or the failure to observe United Nations resolutions, and so forth? Here it is worthwhile to mention how countries are being classified by *WBES 2020*: middle-income, low-income, and fragile. The WB justifies this classification by expressing a belief that, "Countries with similar levels of economic development are likely to be at similar levels of *maturity* and to have comparable capacity for reform" (p. 2, emphasis added).

With such a classification the Bank reaffirms its obliviousness to countries' histories, political constraints, commercial relations, religious issues, land or wealth concentrations, international political relations, and other factors that cannot be sharply differentiated because they might affect countries at any level of development regarding their center or periphery position within the movement of capital. Indeed, with this invocation of "maturity" the Bank reinforces the old nonsense that all countries would be following the same growth path. For instance, a middle-income country in Asia and a middle-income country in Latin America, despite all their cultural, environmental, and political differences, would have equivalent capacity for reform. As is well known, within countries there are regions, counties, and even neighbourhoods with distinct problems demanding diverse forms of support. So, the "one-size-fits-all" perspective, a consequence of this "similar level of maturity" discourse, is another of the Bank's gospels.

The omission of "high-income" countries in this country-level classification scheme demonstrates that the Bank's proposed education reforms target more directly the above three groups of countries (middle-income, low-income, and fragile) by using the model of high income countries—supposedly the most mature.

Regarding the "fragile" classification, this is also problematic if based on the existence of armed conflicts, the occurrence of natural disasters, or other catastrophes. This is a very unsustainable and weak classification, dependent upon circumstantial and changeable factors. For instance, at the beginning of 2010 there were fewer areas and countries enmeshed in conflict that would warrant such a classification than existed following the start of several conflicts at the end of 2010 and the beginning of 2011. How to plan a 10-year strategy based on such a changeable, unexpected condition? How can a country deal with such a situation? How can the international community help or, we may ask, is it really willing to help?

This *WBES 2020* reasoning reflects a persistent lack of historical perspective within Bank strategies. Once more, not a word is mentioned about the historical accumulation process; that is, how rich countries became rich by plundering other nations' natural resources (land, minerals, timber, petroleum, water, and even their knowledge—through the "brain drain" and acquisition of patent rights to native species); not a word about how "development" has contributed to the increase of poverty and environmental depletion and helped the rich (national and international groups) to become richer; not a word about the continuously unfair terms of trade, with quotas and tariffs on primary products when low-income and middle-income countries are the main producers. Not a word about the adoption of the structural adjustment loans (SALs) and the huge transfers of money from the South to the North during the "lost decade" (the 1980s) when the former countries transferred to the latter countries the equivalent of six Marshall Plans (George, 1992, p. xvi). There is also not a word about the effects of the pressure and sanctions for opening markets, leading to the destruction of many national and local businesses, as well as widespread unemployment and increased dependence on the supply of basic foods, while at the same time pressuring for the adoption of cuts in budgets affecting most social areas—all this to the detriment of people's nutrition, health, education, and well-being.

The Bank, using an authoritative argument, continues to endorse a kind of linear relationship between the economy—more precisely, GDP growth—and improved results in international standardized tests, such as PISA (Programme for International Student Assessment), TIMSS (Trends in International Mathematics and Science Study, and PIRLS (Progress in International Reading Literacy Survey)."[O]ne influential study [Hanushek & Woessmann, 2008] estimates that an increase of one standard deviation in student reading and math scores on international assessments of literacy and mathematics is associated with a 2 percentage increase in annual GDP per capita growth" (World Bank, 2011a, p. 2).

Certainly this belief fails if one recalls, for instance, that Cuba has excelled in many of these international measurements and yet it did not increase its "annual GDP per capita growth." This assertion about GDP growth seems to be challenged by another *WBES 2020* statement: "[A]ccording to the International Monetary Fund (2010), output growth in emerging and developing economies is expected to be 7.2 percent in 2010, and 6.4 in 2011—more than twice the projected output growth of rich economies (p. 9). Thus, if the Bank's rationale regarding the link between education and GDP growth is held to be true, "emerging" and "developing" countries presenting such a huge GDP growth should be taken as "best performers," and they should be exporting their education systems, rather than being pushed to reform them.

However, public education systems in "emerging" and "developing" countries have been suffering severe budget constraints and there is a clear shift towards a service-delivery perspective on education instead of looking at it as a human and social right. This service rationale, strongly advocated by the World Bank since its 1999 education sector strategy (World Bank, 1999), reinforces education as a very promising commodity for private providers. Indeed, after the recent financial crisis, with low or decreasing possibilities of profiting from traditional areas of capital investment (banking, industries, transportation, etc.), education is seen as a chief venture for capital investments and profits. In this venture, capital can reap public funding by offering "services" such as school management and monitoring, teacher training (not education), student testing schemes, health and nutrition services, textbooks, curriculum design lined up with standardized tests, and information and communication technologies (ICTs), including equipment, software—all without incurring large risks. However, capital, with its inherent for-profit behavior, must reduce as much as possible its costs, and in education this implies changing the meaning and way of dealing with education, fostering a businesslike approach, seeking to encompass new markets, and offering standard and measurable "services," including a full package to foster market-driven education reform at a fast pace.

## THE "NEW" EMPHASIS AND STRATEGIES

Besides the use of authoritative arguments, the Bank continues to present a trend toward generalization with statements prefaced by "research finds," "research shows," "ultimately what matters is," and "research and field experience indicate," usually referring to World Bank-funded studies and/or private sector supporters. Two of the most frequently mentioned Bank researchers are Harry Anthony Patrinos (Bank staff), known for his advocacy of Ed Invest, International Finance Corporation (IFC), demand-side finance, and public-private partnership, and Eric Hanushek (Bank consultant), a supporter of linking resources, performance, outcomes, and accountability to international assessments and measurements in education. Both authors can be seen as genuine representatives of the neoliberal ideology in education.

It is worthwhile to comment that the above-mentioned authors have also been contributing to other international institutions, programs, and think tanks backing education reforms, such as OECD, PREAL, and the Brookings Institution as top researchers or consultants. Thus, the resemblance of many reports from the World Bank, OECD, and PREAL is not a surprise. Nor is it a surprise that when explaining "a new Strategy," the document utters laudatory notes regarding the importance of the IFC and the role of the private sector in education, with the Bank identified as supporting it with "financing, technical assistance and ... *ideas*" (p. viii, emphasis added). Also not a surprise is that several business procedures and statements such as "what matters is measurable outcomes"; "funding must be attached to results, efficiency, productivity"; "measurably better results"; "competition; comparison; best performers; low performers; incentives; sanctions; international best practices" are present throughout *WBES 2020*, evincing its strong market-driven bias.

The World Bank is far from being unpretentious, and once again claims, as proposed in the 1999 educator sector strategy and elsewhere, to be the Knowledge Bank, aiming at seizing much more leverage on worldwide education than ever: "[T]he Bank likes to think of itself as a 'knowledge bank,' and has aspirations to be both a generator of new knowledge and a synthesizer of existing knowledge" (World Bank, 2011a, p. 34).

In order to accomplish the above-mentioned aspirations, the Bank's "new" education strategy envisions "promoting country-level reforms of education systems and building *a global knowledge base powerful enough to guide* these reforms" (p. iv, emphasis added). The "Knowledge Bank" clearly defines reform directives:

[P]olicies and regulations on quality assurance, learning standards, compensatory programs, and budgetary process need to be transparently implemented and enforced .... Compliance with these policies and regulations must be monitored and noncompliance sanctioned. (p. 19)

[I]n ongoing programs or projects with results-oriented financing, disbursements are conditioned on the delivery of specific outputs or services, changes in government rules, changes in incentives structures, and changes in specific policies. (p. 44)

The new World Bank's System Assessment and Benchmarking for Education Results (SABER) must be seen in this scenario.

## SYSTEM ASSESSMENT AND BENCHMARKINGFOR EDUCATION RESULTS—SABER

SABER, a supposedly "evidence-based program," is going to bring about "what is the knowledge on what matters most to improve the quality of education," as well as "what reforms are needed" to strengthening the performance of countries' education systems, "against global standards and best practices." It is going to "put world class expertise," based on the "best global evidence" to help countries' policy-makers in identifying "potential leverage points" in order to "improve system performance and results" (World Bank, 2011b, p. 1).

To accomplish this task the SABER program has defined 13 policy domains: Assessment, Early Child Development, Education Finance, Education Technology/ICT, Engaging the Private Sector, Equity and Inclusion System, Information Systems for Planning and Policy Dialogue, School Autonomy and Accountability, School Feeding, School Health and Nutrition, School Quality Assurance, Teacher Policies, Tertiary Education, Tracking/Extending Learning Opportunities, and Workforce Development. For each one of these policy domains, SABER is going to produce a conceptual framework and diagnostic tools, country reports, case studies, prototype project concept notes and corresponding results frameworks, and finally a knowledge-based website on each domain as well as construct a "Global Education Benchmarking Tool" to define "what can be reformed for *any* country to get better results from their education system" (World Bank, 2011b, p. 2, emphasis added).

In this chapter it is impossible to look at all 13 policy domains; moreover there was nothing available at the World Bank's SABER homepage on three of the 13 domains: equity and inclusion systems, school quality assurance, and tracking/extending learning opportunities. The policy domain occupying the largest space in the homepage, with eight pages, was "Engaging the private sector." Additionally some of the mentioned policy domains present links to larger papers detailing their conceptual frameworks or objectives.

Here I am going to deal with three policy domains of *WBES 2020*: assessment, education finance and engaging the private sector, and teachers, and briefly present some concepts, such as education practice appraisals, recommendations, and conditionality attached to aid concession formulated by the World Bank in its SABER homepage and specific reports.

### *SABER—Assessment*

SABER aims at promoting "stronger assessment systems that contribute to improved education quality and learning for all" and helping countries to develop "more effective assessment systems." To do so, SABER will make available the "latest evidence for 'what works' in creating effective assessment policies and systems" (World Bank, 2011c, p. 2). The assessment framework paper (Clarke, 2011) defends the link between the increase in scores on international assessments (such as TIMMS and PISA) and GDP growth, as well as emphasizes the benefits of reduced costs and efficiency of the above-mentioned measuring instruments. Clarke (2011, p. 2) argues: "[T]esting [has] shown to be among the least expensive innovations in education reform, costing far less than increasing teacher's salaries or reducing class size, but having a higher ratio of benefit to costs."

Indeed, this quote seems to propose that countries will be better off if they choose to make a trade-off favoring the adoption of tests, mainly large-scale assessments, and rejecting teacher salary increases or class size reduction. These ideas can only come from economists, not from teachers/educators, who deal daily with students, classroom and school particularities, and individual and collective arrangements. Did any of these World Bank education policy makers or economists teach, work, or spend some months in regular schools at any time throughout their careers? Or is it that, using a lot of calculations, they write down their policy advice based on cold cost/benefit analyses, very far from schools and education reality?

Although a strong defense of such a "sound, effective and sustainable" assessment system based on international standards and tests, SABER's assessment framework paper (Clarke, 2011), referring to a 1995 Greaney & Kellaghan study, recognizes that such examinations can harm students from disadvantaged groups. Indeed, it is possible to say that it can harm, by excluding all (teachers, schools, and countries) that do not subscribe to "better performance" based on an international testing perspective.

"These kinds of examinations have shown to disproportionately negatively impact students from disadvantaged groups by limiting their opportunities to proceed to the next level of the education system or avail themselves of certain kinds of educational opportunities" (Clarke, 2011, p. 7). [Or, more clearly] "they may be excluded from the education of their choice (or any kind of education at all) on the basis of their performance" (Clarke, 2011, p. 11).

Notwithstanding the contradiction between using tests and the recognized exclusionary nature of performance-based tests, SABER's assessment framework paper, drawn by Western-oriented experts, in their majority economist-minded educators and test developers, continues to enhance their use not only as the key mechanism to evaluate student learning, but also to control school and educators. Research shows a weak but positive link between the uses of large-scale assessments to hold accountable schools and educators and better student learning outcomes" (Clarke, 2011, p. 7).

In order to forge such a link, SABER's Assessment Framework asserts that it is necessary to align curriculum, subject, and performance criteria with desired learning outcomes, as well as engage teachers and students. Thus, everybody must agree that all education and all schoolwork must be guided by international assessments; otherwise they will fail. And to get such an agreement, government intervention is needed to "create an enabling environment" or "assessment culture," in which assessment "has clear mandate and solid structure." After imposing this reduced idea of evaluation, and establishing the "needed" alignment (curriculum, teachers' work, selection, training, promotion, student requirements, classification, etc.), governments must leave the implementation to private providers, using public-private partnerships (Clarke, 2011, p.15).

*SABER—Finance*

Subsequently, the SABER finance framework (World Bank, 2011d) reinforces the idea that the best practices in education finance are those that align funding with education outcomes. Thus, SABER Finance eagerly defends performance-based budgets as a way of creating fiscal incentives to improve results. Such a performance-based finance is seen as a neutral—not biased—apolitical instrument, providing "transparency and accountability." The full adherence of countries to this model would signal "good governance." The SABER finance framework also states the need to train school leaders, mainly "if they have *prior experience* as educators" (Vegas et al., 2011, pp. 10-11, emphasis added). Following this reasoning, what is needed is to change school leadership by adopting an economist's view of education and displacing remaining pedagogical/academic/education perspectives.

The World Bank's SABER finance framework also tries to lessen the importance of countries devoting more resources to education, stating that "beyond a certain threshold, how funds are spent is more important than how much they are" (Vegas et al., 2011, p. 8). This kind of rationale aims at making countries supposedly more "productive", more "efficient," that is, doing the same or more with equal or smaller resources. Such reasoning avoids pressures on government budgets and also allows private sector "services" in education. Indeed, recalling the Bank's country classifications (latent, emerging, established, and mature), those classified as latent or emerging—that is, those at the bottom of the "best performers" scale—probably encompass the majority of the worldwide economically disadvantaged population. So these countries need to devote more resources to building or strengthening public social networks, allowing their population to have access to quality schools and health systems, potable water, sewer facilities, reliable transportation, etc.

The SABER finance framework also criticizes teachers' absenteeism in schools and the lack of punishment mentioned in their records or any cut in their salaries (Vegas et al., 2011, p. 10). This criticism seeks to weaken or ban the long-established status of teachers as civil servants. As civil servants, teachers in many countries have specific rules to be hired, fired, promoted, paid, and retired. Most of those civil servants are also unionized and can fight—by promoting protest marches or even strikes—not only to get higher pay, better working conditions, and protection of their acquired rights, but also to stand for an education perspective aimed at empowering all people as citizens conscious of their rights as human beings, and with the knowledge, intellectual autonomy, and means to express their concerns, desires and needs. Surely, this standpoint clashes with the Bank's market-driven perspective, based on the premise of linking resource allocation and disbursement with expected education outputs, chiefly reduced to improved results in international standardized tests established by such entities as the Knowledge Bank and OECD.

*SABER—Engaging the Private Sector*

SABER also manifests concerns about teachers, especially in regards to hiring, rewarding, and firing policies (World Bank, 2011e). Indeed, it places the private sector's methods of dealing with teachers as better than those of the public sector, because it is more "flexible". In other words, it is possible to say that teachers can be hired and fired more easily; that is, hired without the need of organizing a public competition and fired if they do not achieve the expected outcomes as, for instance, students' improvement in international test scores. Further, the SABER document states that, "Flexibility in teacher contracting is one of the primary motivations for engaging the private sector" (World Bank, 2011e, p. 4).

This affirmation seeks to reduce expenditures on teachers while fostering other expenses such as the creation of testing schemes and spending more on ICTs, as well as making room to expand the hiring of private sector providers to design curriculum, evaluate students, train teachers, produce education software, and books.

The document mentions other benefits of engaging the private sector in education, such as stimulating competition among public and private schools to attract students, as well as bringing about cost reductions with quality assurance by fostering the use of bidding contracts with minimum quality standards and measurable outcomes attached. It states that both private sector features would improve the quality of education. Indeed, its reasoning justifies the reaping of public resources by private providers that see and deal with education largely as a promising profitable commodity, with the intention of increasing their own wealth.

In order to achieve this goal, private providers will be willing to reduce education costs as much as possible, implying attacks on teachers' civil service status and changing the meaning and manner of dealing with education by fostering a business-like approach to offer a cheaper, limited, standardized, and measurable training "service," rather than a comprehensive education.

*SABER—Teachers*

The first point to observe in SABER's focus on teachers is that it is confined to public schools (World Bank. 2011f). Does that mean that private schools do not need to improve their teachers' goals or policies, or that private teachers must not become a matter of public intrusion into private business? Or even that this is a clear sign that the Bank really wants to change public school teachers' methods and thinking on education, curriculum, evaluation, schools, intellectual autonomy, democracy, etc.?

The SABER document on teachers refers to, "core teacher policy goals to which *all education systems* should aim" in order to produce "effective teachers" (p. 2, emphasis added). So, once more, the Bank adopts a "one-size-fits-all perspective," despite its denial in some parts of *WBES 2020*. The eight policy goals are:

> Setting *clear expectations* for teachers, Attracting the best into teaching, Preparing teachers with *useful* training and experience, Matching teachers' skills with students' needs, Leading teachers with *strong principals, Monitoring* teaching and learning, Supporting teachers to improve *instruction,* Motivating teachers *to perform.* (World Bank. 2011f, p. 2, emphasis added)

These goals completely disempower teachers and disqualify their work and careers by: reducing their education to being trained in useful skills, permitting an assault on their civil service rights (hiring, sabbatical leaves, and retirement benefits), compelling them to develop their teaching work to improve student results in international assessment tests, fostering submission to authoritarian and inflexible principals, using measurement instruments to scrutinize teaching and learning, and fostering competition and fear of punishment or even dismissal to make teachers accomplish defined goals. The document justifies the choice of the above eight goals by arguing that "they are related to either student or teacher performance; they are priorities for resource allocation; they are actionable (i.e., governments can have a direct influence on them through policy reforms)" (p. 2).

Finally, countries are classified based on their adherence to and improvement in each of these education goals, from latent through mature, with those countries with greatest adherence/improvement being classified as mature. Once more the World Bank recalls the flawed maturity argument.

The SABER document on teachers also defines 10 core teacher policy areas: Requirements to enter and remain in teaching, Initial teacher preparation, Recruitment and employment, Teachers' workload and autonomy, Professional development, Compensation (salary and non-salary benefits), Retirement rules and benefits, Monitoring and evaluation of teacher quality, Teacher representation and voice, and School leadership. These areas are thought to be restructured by taking the private sector's method of dealing with teachers as the main model.

Here it is fundamental to restate that these goals and policy areas for teachers intended by the Bank to guide restructuring are akin to the OECD rationale and drive, as expressed in its teachers report *Teachers Matter: Attracting, Developing and Retaining Effective Teachers* (OECD, 2005), which is also being used by other programs for education reforms, such as the PREAL in Latin America (see PREAL/BID 2004; **Vaillant & Rossel, 2010**). They can also be found in Hanushek et al. (1994), a book resulting from the Panel on the Economics of Education (PEER), organized by Hanushek and published by liberal think tank, the Brookings Institution.

Despite the strict guidelines and enforcement practices (financing conditioned to reform implementation and enhanced results in international standards, evaluation/measurement procedures, and the fact that the "right" knowledge will be the one that builds, collects, amasses, and spreads according to the SABER program), the Bank continues to affirm a supposedly democratic and open framework, respecting countries' differences and leaving them hypothetical choice options: "Given the immense differences among countries, it would be unwise to prescribe a one-size-fits-all strategy" (p. 35).

But *WBES 2020* will contribute to taking control and autonomy over academic work from students, parents, teachers, schools, and community, placing it in the hands of a small group of experts connected with selected international organizations and programs, such as OECD, UNESCO, regional development banks, PREAL, and the World Bank's Knowledge Bank and SABER, as a new initiative to guide, supervise, finance and control all aspects of education.

## FINAL REMARKS

The World Bank with its new "Learning for All" strategy, in which education is reduced to "learning," and learning reduced to improved results in international standardized tests, contributes to fostering the commodification, sterilization, and standardization of knowledge.

Based on such a restricted, limited, and commercial view of education and learning, the academic work will thwart the existence of references to and linkage with the local reality and peoples' lives. Teachers, students, parents and all the national/local academic researchers who think about the everyday problems their education systems face—continue to be ignored and discarded as active intellectual actors.

*WBES 2020* reaffirms the Bank's desire to act as the "knowledge bank," geared to define, guide, enforce, and monitor education reforms as well as to punish non-compliance. In order to achieve this goal, the Bank created its SABER program, with the intention of establishing "a Global Education Benchmarking Tool." Surely, with this program there will be an immense outside influence controlling what must happen inside classrooms, what must be taught, and at what pace it must

ANGELA C. DE SIQUEIRA

be done to be measured at a specific time and date. Therefore, it constitutes a serious peril to democracy, which presupposes diversity, not homogeneity.

It is pertinent to mention that the word SABER, which in the Portuguese and Spanish languages, means "to know," was the choice acronym for this key Bank program supporting *WBES 2020* implementation. Was it a mere coincidence or an intended choice? Surely it is a suitable name for the "knowledge bank" that always knows everything and that with all its achieved wisdom can give advice and even demand compliance with best performance indicators or deny financial resources, hamper promotions and new hiring, and demand certifications.

Moreover, this "Learning for All" strategy is very far from contributing to a true education of people, empowering them as citizens conscious of their rights as human beings and providing them with knowledge, intellectual autonomy, and ways to express their concerns, desires, and needs. To do so would mean offering opportunity and conditions to every human being to develop his/her potential as "a philosopher and artist, a technician and a politician" in order to be placed "in a government position or in control of those in a decision-making position" (Gramsci, 1971).

Finally, it seems that the World Bank continues to lack an interest in and humble posture toward learning rather than imposing and selling "a best performer education reform agenda" from a distinct social and cultural milieu.

## REFERENCES

Clarke, M. (2011). *Framework for building an effective assessment system*. READ/MAPS Discussions Paper, 1/12/2011. Washington, D.C.: The World Bank Group.
http://siteresources.worldbank.org/EDUCATION/Resources/278200-1121703274255/1439264-1294964677637/Framework_Paper.pdf
George, S. (1992). *The debt boomerang. How Third World debt can harm us all*. Boulder: Pluto Press with Transnational Institute.
Gramsci, A. (1971). *Selections from the Prison Notebooks*. (Translated and edited by Quintin Hoare and Geoffrey Smith.). New York: International Publishers.
Greaney, V. & Kellaghan, T. (1995). *Equity issues in public examinations in developing countries*. Washington, D.C.: World Bank.
Hanushek, E., Benson, C., Freeman, R., Jamison, D., Levin, H., Maynard, R., Murnane, R., Rivkin, S., Sabot, R., Solmon, L., Summers, A., Welch, F., & Wolfe, B. *Making schools work: Improving performance and controlling costs*. Washington, D.C.: The Brookings Institution.
Hanushek, E. & Woessmann, L. (2008). The role of cognitive skills in economic development. *Journal of Economic Literature, 46*(3), 607-668.
OECD. (2005). *Teachers matter: Attracting, developing and retaining effective teachers*. Paris: OECD.
PREAL/BID. (2004). *Maestros en América Latina: Nuevas perspectivas sobre suformación y desempeño*. Santiago: Editorial San Marino.
Vaillant, D. & Rossel, C. (2010). *El reconocimiento de la docencia efectiva: la premiación a la excelencia*. N° 48. Santiago: PREAL.
Vegas, E. et al. (2011). *SABER—Finance. Objectives and conceptual approach*.
http://siteresources.worldbank.org/EDUCATION/Resources/278200-1290520949227/7575842-1299533754312/Summary_Paper.pdf.
World Bank (1999). *Education sector strategy*. Washington, D.C.: The World Bank Group World. Human Development Network.

80

World Bank (2011a). *Learning for all: Investing in people's knowledge and skills to promote development. World Bank Education Sector Strategy 2020.* Washington, D.C.: The World Bank.

World Bank. (2011b). *SABER—System assessment and benchmarking for education results.* http://go.worldbank.org/C36SDN4CS0

World Bank (2011c). *SABER—Assessment.* http://go.worldbank.org/DWZB0TMTS0

World Bank. (2011d). *SABER—Finance.* http://go.worldbank.org/L5Y0A31000

World Bank. (2011e). *SABER—Engaging the private sector scale.* http://go.worldbank.org/R9HRQ82UG0

World Bank. (2011f). *SABER—Teachers.* http://go.worldbank.org/MU6QMF8340

*Angela C. de Siqueira*
*College of Education*
*Universidade Federal Fluminense, Brazil*

## CHAPTER 6

MARK GINSBURG

# TEACHERS AS LEARNERS: A MISSING FOCUS IN "LEARNING FOR ALL"

## INTRODUCTION

As indicated in its title, *Learning for All: Investing in People's Knowledge and Skills to Promote Development*, the World Bank Group Education Strategy 2020 focuses on learning for all. The document (World Bank, 2011) states that the "Bank's mission in education" is "learning for all" (p. xi) and explains that:

> The World Bank commits to supporting educational development, with a focus on *learning for all* ... for a simple reason: growth, development, and poverty reduction depend on the knowledge and skills that people acquire, not just the number of years that they sit in a classroom ... The "for all" part of the strategy's goal is crucial ... [because it] promotes the equity goals that underlie the education MDGs [Millennium Development Goals] ... by linking them to the universally shared objective of accelerating learning ... The new education strategy is built on the premise that *people learn throughout life*, not simply during the years they spend in formal schooling. (pp. 11-12; emphasis in original)

Thus, the title and some parts of the text of the 2011 strategy document highlight the importance of "learning", but the focus on learning" (or, more precisely, learning outcomes) is not really new. As we will see, these issues also appear in previous World Bank strategy documents (1995 and 1999).

What concerns me, however, is that an important group of people—teachers— are not included as part of the "all" when it comes to the focus on learning. As Leu and Ginsburg (2011, p. 1) state, "teachers and the quality of their teaching are now widely recognized as the most critical of many important factors that combine to create overall quality of education (see also Craig et al., 1998; Darling-Hammond, 2000; Good et al., 2009; UNESCO 2006). Fifteen years ago Villegas-Reimers and Reimers raised a similar concern in their article, "Where are 60 Million Teachers? The Missing Voice in Educational Reform around the World." Specifically, Villegas-Reimers and Reimers (1996, p. 470) criticize the World Bank's (1995) *Priorities and Strategies for Education* document for not "addressing teachers,

*S.J. Klees et al. (eds.), The World Bank and Education, 83–93.*

their selection, training, supervision or participation in the reforms" at the core of its "six key options ... to reform education systems." They also lament the fact that little attention is given to teacher learning:

> It is better to think of an education system as a living organization, where individuals (teachers, parents and students) can grow ... and [be] ready to face new problems .... The key question in this perspective then becomes how can one help reforms learn from teachers, and how can reforms help *teachers learn*. The current emphasis of school reform on learning is well founded if it includes not just student learning but *teacher learning* as well. (p. 484; emphasis added)

In this chapter I trace how teachers—and, especially, teacher learning—are or are not included as a focus in key World Bank education sector strategy documents (1995, 1999, and 2011). Based on content analysis of these documents, I show that teachers have not been ignored, but that issues of teacher learning are rarely treated. Indeed, while brief discussions about teacher learning appear in the 1995 and 1999 publications, no such references can be found in the 2011 text. Instead of focusing on teachers as learners and promoting learning for teachers, the World Bank strategy documents treat teachers as a human capital, a resource or input that is required for the process of producing student learning outcomes. I then review some of the literature discussing why teacher learning is important and how schools and education systems can become learning organizations or learning communities for all, teachers as well as students. Finally, I consider why the World Bank strategy documents tend to ignore or downplay the importance of teacher learning.

TEACHERS AND TEACHER LEARNING IN WORLD BANK
STRATEGY DOCUMENTS

In this section I report on a content analysis of three strategy documents published by World Bank in the last 16 years: (1) *Priorities and Strategies for Education: A World Bank Review* (1995), (2) *Education Sector Strategy* (1999), and (3) *Learning for All: Investing in People's knowledge and Skills to Promote Development* (2011). This analysis involved counting the number of sentences or phrases in which the words, teacher(s),[1] appeared as well as a classification of such references into the following themes:

a) teacher as *human resource* for education (including input, student-teacher ratio, teacher knowledge/skills),
b) teacher as *employee* (including issues of hiring/firing, salary, conditions/ benefits, attendance, supervision, assessment),
c) teacher as school/classroom *staff member* (decision-making, relating to community),
d) teacher as member of an organization/*union,*
e) teacher as *recipient of pre-service* education/training,
f) teacher as *recipient of in-service* education/training, and

g) teacher as *learner/inquirer*.

Note that I distinguish between references to teachers needing pre-service education (e) or in-service training (f) and discussions of teacher learning or teachers as inquirers (g). The latter focuses on the *process* of teacher learning, while pre-service and in-service are treated either as a *product/output* (i.e., teachers being or needing to be trained) or as an *input* (i.e., trained teachers contributing to student learning/achievement).

*Priorities and Strategies for Education (1995)*

In the introductory "Summary" section of the 1995 strategy document, we learn that:

> This paper synthesizes World Bank work on education since publication of the last sector policy paper, in 1980, and considers options for the Bank's borrowing countries .... Investment in education contributes to the *accumulation of human capital*, which is essential for higher incomes and sustained economic growth. Education—especially basic (primary and lower-secondary) education—helps reduce poverty by increasing the productivity of the poor, by reducing fertility and improving health, and by equipping people with the skills they need to participate fully in the economy and in society. More generally, education helps strengthen civil institutions and build national capacity and good governance—critical elements in the implementation of sound economic and social policies. (pp. 1-2)

And Chapter 4, "Improving Quality," explains "the quality of education is defined both by the *learning* environment and student *outcomes*," [ii] and argues that "education outcomes can be improved through four important actions: (a) setting standards for performance; (b) supporting inputs known to improve achievement; (c) adopting flexible strategies for the acquisition of inputs; and (d) monitoring performance" (p. 73; emphasis added). On the next page the document identifies "a teacher who knows and can teach the subject" (p. 74) as one of five types of inputs for achieving learning outcomes and devotes approximately one page (out of 15) to a section focused on research documenting how "teachers' knowledge and skill" contributes to student learning outcomes, although this issue is mentioned in other places as well.

In Part II of its 1995 strategy document, the World Bank identifies six key reforms:

> which taken together will go a long way toward enabling low- and middle-income countries to meet the challenges in access, equity, quality, and pace of reform that they face today. These reforms are a higher priority for education; attention to [learning] outcomes; [iii] concentration of efficient public investment on basic education, coupled with more reliance on household financing for higher education; attention to equity; household

involvement in education systems; and autonomous institutions that will permit the flexible combination of instructional inputs. (p. 89)

*Table 1. Frequencies and Percentages of Various Categories of References to Teachers*

| | Priorities & Strategies for Education (1995) | Education Sector Strategy (1999) | Learning for All (2011) |
|---|---|---|---|
| *Teacher as:* | Number of specific references (% of total references to teachers) | | |
| *Human resource for education/student learning (input, student-teacher ratio, knowledge/skills)* | 57 (36%) | 27 (34%) | 21 (27%) |
| *Employee (issues of hiring/firing, salary, conditions/benefits, attendance, selection, supervision, assessment/accountability)* | 32 (20%) | 13 (16%) | 34 (44%) |
| *School/classroom staff member (decision making, relating to community)* | 26 (16%) | 5 (6%) | 4 (5%) |
| *Professional organization/union member* | 10 (6%) | 3 (4%) | 0 (0%) |
| *Recipient of pre-service education/training* | 15 (9%) | 12 (15%) | 7 (9%) |
| *Recipient of in-service education/training* | 27 (17%) | 17 (21%) | 11 (14%) |
| *Learner/inquirer* | 3 (2%) | 3 (4%) | 0 (0%) |
| *TOTAL references to teachers (per page)* | 160 (1.03) | 80 (0.95) | 77 (0.88) |
| *TOTAL pages analyzed in document* | 155 | 84 | 88 |

As can be seen in Table 1, this World Bank document includes just over one reference to teacher(s) per page (i.e., 160/155), though clearly those references are not equally distributed across the pages of the report. Moreover, more than one-third (57/160 or 36 percent) of these references concern teachers as human resources, that is, inputs that are discussed in parallel with other inputs such as school facilities and textbooks. If one combines these with references to teachers as employees (i.e., issue of hiring/firing, salary, conditions/benefits, attendance, selection, supervision, assessment/accountability), which may be seen as an extension of the focus on teachers as human resources, we have over one-half (89/160 or 56 percent) of the references to teachers. Two other categories, teacher as school/classroom staff member (26/160 or 16 percent) and teacher as recipient of in-service training (27/160 or 17 percent) each constituted about one-sixth of the references to teacher(s).

However, as Table 1 shows, there were 3 (2 percent) out of 160 references to teachers (in 155 pages of text) that could be categorized as addressing the issues of teachers as learners/inquirers. [iv] The first example comes from Chapter 4, "Improving Quality." Here the document provides more detail regarding in-service training, citing a range of US-based research literature that focuses on strategies for promoting teacher learning:

> Recognized effective elements of in-service training include exposure to new theory or techniques, demonstrations of their application, practice by the teacher, feedback to the teacher, and coaching overtime .... As these elements suggest, in-service training is most effective when [what teachers learn] is linked directly to classroom practice by the teacher ... and provided by the head teacher .... (p. 83)

The other two, consecutive references to teachers as learners/inquirers, appear in Chapter 10, "Autonomous Institutions:"

– Clusters of schools, sometimes called nucleos or school learning cells, facilitate professional interaction among teachers and decision-making about instruction, ... [which] may be more important than decision-making authority for [teacher] motivation and learning .... (pp. 129-130)

– Periodic conferences and workshops can provide opportunities for teachers representing different clusters to share what they are doing with their colleagues, ... [and, thus, for example, help them learn how] to develop new curricular materials in local languages .... (p. 130)

*Education Sector Strategy (1999)*

Near the beginning of its "Executive Summary" of the 1999 strategy document, the World Bank states:

> The long-term goal in education is nothing less than to ensure *everyone* completes a basic education of adequate quality, acquires foundation skills— literacy, numeracy, reasoning, and social skills such as teamwork—and has *further opportunities* to learn advanced skills throughout life, in a range of post-basic education settings .... Whatever the education situation and needs in a country, access to quality teaching and learning must be a pre-eminent concern ... [in relation to] people ... gaining the knowledge, skills, and values they need .... There must be, in policy and actions, an unrelenting *concentration on learning.* (1999, p. vii; emphasis added)[v]

In seeking to address this long-term goal, the World Bank (1999, pp. 29-35) spells out four global priorities: (a) basic education for girls and for the poorest; (b) early intervention: early childhood development and school health; (c) innovative delivery: distance education, open learning and the use of new technologies; and (d) selected areas of system reform: standards/curriculum/achievement assessment, governance and decentralization, and providers and financiers outside of government.

Looking at Table 1, we see that the 1999 document contains on average slightly under one reference to teacher(s) per page (80/84). Of these references, just over one-third (27/80 or 34 percent) are categorized as focused on teachers as human resources/inputs and an additional 16 percent (13/80) of the references concern teachers as employees. Indeed, there is an entire, though brief section devoted to "teachers and teachers' organizations" in Chapter 4: "Partnering: A World of Opportunities." The one paragraph in this section contains the following:

> Teachers' commitment to improvement is essential if change is to have a real impact on [student] learning. Teachers, and the local, national and international organizations that represent them, must therefore have the opportunity to participate not only in implementing reform, but also in developing new programs .... The interests of teachers, as workers, have to be considered in relation to the preeminent interests of students and their parents, as consumers. (p. 19)

Additionally, while 12 (15 percent) and 17 (21 percent) of the 80 references to teachers are linked to the general ideas of pre-service and in-service training, respectively, only 3 (4 percent) references even briefly address issues of teachers as learners/inquirers. The first reference to teachers as learners occurs in Chapter 2, entitled "The Vision: Quality Education for All." The 1999 strategy document explains that "improving quality education will require countries to deal with a number of crucial issues," the first of which involves paying "especial attention" to:

> the processes of teaching and learning. Given the impact that classroom teachers can have on students' attainment and the share of most education budgets that go to pay teachers' salaries, an education policy that highlights the importance of quality teaching—where teachers have the opportunity for regularly upgrading their skills in order to maintain mastery of their subject area—is likely to bear fruit. (p. 8)

The second such reference appears in Chapter 5: Moving Forward: The Bank's Role Thus Far, in a section entitled "a changing focus":

> The most dramatic change has been the investment shift from "hardware" to "software," ... [which] covers many aspects of the education system, including: ... technological innovation (e.g., WorldLinks for Development, aiming to establish ... on-line [learning] communities for students and teachers in 1500 secondary schools around the world by the year 2000. (p. 25)

The third example of teachers as learners is also associated with the use of information and communication technology. In Chapter 6: Moving Forward: What the Bank Will Do, the document includes a box presenting "four examples of innovative use of media and technology," including the following one:

> The Development Education Program (www.worldbank.org/depweb/) offers a website for teachers and students who want to study social, economic, and environmental issues of sustainable development around the world. The program uses learning modules, maps, charts, data tables, case studies, photos, outreach activities, teachers' materials, on-line student newspaper, and much more. (p. 33)

### Learning for All (2011)

The 2011 strategy document includes less than one reference to teacher(s) per page. As shown in Table 1 there are 77 such references in a document that contains 88 pages.[vi] Additionally, it is important to note that, unlike the 1995 and 1999 strategy documents, the 2011 publication has no section labeled as focusing specifically on teachers.

Moreover, as is shown in Table 1, there are no references that can be categorized as focused on teacher learning or teachers as learners/inquirers, and there are only a few references to teachers as recipients of pre-service training (7/77 or 9 percent) and in-service training (11/77 or 14 percent). The large majority of references to teachers were categorized either as teacher as human resource (21/77 or 27 percent) or as teacher as employee (34/77 or 44 percent), in combination representing almost three-fourths of the references to teachers (55/77 or 71 percent). For instance, the 2011 strategy document describes the system approach it will employ, referring to one of the system tools, "Teacher Policies around the World, which has been launched as a prototype, together with the publication of the strategy" (p. xiv). In a footnote the World Bank (2011) explains that "[t]he system tool on teacher policies builds evidence on policies and practice regarding teacher recruitment, selection, training, evaluation, incentives for performance, pedagogy, and professional development" ( p. 97).

## WHY TEACHERS AS LEARNERS RECEIVE LIMITED ATTENTION IN WORLD BANK DOCUMENTS

Here I consider two possible reasons for the limited attention to teachers as learners/inquirers in the World Bank Strategy documents. The first is that there might not be research or other literature on which the Bank could draw to develop this topic. The second revolves around how teachers (and others) are conceived within the dominant theoretical perspective informing the World Bank's writings and other activities: human capital.

### Teachers as Learners and Schools as Learning Organizations/Communities

The limited attention to teachers as learners/inquirers in the World Bank's 1995 and 1999 strategy documents and the total absence of such in its 2011 strategy document are surprising given the attention to such issues in the education and teacher education literature. For example, the ideas Peter Senge presented in his 1990 book, *The Fifth Discipline: The Art and Practice of the Learning Organization*, caught the imagination of leaders in education, business, and other professional fields. And Senge's subsequent publication, *Schools that Learn: A Fifth Discipline Fieldbook* (2000), only increased the influence of his ideas on educators and teacher educators. As Westheimer (2008) recounts, Senge initially "urged corporate America to consider developing 'learning organizations'" (p. 768) and then encouraged education reformers to "imagine a successful school-based learning community ... [as] a meeting ground for learning—dedicated to the idea that all those involved with it, individually and together, will be continually enhancing and expanding their awareness and capabilities" (p. 762).

Furthermore, in his chapter on "Learning among Colleagues" in the *Handbook of Research on Teacher Education*, Westheimer (2008, p. 756) argues—and provides evidence to support the claim—that "teachers cannot possibly create and sustain productive learning environments for students when no such conditions exist for teachers."[vii] Cochran-Smith and Demers (2010, p. 34) elaborate the issues in their chapter on "Research and Teacher Learning: Taking an Inquiry Stance" in *Teachers as Learners: Critical Discourse on Challenges and Opportunities*:

> A central aspect of teacher learning from an inquiry stance is learning in the company of ... new and experienced teachers as well as teacher educators and other partners .... In inquiry communities, everybody is regarded as a learner and a researcher rather than some people designated as the experts with all of the knowledge and others designated as being in need of that knowledge. Inquiry communities are designed to pose questions, gather and analyse data in order to make decisions about instruction and practice.[viii]

### Human Capital or Human Beings?

It is not news that the World Bank draws upon and promotes human capital theory (e.g., see Psacharopoulos, 1995). Thus, one would expect to see connections with human capital theory in the strategy documents analyzed in this chapter. For instance, one of the quotes presented above from the 1995 World Bank strategy document includes the following words: "human capital ... helps reduce poverty by increasing ... productivity" (World Bank, 1995, p. 1). Similarly, World Bank (1999) argues that "for the poor ... human capital [i]s the main, if not only, means of escaping poverty" (p. 1) and "human capital development → productivity" (p. 5). These statements are mainly concerned with the importance of developing through formal education the human capital of students as future workers, which is the main focus on education within human capital theory (Levinson, 2002; Woodhall, 1997).

However, the 2011 strategy document explicitly signals that teachers themselves should be understood as human capital, thus contributing to the "production" process in schooling. For instance, in the excerpt below, note how policies related to teachers are listed along with financial capital and buildings (a form of fixed capital): "An education system has several core policy domains that ... include: a) ... laws, rules, and regulations that determine how *teachers* are recruited, deployed, paid, and managed; b) how *fiscal resources* are allocated and spent; and c) how *schools* ... are established and supervised ... (World Bank, 2011, p. 17, emphasis added).

This excerpt from the 2011 strategy document is illuminative, in that human capital is defined as "the concept based on the belief that the role of workers in production is similar to the role of machinery and other forces of production" (Johnson, 2000, p. 46; see also Becker, 1993). As Schultz (1961, p. 3) argues, "human beings are incontestably capital from an abstract and mathematical point of view." In this approach teachers (and other workers) are commodified, treated—at least conceptually—as things to be bought, sold, traded, or invested in (see Marx, 1859). Indeed, even Schultz (1961, p. 2) recognized the potential problem of the concept of human capital, in that "it seems to reduce man [i.e., human beings] ... to a mere material component, to something akin to property."

One explanation of the limited focus in World Bank strategy documents on teachers as learners, therefore, derives from this commodification of teachers' labor (and, indeed, of teachers themselves). Attention to teachers' learning (a process that enhances the value of their human capital) might be considered as tangential to an education sector strategy document as the processes of enhancing financial capital (e.g., collecting taxes) or enhancing fixed capital (constructing buildings).

## CONCLUSION

In contrast, if one begins with a concept of teachers (or, for that matter, students) as human beings then the *process* of learning and human development becomes very relevant. From this starting point, one would be less likely to focus only on the *product* of learning, treating teachers as a material component or as commodity. If teachers were conceived of as human beings, with special attention to teachers as learners, then strategic attention by the World Bank, other international organizations, and governments would be given to how education systems and policies need to be reformed to encourage and facilitate teacher learning. This would mean taking seriously the idea that schools and school systems should be learning communities for teachers as well as students.

## NOTES

i   I counted only instances in which primary and secondary school teachers were mentioned, not including the few references to higher education instructors.

ii  Note how the World Bank's 1995 document emphasizes learning outcomes, thus anticipating its 2011 special focus on learning.

iii In Chapter 6, "Attention to Outcomes," the document clarifies that "the emphasis solely on years in school is misplaced. More appropriate would be an emphasis on knowledge and skills" (World Bank, 1995, p. 95).

iv  The existence of these three references to teachers as learners in the 1995 World Bank Strategy document provides a minor contradiction to the above-noted conclusion reached by Villegas-Reimers and Reimers (1996).

v  Note how the World Bank's 1999 document emphasizes "learning" and "quality" education for "everyone," thus anticipating its 2011 focus on "learning for all."

vi  However, I should note that 2011 Education Strategy gives considerably more attention to teachers than was the case for the previously circulated document, "Concept Note for the World Bank Education Strategy 2020" (World Bank, 2010a), which was the focus of the first phase of external consultations (for a report on the consultations, see World Bank, 2010b). In the 15-page "Concept Note," only three brief references are made to teachers as an occupational group, concerning retrenchment (p. 4); shortages (p. 6); and recruitment, hiring, training, and management (p. 7).

vii  However, Westheimer (2008, p. 768) also identifies some of the obstacles to fostering professional learning communities: teacher isolation, lack of time, school architecture, and external pressures such as standardized testing of students.

viii  As Cochran-Smith and Demers (2010, p. 28) explain, an inquiry stance offers a challenge to the dominant discourse during the current "era of accountability" in which emphasis is given to "scripted curricula and teacher-proof materials designed to compensate for a weak teaching force. On the contrary, inquiry-centered teaching and teacher preparation are based on the twin premises that teaching and teacher preparation are intellectual rather than technical activities and that most educators are capable of inquiring into practice, posing and answering questions, generating local knowledge within learning communities, and making complex decisions about teaching and learning."

## REFERENCES

Becker, G. S. (1993). *Human capital: A theoretical and empirical analysis, with special reference to education.* 3rd ed. Chicago: University of Chicago Press.

Cochran-Smith, M. & Demers, K. (2010). Research and teacher learning: Taking an inquiry stance. In O. Kwo (Ed.), *Teachers as learners: Critical discourse on challenges and opportunities.* Hong Kong: CERC and Springer, pp. 14-43.

Craig, H., Kraft, R., & duPlessis, J. (1998). *Teacher development: Making an impact.* Washington, D.C.: USAID and World Bank.

Darling-Hammond, L. (2000). How teacher education matters. *Journal of Teacher Education, 51*(3), 166-173.

Good, T., Wiley, C. & Florez, I. R. (2009). Effective teaching: An emerging synthesis. In L. Saha & A. G. Dworkin (Eds.), *International handbook of research on teachers and teaching* (pp. 803-816). New York: Springer.

Johnson, A. (2000). *The Blackwell dictionary of sociology.* Oxford, UK: Blackwell Publishers.

Leu, E. & Ginsburg, M. (2011). *First principles compendium: Designing effective education programs for in-service teacher professional development.* Washington, D.C.: American Institutes for Research, EQUIP1, and USAID.

Levinson, D. (2002). Human capital theory. In D. Levinson, P. Cookson, & A. Sadovnik (Eds.), *Education and sociology: An encyclopedia* (pp. 377-379). New York: RoutledgeFalmer.

Marx, K. (1859, 1977). *Contribution to a critique of political economy.* Moscow: Progress Publishers.

Psacharopoulos, G. (1995). *Building human capital for better lives.* Series: Directions in Development. Washington, D.C.: World Bank.

Schultz, T. (1961). Investment in human capital. *American Economic Review, 51*(1), 1-17.

Senge, P. (1990). *The fifth discipline: The art and practice of the learning organization.* New York: Doubleday.

Senge, P. (2000). *Schools that learn: A fifth discipline fieldbook for educators, parents, and everyone who cares about education.* New York: Doubleday.

UNESCO Institute for Statistics. (2006). *Teachers and educational quality: Monitoring global needs for 2015*. Montreal: UNESCO Institute for Statistics.

Villegas-Reimers, E. & Reimers, F. (1996). Where are 60 million teachers? The missing voice in educational reforms around the world. *Prospects, 26*(3), 469-492.

Westheimer, J. (2008). Learning among colleagues: Teacher community and the shared enterprise of education. In M. Cochran-Smith, S. Feinman-Nemser, D. J. McIntyre, & K Demers (Eds.), *Handbook of research on teacher education*, 3rd edition (pp. 756-783). New York: Routledge and Association of Teacher Education.

Woodhall, M. (1997). Human capital concepts. In A. Halsey, H. Lauder, P. Brown, & A. S. Wells (Eds.), *Education, culture, economy and society* (pp. 219-223). New York: Oxford University Press.

World Bank. (1995, August). *Priorities and strategies in education: A World Bank review*. Washington, D.C.: World Bank.

World Bank. (1999, July). *Education sector strategy*. Washington, D.C.: World Bank.

World Bank.(2010a, February).Concept note for the World Bank Education Strategy 2020.Washington, D.C.: World Bank.

World Bank (2010b, 31 August). Report on Phase I External consultations. Washington, D.C.: World Bank.

World Bank. (2011, 12 April). *Learning for all: Investing in people's knowledge and skills to promote development. World Bank Group Education Strategy 2020.*Washington, D.C.: World Bank.

*Mark Ginsburg*
*FHI 360 (formerly Academy for Educational Development)*
*College of Education, University of Maryland*
*Teachers College, Columbia University, U.S.A.*

## CHAPTER 7

CRAIN SOUDIEN

# "QUALITY'S" HORIZONS

*The Politics of Monitoring Educational Quality*

## INTRODUCTION

The latest World Bank strategy document, *Education Strategy 2020* (*WBES 2020*, hereafter), is likely to evoke a great deal of discussion around the world because of the emphasis it places on education quality. *WBES 2020* says, for example: "Growth, development, and poverty reduction depend on the knowledge and skills that people acquire, not the number of years they sit in the classroom" (p. vii). It makes a distinction, moreover, between physical access to education and the access education provides to personal growth and development. Critical about this development is that it brings the World Bank into a discursive space with which it is not traditionally associated—that of the debate around the purposes of education. The opening paragraph of the Bank's executive summary of *WBES 2020, Learning for All: Investing in People's Knowledge and Skills to Promote Development*, appears to lift the Bank out of its preoccupation with particular kinds of skills and competencies. It refers to the "human mind": "The human mind makes possible all other development achievements, from health advances and agricultural innovation to infrastructure construction and private sector growth. For developing countries to reap these benefits fully—both by learning from the stock of global ideas and through innovation they need to *unleash the potential of the human mind*" (p. 1, emphasis added). The document elsewhere emphasizes, too, that the Bank's strategy "is built on the premise that *people learn throughout life*, not simply during the years that they spend in formal schooling" (p. 25, emphasis in the original). Interestingly, it goes on to say that

> Learning outcomes have typically been measured in terms of reading and numeracy skills, but the knowledge and competencies that help people live healthy, productive and satisfying lives are much broader ... Education is not only about reading, writing, and arithmetic (the "3 Rs"). Social, communication, teamwork, critical thinking, and problem-solving skills are invaluable for people to function well at home, in their communities, and at work. (p. 26)

Implicit in these statements is a generous sense of human possibility—the stock of global ideas—and even of the great power of education to unleash the power of the

*S.J. Klees et al. (eds.), The World Bank and Education*, 95–107.

human mind. As the world confronts the challenges of global hunger, the desecration of the planet, social inequality, disease, conflict and violence between people and countries, corruption in the corporate and political arena, abuse of power and, particularly for young people, the indignity of a lack of meaningful lives and their consequent vulnerability to conscription into the anti-social formations of gangs, fundamentalist movements, and even the supposedly respectable legions of war in many countries, the importance of quality education is profound. It is profound, moreover, for young people everywhere, not only in the so-called low-income world. It is important that youth everywhere receive an education "that (will) unleash the power of the human mind" to help them understand the full complexity of the world in which they live and to act in ways that promote global justice and development in forms that are inclusive (p. 12). The language invoked by *WBES 2020* is, therefore, deeply significant.

And yet, there is much in *Learning for All* that is puzzling. The Bank's signature discourse—a narrow definition of skills and knowledge—remains prominent. The questions, "What are the strengths of our system? Where are the weaknesses? Are children and youth acquiring the knowledge and skills that they need?," posed regularly throughout the document, are invariably answered in an economistic way.

What then, one needs to ask, does the Bank mean when it speaks of quality? What is *in* the quality it is holding up that countries should strive to achieve? The question is serious because of the simple question of justice. Implicit in the Bank's approach to quality is the assumption that the questions of what is valued in different parts of the world and of what is deemed to be worthy of promoting and defending in what is taught and learned are finished questions. Quality in these formulations is a universal "given."

This paper begins with a deep concern with the idea of quality as a "given" and argues, instead, that it is a choice. These choices are never apolitical. What this paper does is attempt to surface the nature of the politics inherent in the Bank's choices. Towards this attempt, the paper begins with a brief review of the quality discussion. The purpose of this discussion is to make clear how "quality" as a value is being addressed in the education community. Thereafter, the paper looks to those sites to which the Bank defers for quality: the Trends in International Mathematics and Science (TIMMS) and Progress in International Reading Literacy (PIRLS) tests, and particularly their framework documents, to understand what it means by "quality."

## A POINT OF DEPARTURE IN THINKING ABOUT QUALITY

There are many ways of approaching the question of quality in education. These approaches are evident in the very different kinds of literature that exists around it. The discussion below will quickly review this literature for the purpose of showing that not only is quality *not* a self-evident proposition but that it is immensely contested.

The literature that most prominently addresses itself to questions of quality is that of assessment. In this literature it is in the area of standard-setting where quality is most directly discussed. Standard-setting is the exercise of determining what levels of attainment are acceptable in a test or examination. How much should a learner know and to what depth? (Placier et al., 2002, p. 282). Sophisticated versions of the notion of the standards or levels that should be applied and what students should be required to demonstrate in tests, talk of the derivation of "objective" standards through "rigorous" interrogation of questions. This interrogation evaluates a question and so seeks to determine what a defensible standard is in terms of the cut-off for minimally acceptable levels of competency (see Black & Wiliam, 2007, p. 37; Tamir, 1990). On the basis of this a reasonably clear and meaningful description of a "standard" for a question can be determined both quantitatively and qualitatively. What such processes of determination make possible is the classification of performance and its calibration into levels, such as that of "low," "intermediate," and "high." It is from this calibration that quality is then inferred. For researchers working in this area, the integrity of the techniques used in determining quality is supremely important (Black & Wiliam, 2007, p. 35).

A second body of literature that is pertinent to the discussion focuses on quality as a policy commitment. In this literature there are currently, as Sayed and Ahmed (2011, p. 104) explain, three identifiable approaches to the question. The first is essentially the human capital approach. Premised on the idea that educational quality is a prerequisite for economic development, it makes the argument that a modern economy has to invest in a high-quality educational system. Quality in this approach is the level of skill that a learner is able to demonstrate. The second is a human rights approach that is concerned with equity and equality. In this approach quality is understood to be a skill too. The focus, however, now falls on how these skills are distributed. The argument that is made is that the skills that are valued in an educational system constitute a basic right to which all learners are entitled. The policy focus of this approach is on creating the systemic conditions for realizing learners' rights to quality through an emphasis on the provision of enabling structures and contextual environments. A third approach, drawing on the work of AmartyaSen and Nancy Fraser, emphasizes the "voice" of all the stakeholders within a social context and those things they themselves value. Its central feature is the participation of people themselves in defining—giving voice to—what quality constitutes. In this approach the idea of human flourishing is important. Quality is substantively what people value. To get at it, Sen's concept of capabilities is crucial. He describes capabilities "as any potential functioning which is valued. A distinction is also made between capability and functioning as capabilities may not be realized" (Sayed & Ahmed, 2011, p. 104; and also see Sen, 1999, p. 15).

A third and related body of literature to the issues raised by Sen is the philosophical literature. Soudien (forthcoming) has elsewhere attempted to summarize the major issues at stake among those in debate in this body of writing. Still concerned with rights but much more focused on questions of content, such as what is in bench-mark tests and the fairness of what is there, this literature is represented by liberals and their critics. The former argue that it is permissible to have variations in standards among places and regions of the world, but that there are "limits to the level and kind of regional differences that can be permitted" (Howell, 1998, p. 7). In this argument a universal standard is necessary. Everybody has an unqualified right to access it. Without it their capacity to participate fully in public life is impaired. Howell, drawing on Rawls, describes the kind of education which is premised on this definition of quality as a Type A good or standard which is not dependent on any contingent fact about individual citizens or group, but is rather a necessity without which any liberal society would be unworkable. Permissible, on the other hand, are what Howell refers to as Type B goods, which, in a Rawlsian sense, allow for contingency. They represent the interests of sub-groups.

Critics of this differentiated approach to quality argue that the very basis of what is considered universal and contingent is fraught with difficulties. One such critic, Sison (1998, p. 3), writing in direct response to Howell (1998), argues that all the notions of types, both A and B, are unsatisfactory because all the "practical" virtues that are included in all the lists are determined simply by force of political weight: "So, whatever reason cited by either side will necessarily be 'political,' that is whatever its constituents or leaders decide ..." (p. 3). He acknowledges that there is something in the question of how public good issues are resolved in education that merits the discussion of a single test being saved and developed, but cautions that an honest answer to the question, "Whose equity?" would need to be provided (p. 4).

While not addressing these issues specifically, a fourth body of literature can be identified which approaches quality as a deliberately constructed value. This discussion, for reference sake, can be described as a constructivist one. Drawing on a discussion derived from scholars such as Hawes and Stephens (1990) and Stephens (2003), who sought to locate quality as a classroom ideal through the invocation of efficiency (as reaching standards), relevance (to context), and "something special," Nikel and Lowe (2010, p. 594) developed a model that sought to stabilize and give content to what is meant by quality. To achieve this they identified seven dimensions to which a defensible explanation of quality should respond: effectiveness, efficiency, equity, responsiveness, relevance, reflexivity, and sustainability. Important about the model is that it seeks a "contextually relevant balance among the seven dimensions, where 'balance' does not imply a simple equalising across all seven – even if that were conceptually possible. The needs and the possibilities for action within different contexts will vary and decisions must be made over what is desirable and feasible within a specific situation" (Nikel& Lowe, 2010, p. 595). Quality in this view is a fabric constructed not as a distinct end-state but as a commitment sensitive to "situationally grounded" realities which are in constant tension (Nikel& Lowe, 2010, p. 600).

What might one take away from this literature?

The first point to be made is that there are both similarities and differences in the various works on the subject. There is a fair degree of implied agreement in the literatures in their approaches to quality, suggesting the existence of what in the comparative education literature is called the "convergence model." This convergence is significant for the purposes of this discussion in terms of its dependence on assessment experts.

What are the differences? The assessment literature is fundamentally concerned with technical issues. Quality is a value that is determinable statistically. The central criticism to make about this kind of work is that it fails to define quality. Instead what it identifies are metrics for determining performance. Quality in this literature is essentially "high-performance."

For those working with quality as a policy focus, with the exception of those who are interested in the capabilities approach, the discussion is essentially about the economics of quality, its quantity and its distribution. With the exception of the capabilities proponents, they accept the assessment community's view of quality and so don't actually define quality either. Interestingly, the philosophers, while interested in questions of value—*what* the "goods" are that are to be distributed—do not, also, specifically define quality. The constructivists, working both with the questions of distribution and the value of what is to be distributed, are interested in developing frameworks that recognize the basic texture of contradiction within quality-determination processes.

Reviewing this whole corpus, it is argued that the constructivists come at the issues more consciously and see more of the complexity in the situation than most others in the discussion do. They recognize the critique made by some policy-makers that the technical approach to quality is at best a naïve one. They do not, however, shy away from the challenge posed by critics of the liberal school that a universal standard embodied in Type A goods cannot be determined. Interesting about them, is their recognition of the nature of the politics around quality. They are able to distinguish between what they call the "quality movement" on one side, along with the politics that animate it, and the "quality debate" itself on the other side, with its own much more conscious interlocutors. The first, they explain, is a patently neo-liberal movement concerned about a weakened state sector unable to hold its public institutions to account and the consequent necessity for developing instruments for measuring inputs and outputs: "'Accountability' is at the core of the quality movement, where it takes on the status of both a political ideology ... and a practical device for enhancing quality" (Nikel& Lowe, 2010, p. 591). The "quality debate," the second, they recognize, emerges from a configuration of social, economic, and political conditions which are much more complex than the accountability ideologues driving the first. Emerging from these conditions, exemplified in the Education For All (EFA) process and the realization that achieving the Millennium Development Goals without attendant improvements in the quality of the educational process is an empty achievement, is a much more grounded democratic and social justice view of the world (Nikel & Lowe, 2010, p. 592). The value of Nikel and Lowe's work, in relation to all of this, is that it is both open-ended and systematic. With respect to the dimensions of open-endedness it has room for interpreting what is meant by responsiveness, relevance, reflexivity, and sustainability. The Senian capabilities idea is inherent in these sub-dimensions through the use of the criterion of responsiveness. Responsiveness here is meant as an approach that recognizes how "capability deprivation" works (see

Sen, 1999, p. 87). A responsive system will prioritize actions that catalyze the capabilities that count in that political and economic system. Such an approach is sensitive to the specific conditions of the local context. It is aware of the particular forms of knowledge that exist in a particular time and space. It is, in these terms, culturally aware of the politics of the micro and macro-contexts in which it is set. But, it also has room for more systematic analysis in its recognition and identification of the necessity for systems of education to demonstrate effectiveness, efficiency, and equity. Their discussion demonstrates an understanding of the challenges in these ideas but they approach the issues pragmatically enough to recognize that the issues cannot be ignored.

It is suggested here, however, that even Nikel and Lowe do not push the analysis far enough. They make the insightful observation that the quality movement is focused on management issues, while the quality debate has pedagogy as its preoccupation. The point is significant, emphasizing how much the first, coming as it does out of a business paradigm, is vacuous in educational terms. It sees, correctly, how "education" in the quality movement is defined in economistic terms. But Nikel and Lowe do not pay sufficient attention to how the interests of the second are captured and subverted through a dependence on the sophisticated discursive strategies of the first.

Where then might one take this discussion? A way forward is available in the reference made by Nikel and Lowe to the undervalued Delors Report, *Learning: The Treasure Within* (UNESCO, 1999). This report provides, even as it comes from the heart of a modern Europe exploring its identity, a *vision* of education that is more than about the economic. Nikel and Lowe do not explore the fullness of Delors' view of what education should do and be about. Delors' vision is based upon four pillars for learning: (1) to know, (2) to do, (3) to live together, and (4) to be: "It explicitly takes a standpoint opposed to educational policy being driven by valuing education primarily for its economic functions ..." (Nikel& Lowe, 2010, p. 592). Their seven dimensions go only as far as Delors' first and second pillars of learning. Quality, it is argued here, also has to be about his third and fourth pillars: how education addresses the questions of relationships—to live together—and the fundamental ontological question of what it means to be a human being—to be. It is here, at this point, that the Nikel and Lowe approach and indeed much of everything else that is written on quality, is rendered dependent on the technical approaches to quality.

The chapter turns now to the TIMMS and PIRLS frameworks to understand what the scale of the difficulties arising from this dependence are.

## TIMMS, PIRLS: THE WORLD BANKS' "QUALITY"

In light of the discussion above it is now necessary to see what the Bank itself says about quality in education. Early in the executive summary of *WBES 2020*, the Bank says that, "Gains in access have also turned attention to the challenge of improving the quality of education ..." (p. 2). Critically, nowhere after that does it actually spell out what it means by quality. It frequently, throughout the document, refers to "low levels" of skills and "knowledge gaps between most developing countries and members of the OECD"(p. 3). The assumption it makes—apparent for example, in the way it refers to the "impressive performance of Shanghai-China in the recently released PISA (Programme for International Student Assessment) 2009 results" and also in its observation "that the scores of almost every other low- and middle-income country or region were in the bottom half of results, with many lagging behind the Organisation for Economic Co-operation and Development (OECD) average"(p. 4)—is that quality is evident in performance on bench-mark tests. It is referenced similarly elsewhere: "Quality needs to be the focus of education investments, with learning gains as a key metric of quality" (p. 4). It is on the basis of this approach that it then turns to the next idea that, to improve themselves, countries need to invest in "system assessments… and assessments of learning and skills" (p. 6). How might this be done? It will be done, it explains, by "continu(ing) to support the development and use of regular education data. It will support efforts by partner countries to measure both student achievement (i.e., learning outcomes) and the overall performance of education systems on a regular and systematic basis, and to use such data to inform education policies and investments" (p. 39). And so, it says, it encourages country participation in international and/or regional assessments such as PIRLS, PISA, the Southern African Consortium for Measuring Education Quality, and TIMMS, "as a means of building a global database on learning achievement" (p. 62).

What these tests are requires a quick explanation. TIMMS and PIRLS are possibly among the most important of a new wave of international benchmarked tests. Both are projects of the International Association for the Evaluation of Educational Achievement (IEA), an independent, international cooperative of national education research institutions and governmental research agencies dedicated to improving education in the world located at the International Study Center, Boston College (Mullis et al., 2009a). TIMMS has been run five times since 1995 while the PIRLS tests were first conducted in 2001. The former seeks to assess mathematics and science achievement while the latter seeks to measure reading achievement. The process which the IEA used for the construction of its 2011 tests was to build on earlier iterations of the tests. The TIMMS framework, as that of PIRLS, is drawn on "co-operative expertise provided by representative countries from all around the world" (Mullis et al., 2009a, p. 7). It consists of three sub-frameworks, one for Mathematics, another for Science, and a third to take cognizance of context, a contextual framework. The curriculum model used in TIMMS has three aspects, the "intended curriculum, the implemented curriculum and the achieved curriculum. These represent, respectively, the mathematics and science that society intends for students to learn and how the education system should be organized to facilitate this learning" (Mullis et al., 2009a, p. 10). An important step in the development of the general framework is the TIMMS Encyclopedia. The 2007 version of this Encyclopedia provided information from the participating countries about their national contexts for mathematics and science education and included descriptions of their curricula. It is complemented by the Mathematics and Science Reports, which contain information about countries' curricula and the efforts taken in countries to help learners with the actual curriculum. Building on the TIMMS 2007 framework, the 2011 framework gave participating countries regular opportunities to review and comment on the frameworks and was formally discussed at meetings at the International Study Center. Each country was represented by a national research coordinator (NRC) "to work with the international project staff to ensure that the study is responsive to the country's concerns .... The NRCs also consulted their national experts and responded to questionnaires about how best to update the content and cognitive domains for TIMMS 2011" (Mullis et al., 2009a, p. 12). Thereafter the frameworks were reviewed "in-depth by the TIMMS 2011 Science and Mathematics Item Review," were sent back to the NRCS, and updated finally (p. 12). An important difference noted as a result of this review process for 2011 was the emphasis on "quality of measurement" and "on increasing the utility of results for participating countries. This includes assessing content appropriate to the students and important to their future lives ..." (p. 12).

> The PIRLS 2011 assessment framework evolved in a similarly collaborative way. It was adapted from widely accepted earlier versions of the PIRLS framework, (and) resulted from a collaborative process involving many individuals and groups—notably the PIRLS Reading Development Group (RDG) and the National Research Coordinators of the more than 50 participating countries. All told, the framework underwent several iterations in response to the comments and interests of the PIRLS countries and the reading research community, and embodies the ideas and interests of many individuals and organizations around the world. (Mullis et al., 2009b, p. 2)

In both TIMMS and PIRLS, clearly, important sectors of the educational community were involved and endorsed the form and substance of the tests. In both their frameworks, the point is made repeatedly that the tests were "endorsed by society" or "required by society and/or valued by the individual" (Mullis et al., 2009a, p. 11).

In assessing what is before the world now with these tests, it is clear that a convergent process has occurred, even among scholars who raise the question of the distribution of quality. The criticism of scholars such as Vinson and Ross (2000) notwithstanding, a high-level consensus around quality has descended on the world. Behind it, as Andere (2008, p. 5) has argued, lies the belief that there are intrinsic values in good educational practice.

But, as critical assessments of the benchmarking experience around the world suggest, there are major problems at a number of levels in the processes involved in setting up and applying benchmark tests. The discussion below focuses on some of these challenges.

## BENCHMARKING QUALITY: ITS CHALLENGES

The benchmarking movement received a huge boost in 1958 when a group of international scholars met in Hamburg, Germany, to look at how student learning around the globe could be measured: "They saw the world as one huge educational laboratory, with each country acting as its own naturally occurring experiment. If tests could gauge the effects of those experiments, the researchers reasoned, the results might yield a bonanza on how best to teach children" (Viadero, 2006, p. 1). TIMMS was one of the creations of this meeting. Significantly, participant scholars interested in promoting the idea of a global assessment of learning argue that it hasn't yet delivered on its own promise, with one, Judith Torney-Purta, remarking that TIMMS had "become a sort of cognitive Olympics instead" (Viadero, 2006, p. 1). The problem, according to Torney-Purta, is that the program "seemed to miss out on becoming a major contributor of international studies in identifying effective practices and adapting them" (Viadero, 2006, p. 1). The response of the IEA to this analysis is also significant. Its chairman, Seamus Hegarty, said: "What we've got to do more of now are two things. We've got to ensure better, more systematic secondary analyses, and we've got to relate our findings to policy interests" (Viadero, 2006, p. 1).

The situation is more complex. This complexity relates to (1) the assumptions which provide the rationale for the tests, (2) their design and construction, and finally (3) the value which they add to the question of quality.

The first point to make is that the question remains open about the relationship between the kinds of skills that the tests measure and their impact on economic development. The basic claim made in *WBES 2020* is that "growth, development and poverty reduction depend on the knowledge and skills that people acquire" (p. 3). The evidence for this is mixed. Recent studies show quite divergent results. One study based on data from TIMMS 2003 for Lithuania (Mikk, 2005) suggests a strong relationship: "The correlation analysis revealed a strong relation between TIMMS results and the economic development of countries ... (an) in-country comparison revealed a positive correlation between these variables." A more recent study (see Chen &Luoh, 2011) asked the question directly about the link between test scores for mathematics and science and labor force quality. It concluded, "we have investigated whether mathematics and science test scores are able to account for cross-country income differences. After adding more direct measures of labor-force quality in the regression analysis, we have shown that the strong link between test scores and cross-country income differences is broken" (p.138). There is a great deal more to talk about here, but it involves the unproblematized syllogism that high educational performance ineluctably produces economic development.

Secondly, there is sufficient evidence in the analysis of the process behind the development of the tests to emphasize how problematic the convergence theory is. Andere (2008, p. 5), for example, on the basis of an analysis of the PISA process concluded that there were indeed convergences taking place around the world, but that the convergences were only with respect to some inputs and outputs: "Policies, which in themselves are understood as processes or production functions of education, have not converged; nor do they seem to be converging" (Andere, 2008, p. 5). The conclusion to which he comes is that it is not possible from the tests to establish causal relationships at all between inputs and outcomes that apply to all systems. This conclusion is given weight by the analysis of Bouhlila (2011, p. 339), who undertook a comparison of the "intended curriculum," one of the analytic frames used by TIMMS, and found that of the 39 topics specified in the mathematics framework and the 46 topics in the science framework a significant percentage had *not* been covered in some of the countries participating in the test. In mathematics Morocco had covered 22 out of the 39 topics, while in science Tunisia had covered 14 out of the 46 items (Bouhlila, 2011, p. 337). Looking also at trends in performance on the tests, Rutkowski and Rutkowski (2009, p. 143) found that countries that had participated in what had been all three cycles of the TIMMS test up to that time could be clustered regionally: "… response patterns for these mathematics items followed a distinct geographic, cultural and linguistic pattern." They identified a cluster consisting of European countries, another of East Asian countries, and also an English-speaking cluster. Convergences certainly exist, but at a much more regional level than the global scale suggested by the TIMMS process. At the more technical level, scholars such as Dempster and Reddy (2007) complained that the tests were constructed with the use of unnecessarily complex language.

The point to be made is that the tests would struggle to meet the criteria framed by Nikel and Lowe, and, much more substantially, the question of the issues raised by Delors. To be sure, the test design process is inclusive to the degree that countries have the opportunity to include their own questions. But there is sufficient disagreement in the literature to be cautious about the claims to universality in the test. There is, what is more, some basis for making an argument about the inability of the tests to address what might be called the "higher order" dimensions of quality. There is little in the frameworks of either TIMMS or PIRLS that speak to the challenges of relationships and of the ontological. They are entirely about instrumental knowledge. What the world is left with, as a result, is a dependence on a convergence-framed understanding of what quality is all about.

CONCLUSION

In terms of the discussion, it is not an unreasonable point to be making that the kind of quality projected in the benchmarking movement has to be viewed much more critically. Respectful as the testing movement is of difference in context, the underlying curricular assumptions about the inevitability of the convergence model that are circulating in governments everywhere in the world are a cause for concern. While the results of the TIMMS and PIRLS tests certainly present countries and their governments with much food for thought, the nature of their challenge needs to be understood. TIMMS and PIRLS—and the World Bank, by dint of its dependence on them—have an approach to quality that is not sufficiently capacious and that is even exclusionary at several levels.

The first level is the design level. What the intended curriculum is—the obligatory corpus of fundamentals—is an immensely significant question. While the gains that have been made in the design processes surrounding the tests need to be acknowledged and the immense challenges of eliciting an agreement between "experts" from around the world recognized, particularly those of the kinds of cognitive demands that need to be made on young people at key stages of their learning lives, the point needs to be made that the tests and the intended curricula off which they draw are political. They do not represent a neutral and objective set of commitments about what "good" education is all about. The issues of what students have to learn and how they will learn it and, these—bringing the practices of standardization, and the ideals of equity, diversity, and justice into the frame simultaneously—remain deeply contested. Even in the relatively consensual space of mathematics, where symbolic thinking based on cardinality is almost, but not totally, replicated in the ancient computational cultures of China, India, the Middle East, Greece, and Rome, and so presents to the world a form of universality, the argument is made by sophisticated mathematics educators that the pathway from the statement of a mathematical problem to its solution is susceptible to cultural variability (see Davis, 2010). In the PIRLS framework, one has the use of a charming Dr. Seuss-like tale by Franz Hohler, *An Unbelievable Night,* as an exemplar of what children could be tested on, and one has to express some anxiety about the clear middle-class cultural capital embedded in the test. Standards, therefore, need to be understood and repeatedly presented as intellectual settlements to forestall the basic assumption made by the TIMMS and PIRLS stakeholders and by the World Bank that the world has at its disposal a fully accepted consensus on what constitutes quality. The central loss in this consensus is epistemological. The world has no idea of what stocks of cultural knowledge it is forsaking. It does not know what insights into the human condition and of human beings' relationship with their physical environment exist in the ways of knowing of marginal groups in the non-metropole parts of the world. It can only celebrate what it has chosen to privilege. What the implied neutrality of the Bank and its associates comes down to is the idea the idea that a corpus of knowledge has now been identified that serves the entire globe equally and equally satisfactorily. The author (Soudien, forthcoming) has made the point that this idea is premised on an idea of development which is the direct result of firstly the primacy of science. Kamens and McNeely argue (2010, p. 11) that what is actually being observed here is the "hegemony of science … which contributes to the sense of a rationalized global world in which everyone is subject to the same kinds of causal laws."

Perhaps equally critical about the hegemonic idea of quality that has emerged is the simple reality that it is as yet conceptually unable to address the higher order dimensions of education, the relational, and the ontological. Benchmarking in TIMMS and PIRLS has yet to breach the horizons of quality as they shape up in the important areas of life relating to capacity for judgment-making. Even the imperfect levels reached in PISA are levels that have yet to be realized elsewhere. There is not sufficient evidence in the range of benchmarking tests available anywhere that there is either a sense of understanding or the courage to acknowledge this as a central obligation of good education.

In light of these arguments, it needs to be recognized how problematic the quality is to which the Bank refers. It is problematic because it is premised on the notion that the world has before it now unambiguous tools for determining quality and that the Bank is in a position to advise the world's "poor" on what it should do to improve themselves. Clearly, the Bank has a great deal to offer the world's poor, but it really is not in possession of all the tools and much less the perspectives to understand and act on the challenges facing them.

## REFERENCES

Andere, E. (2008). *The lending power of PISA: league tables and best practice in international education.* Hong Kong: Comparative Education Research Centre.

Black, P. & Wiliam, D. (2007). Large-scale assessment systems design principles drawn from international comparisons. *Measurement, 5*(1), 1-53.

Bouhlila, D. (2011). The quality of secondary education in the Middle East and North Africa: What can we learn from TIMMS' results? *Compare: A Journal of Comparative and International Education, 41*(3), 327-352.

Chen, S. & Luoh, M. (2011). Are mathematics and science test scores good indicators of labor-force quality? *Social Indicators Research, 96*(1), 133-143.

Davis, Z. (2010, November). On generating mathematically attuned descriptions of the constitution of mathematics in pedagogic situations. Unpublished paper presented at the Kenton, South Africa Conference.

Dempster, E. & Reddy, V. (2007). Item readability and science achievement in TIMMS 2003 in South Africa.*Science Education, 91*(6), 906-925.

Hawes, H. & Stephens, D. (1990). *Questions of quality: Primary education and development.* Harlow, UK: Longman.

Howell, C. (1998). Liberalism, primary goods and national education standards. http://www.ed.uiuc.edu/eps/PES-Yearbook/1998/howell.html

Kamens, D. & McNeely, C. (2010), Globalization and the growth of international testing and national assessment.*Comparative Education Review, 54*(1), 5-25.

Mikk, J. (2005). Economic and educational correlates of TIMMS results. Paper presented at the International Conference on Economics and Management, Lithuania.

Mullis, I., Martin, M., Ruddock, G., O'Sullivan, C., & Preuschoff, C. (2009a). *The TIMMS 2011 assessment framework.* Boston: International Study Center, Lynch School of Education, Boston College.

Mullis, I., Martin, M., Kennedy, A., Trong, K., & Sainsbury, M. (2009b). *The PIRLS 2011 assessment framework.* Boston: International Study Center, Lynch School of Education, Boston College.

Nikel, J. & Lowe, J. (2010). Talking of fabric: A multi-dimensional model of quality in education. *Compare: A Journal of Comparative and International Education, 40*(5), 589-605.

Placier, M., Walker, M. & Foster, B. (2002). Writing the "show-me" standards: Teacher professionalism and political control in U.S. State curriculum policy. *Curriculum Inquiry, 32*(3), 281-310.

Rutkowski, L. & Rutkowski, D. (2009). Trends in TIMMS responses over time: Evidence of global forces in education. *Educational Research and Evaluation, 15*(2), 137-152.

Sayed, Y. & Ahmed, R. (2011). Education quality in post-apartheid South African policy: Balancing equity, diversity, rights and participation. *Comparative Education, 47*(1), 103-118.

Sen, A. (1999). *Development as freedom.* Oxford: Oxford University Press.

Sison, A. (1998). What liberalism? Which standards? Whose equity? http://www.ed/eps/PES-Yearbook/1998/sison.html

Soudien, C. (2010, November). Building quality in education: are international standards helpful? Paper delivered at the Comparative Education Society of India, Delhi.

Stephens, D. (2003). Quality as basic education. Paper prepared for the UNESCO EFA Monitoring Report Team. Paris: UNESCO.

Tamir, P. (1990). Justifying the selection of answers in multiple choice items. *International Journal of Science Education, 12*(5), 563-573.

UNESCO (1999). *Learning: The treasure within.* Report to UNESCO of the International Commission on Education for the Twenty-First century. Paris: UNESCO Commission.

Viadero, D. (2006). Potential of global tests seen as unrealized: Scholars urged to scour TIMMS, PISA for policy insights. *Education Week, 26*(13), 14-15.

Vinson, K. & Ross, E. (2000). Education and the new disciplinarity: Surveillance, spectacle. *Cultural Logic,* 4(1). http://clogic.eserver.org/4-1/vinson&ross.html

World Bank (2011). *Learning for all: Investing in people's knowledge and skills to promote development.* Washington, D.C.: World Bank.

*Crain Soudien*
*School of Education*
*University of Cape Town, South Africa*

## CHAPTER 8

JOEL SAMOFF

# MORE OF THE SAME WILL NOT DO

*Learning without Learning in the World Bank's 2020 Education Strategy*

Perhaps most striking—and frustrating and dismaying—about the World Bank's 2020 education strategy (World Bank, 2011) is the tension between its title, *Learning for All*, and its content. *Learning for All*, it turns out, has hardly anything to say about learning.

The explicit commitment to learning for all is an imaginative and potentially transformative reconceptualization of a global challenge. For more than two decades, formally confirmed in Thailand in 1990 and reconfirmed in Senegal in 2000, the world has agreed on the importance of education for all. Education is both a right and a necessity. Individual learners, communities, countries, and the global political economy all benefit from broad access to quality education.

Expansively conceived, education for all has most often been narrowly implemented, if that. Nearly everywhere, education for all became schooling for all, ignoring the clear and reiterated commitment to providing learning opportunities for the very young and for those beyond school age. Schooling for all has advanced unevenly, nearly accomplished in some places and still a distant goal in others. As many, including the World Bank, have observed, schooling for all has not achieved education for all: "more schooling, little learning" (World Bank, 2011, p. 3). More children are in school. When they arrive, many find over-crowded classrooms, poorly equipped facilities, insufficient instructional materials, and teachers who are both over-worked and under-prepared.[i] In some settings parents articulate the embarrassingly obvious: what is the point of all the effort to get children into schools where they do not learn?

Learning for all is a creative response. Refocus the education for all campaign away from schooling and toward learning. Insist on different indicators. Recognize that even more important than the number of children in school or the rate of progress through basic education are measures of learning. Understand that learning is not simply acquiring disconnected bits of information to be recalled on demand but must be rooted in curiosity, concept development, systematic experimentation, structured comparison, scientific analysis, creative insight, problem-solving, and more. Here, then, was an opportunity for the World Bank to support efforts to move global education's center of gravity away from schooling

*S.J. Klees et al. (eds.), The World Bank and Education, 109–121.*

toward the emancipatory and empowering potential of education. International cooperation to end poverty could become something more than a slogan.

An opportunity lost. The World Bank's 2020 education strategy (*WBES 2020*) makes "learning" a catchy title, not a carefully grounded, systematically analyzed, and creatively developed objective. When we look for guidance on how schooling and education are to be different, we find instead inattention to the learning process and more of the same schooling. More of the same will not do.

## RESEARCH ON LEARNING

Quite reasonably, *WBES 2020* insists that policies and practices be evidence-based. Relevant research is to inform the analytic framework that identifies problems and points to promising solutions. Relevant research is to guide choices among alternative public policies. Relevant research is to develop and apply the indicators necessary for monitoring and assessment. Research on learning is not the obscure preoccupation of ivory tower gnomes but the essential foundation for practical action. In my chapter on research and the knowledge environment, I have addressed the development of the education research community in Africa. Strengthened research capacity in Africa is in the global interest and requires moving beyond funding individual researchers to supporting the interrelated activities necessary to establish and sustain an innovative and productive research environment.

Research on learning is an important foundation for developing a strategy to achieve learning for all. What, for example, does research tell us about the roles of teachers and about different sorts of professional preparation for teachers? How does focused research help us understand better the difference between teaching as telling and teaching as motivating learning? For a third example, what has recent research found about the roles, both promising and problematic, of school committees?

Research findings, of course, are regularly disputed. That is an essential part of the process of testing observations, conclusions, and analytic frameworks against relevant evidence. Hence, *Learning for All*—a statement by the World Bank on what is to be done—should reasonably be expected to review the relevant research and to indicate the studies and findings that have guided its recommendations. Alas, not. Since *WBES 2020* does not include that demanding and critical review of research on learning, with careful attention to context and conditions, readers can determine only by inference which research the World Bank deemed relevant and persuasive. Sweeping claims and confident recommendations stand ungrounded. Those who are to implement the proposed strategy must remain unclear on why that strategy has been recommended and why it is expected to be effective.

Even worse, as I have noted in my discussion of creating the knowledge environment for *Learning for All*, for the most part, the World Bank talks with itself. It continues to rely on the research it has undertaken and commissioned, with very little documented attention to the much larger body of research on learning and schooling.

## LEARNING MODEL

How, then, to achieve learning for all? For the World Bank, learning is the acquisition of knowledge and skills. But that has been the articulated objective of the schooling that *WBES 2020* finds inadequate. While the title suggests a new departure, the content of the World Bank's education strategy offers more of the same. In a document titled *Learning for All* we find neither a focused discussion of learning nor a clear explanation of why the World Bank has adopted a particular understanding of learning—acquiring knowledge and skills (World Bank, 2011, p. 12)—and rejected other perspectives. As well, here as in other documents the World Bank regularly uses the term "knowledge" when in common language it means "information." That conflation of the two terms reinforces the notion of learning as a process of acquisition rather than a process that involves acquiring, appropriating, using, manipulating, and generating information.[ii]

That understanding of learning as acquisition leaves little space for attention to learning as the initiative, actions, and responsibility of the learner and to competences like framing problems, developing concepts, drawing inferences that educators insist are the most consequential components of the learning process. Notwithstanding occasional references to learning as an active process, the learning model embedded in *WBES 2020* corresponds closely with what Paulo Freire characterized as the banking model of education (Freire, 1970). Education's task is to transfer wisdom—information, knowledge, and how to use them—from those who have it to those who do not. Teachers are the wise, at least more wise than their students, and students are the empty vessels ready to be filled. If that process works well, learning is like systematic savings. Regular small deposits into the account, that is, the student, are to be accumulated, refined, and protected. Eventually, students draw on those deposits as they move beyond school. The more effective the teacher, the larger the deposit. The more responsive the student, the better able to use and extend that deposit in the future. Especially successful students become teachers, or managers, or decision or policy makers, restarting the cycle.

For that to work, the entire education system must incorporate that learning model, Not only teachers, but teacher education, textbooks and other instructional materials, pedagogy, classroom organization, examinations, even the rules that regulate school social behavior must reflect that understanding of the learning process. As many observers have noted, education systems across Africa regularly do.[iii]

Fundamentally disempowering—the teacher is the primary actor, not the learner—that learning model functions to reinforce the role of schools in reproducing their larger society's cleavages and hierarchies.[iv] A more detailed exposition of the importance and consequences of that learning model is beyond the scope of this chapter. Essential here is to understand that inattention to the learning model and to research about the learning process obscures both the influence of the learning model and its conservative cast. A façade of technical precision obscures its driving ideology, presenting as normal, given, everyday, a part of nature, what is in practice an externally initiated and funded effort to mold the institutions that mold society. Those institutions instruct students to become more competent at following well-trod paths, not creating new pathways, to be accommodating, not critically demanding, to rely on received wisdom rather than risking innovation.

## SCHOOLING MODEL

Along with a learning model, embedded within *WBES 2020* is a related schooling model. That it is far more implicit than explicit masks its role and influence. This, too, is a striking gap in *WBES 2020*, which regularly notes that attention to education inputs is insufficient and that a high priority objective is to reform the education system. In *WBES 2020*, the education system is characterized as a network of accountability relationships that includes a very broad range of learning opportunities and a comprehensive set of beneficiaries and stakeholders (pp 15-17). Affirming that education is a system, that education reaches far beyond schools, and that education matters to everyone in society is welcome progress and essential to developing a platform for exploring why, in so many settings, schooling does not foster learning. At the same time, in *WBES 2020* the World Bank's attention to the education system primarily serves to call for emphasis on how the system is managed and financed, for an increased private sector role, and for a tighter link between inputs and outputs. The learning crucible, the settings where learners and teachers interact, where learning must occur, remains unaddressed.

Most often, education appears as a depersonalized and neutral tool, to be wielded by appropriate experts to achieve specified objectives that are assumed to be unexceptional and unchallenged, technical but not political. Yet, public policy is always political, especially education policy. Public policy functions to manage conflicting societal interests and demands, sometimes to reconcile but often to advantage one set over another. Shaped by society, schools are also central to shaping it. Never apolitical, education is periodically sharply contested terrain.

To explore that process let us consider briefly the schooling model that is common across Africa and that is assumed in *WBES 2020*.[v] With important local variations, education in colonial Africa was designed to educate a small elite, initially Europeans and subsequently Africans expected to assume significant roles in colonial society.[vi] Notwithstanding articulated differences in the philosophy and practice of colonial rule, all colonizing powers recruited and depended on Africans to collect taxes, manage conflict, provide services, and staff the middle and lower layers of the colonial administration. For most Africans most of the time, the immediate face of colonial rule, including, for example, their teachers, nurses, and police, were African. Colonial schools were expected to produce that African elite. I use "produce" intentionally here, since schools were not expected to be liberating or self-actualizing but rather to serve an instrumental colonial need. That schools also nurtured an anti-colonial leadership reflects the imperfections and contradictions of colonial education, not its intended purpose.

The common education pyramid, with many students in the lower grades and far fewer in the upper levels, characterized colonial education well. Its operating strategy was restriction and selection, not mass education. To play its role, it had to track and select, and then track and select again. For that system to survive, those few who made it to the top had not only to succeed academically but also to believe that their success was due to their own ability and effort. Equally important, those who did not progress far had to understand that their exclusion was due to some combination of their lack of ability, their failure to work hard, and perhaps bad luck. Essential was the shared understanding that schools were neutral instruments that identified and rewarded academic competence. Differential success was to be explained by differences in individual attributes and effort, not by structured inequalities that advantaged, say, Europeans over Africans, males over females, Christians over Muslims, or students from one region over another.

That schooling model survived the colonial transition well. Desegregated and at least nominally nationalized, schools in post-colonial Africa maintained, generally uncritically, the assumptions and organization of their colonial predecessors. Notwithstanding the regularly reiterated commitment to education for all, schooling is designed to educate an elite. While access has expanded, schools continue to focus heavily on tracking and selection. Instructional methods, management of books and other materials, examinations, and authority, responsibility, and accountability within the education system are all far more concerned with the few who will proceed than with providing education for all.

Indeed, despite occasional critiques, that is widely assumed to be what schools should be doing. The hegemony of that idea makes any other role for or organization of schooling hardly conceivable. That, however, generates a sharp tension. The national leadership promises and promotes mass education. Yet, education systems that focus on exclusion rather than inclusion are structurally incapable of providing education for all. The education pyramid widens dramatically at the bottom, but remains a pyramid. Put sharply, enabling more learners to enter a system designed to educate elites cannot achieve mass education.

Achieving education for all requires deep and critical rethinking about the objectives and organization of education systems and schooling. Assuming the schooling model is uncontroversial prevents addressing it critically. Doing so converts "learning for all" from a powerful and powerfully transformative objective into a cloak over the dependent integration of Africa into the global political economy.

## MASS EDUCATION REQUIRES A DIFFERENT SCHOOLING MODEL

Expanding access can achieve schooling for all. Accomplishing that does not secure learning for all. As I have argued, retaining an education system and schooling model designed to educate elites cannot enable all students to become more effective learners. Since *WBES 2020* does not address how schooling must change to make learning for all a realistic objective, let us consider briefly several of the problematic features of the schooling model common across Africa.

What would be different in schools designed to achieve education for all? What would be different if the chart of progression through basic education were not a pyramid but a rectangle—reflecting the expectation that all of those who enter school will still be in school for the final year of basic education?

Contrast a school whose organizing premise is *selection* (education for elites: an ever narrowing group moves up through the grades) with a school whose organizing premise is *inclusion* (mass education: all students who begin the basic education cycle are expected to complete it). The former requires attention to individual readiness: is a prospective student deemed ready to begin school? Historically, readiness tests have often functioned to differentiate young children by race or class, say by insisting that school readiness includes competence in using stairs to reach a second story. Inclusive schools redirect the readiness assessment: is the school ready to teach all of the children who enter the school?

Sifting and sorting—determining who will proceed and who will not—encourages tracking, generally begun early and implemented uncritically. One indicator, often reading skill, is used as a proxy for academic ability. Students are then organized into higher and lower level ability groups, with far-reaching consequences. The groups designated as higher ability commonly receive more teacher attention and resources. Teachers come to expect different outcomes and reduce their expectations for students in the groups designated as lower ability. Not infrequently, the tracking becomes a self-fulfilling prophecy: teachers expect more from and do more for students they believe to have higher ability, which in turn enables those students to do better on the next examination. With lower expectations, less teacher time, and less encouragement, students in the lower ability groups do less well and fall farther behind. In this way, tracking also differentiates the curriculum presented to learners: students identified as low ability are exposed to a truncated (though not necessarily simplified) and less dense and nuanced version of the curriculum used with students in the high ability track. Schools that are not obliged to select have less need for tracking and can organize heterogeneous learning groups. There is significant evidence that all learners, both higher and lower achievers, benefit from that arrangement. Note here why the inattention to relevant research in *WBES 2020* is so problematic.[vii]

Examinations of course are a primary tool in schools concerned with selection. Classroom tests and school-wide and country-wide examinations are intended to measure individual mastery, usually of a designated body of information or set of skills.[viii] National examinations are regularly used to determine which students will proceed to the next level. At the major selection points the results are often public, posted in schools and published in newspapers. Notwithstanding their widely recognized defects, examinations are used to measure individual achievement. Inclusive schools reorient the examinations, using them to assess curriculum, pedagogy, and instructional materials. Since the goal is to enable all students to proceed to the next grade, there is no need to determine who will and will not. Instead, examinations can be used to assess whether or not students are developing competence in, say, basic science, or to compare students' comprehension of alternative text books, or to evaluate a new method of teaching mathematics.

That in turn permits reconceptualizing failure. In selective schools, low examination scores point to individual failure. A particular student is not able to master the material, or has not worked hard enough, or perhaps has missed school to herd the cows. Where there is no need to select out individual students, low examination scores point to inadequate instructional materials or to ineffective teaching methods. Schools designed to educate a small elite regularly use examination results to trace, track, and promote or dismiss students. Schools designed for mass education can use examination results to monitor the learning process, to determine where to focus additional effort and resources, and to inform and guide education reform.

These are of course only a few examples of how schools [re-]designed for mass education might function. They show clearly how the elitism of schooling is embedded in its deep assumptions and institutional arrangements. They remind us that changing education's outcomes, making genuine progress toward learning for all, requires transforming education's values, philosophy, and common practices. Opening the school gates a bit wider and updating the curriculum are insufficient.

The general argument here is that schools designed to educate a small elite cannot achieve education, or learning, for all. Exploring these differences helps us understand how expanding access to those schools will not in itself transform their orientation or consequences.


"ALL"

"The 'for all' part of the strategy's goal is crucial" (World Bank, 2011, p. 12). That the potential of re-focusing global attention from education for all to learning for all is so exciting highlights another dramatic gap in the World Bank's 2020 education strategy. "For all" suggests a future in which there has been great progress toward reducing the inequalities that characterize contemporary education systems. The promise is unequivocal: "The Learning for All strategy promotes the equity goals that underlie the education MDGs" (viii). Yet, like learning, *Learning for All* has little to say about equality.[ix]

As colonial rule ended in Africa, reducing inequality was clearly identified as one of education's tasks. Merit would replace privilege in determining who got ahead. Academic achievement would matter, not race, or ethnicity, or region, or religion, or wealth, or patronage. Over four decades, however, research on education in Africa has regularly confirmed the persistence of inequality, both in society more generally and within the schools' walls.

Schools both reflect and reinforce that inequality. Achieving learning for all requires addressing it. In *WBES 2020* we find some attention to gender inequality, largely to note it and to suggest the utility of a system approach. That is surely a step in a productive direction, though considering girls a group that requires special attention likely impedes efforts to understand why and how gender-based differentiation remains so powerful and so difficult to dislodge.

115

Here too is an unexplored research domain. How do class, race, and gender intersect in the classroom? How, exactly, are inequalities institutionalized in education? What are the roles of subject choices, examinations, and teachers in that? What have been the experiences of schools and academic programs explicitly committed to reducing inequality? What roles have education NGOs and other community groups played?

Most important is addressing the ways in which the very formulation of learning for all functions to perpetuate and reinforce, not reduce, inequality. That the effort to explain gender-differentiated access to school focuses more attention on the distance between home and school than on the gendered nature of power and authority in society demonstrates how framing the issue favors some explanations and excludes others. That framing also influences which research is funded and which findings receive attention. That in turn affects policy and funding. Failing to address the structural roots of inequality makes it impossible to explore the ways in which maintaining an elitist education system not only cannot achieve mass education but also the ways in which it entrenches rather than reduces inequality. Notwithstanding its initial promise and a brief discussion of gender equality, WBES 2020 pushes promoting equity off the agenda.

## REFINING THE APPROACH

As we have seen, *Learning for All* at best deals superficially with learning and inequality ("for all"). It does, however, seek to update and refine the World Bank's approach to education, developed and articulated in a series of policy statements, reviews, and strategies published over several decades. That broad effort to shape the organization and institutional arrangements of schooling has several core elements. I shall focus on Africa.

One is to deprofessionalize the teaching corps, an orientation that is strikingly at odds with efforts in most of the rest of the world. Across policy documents and research reports we are told that teachers need limited subject competence and even less pedagogical expertise. Recruiting and then rushing into the classroom teachers with limited education and little or no professional preparation, variously termed paraprofessionals, community teachers, and contract teachers, does not, the World Bank claims, reduce the quality of instruction or impair students' achievement. Curriculum, examinations, and other education components that matter are the province of specialists, with no direct role for the educators who work directly with the learners. Teachers' sensitivity and innovation are devalued, especially when they depart from system norms and expectations. Teachers' organizations are to be regarded primarily as the protectors of shirking and irresponsibility, to be disempowered, disabled, and disbanded wherever possible.

A second is to apply a technical management approach to classrooms. That is reinforced by the World Bank's general disinterest in classroom interactions. Education's black box can remain opaque, provided there is adequate attention to the outputs that are sought and the inputs deemed necessary to achieve them.

Specified activities are to be monitored and measured, with rewards and sanctions to secure desired results.

A third is to provide energetic support for privatization in multiple forms. Public policy should acknowledge the importance of and create more space for private schooling. WTO rules are interpreted to require countries to tolerate and respect foreign institutions and firms that seek to market education programs. To be increased as well is the number of aided and assisted schools—that is, schools that are publicly financed but privately managed. Notwithstanding its current rejection of the school fees on which it formerly insisted, the World Bank encourages the introduction of direct and indirect fees that function to differentiate schools, including public schools, by resource availability. With uneven support for decentralization, the World Bank generally opposes an increased role in school governance for local and regional councils and other public bodies. Energetic is its support for vouchers and other schemes that move education away from a public good specified by public policy and toward a commodity whose contours are to be determined by individual, household, and increasingly corporate decisions.

The emphasis on privatization and the attention to standards combine in a fourth thread. The focus on standards increases the operating room and influence of the several cross-national testing routines (World Bank, 2011, pp. 7-8 and 41). National examinations are presumably to carry less weight (perhaps a healthy development, though for other reasons) and teacher-set tests none at all. Focusing on measurable outputs, the system approach relies on extra-systemic assessments that largely ignore and devalue the learning indicators that lie within the learning process and that can generate organic learning about learning. As well, that combination encourages recourse to the international assessment entrepreneurs increasingly engaged to certify achievement and confirm successful completion, for example the University of Cambridge and the Princeton Testing Service.

In this too, more of the same.

## CONSTRAINING NOTIONS OF RESEARCH AND EVIDENCE

A potentially innovative departure thus proves very frustrating. *Learning for all* does take us beyond the expansion of access that has characterized most of the education for all campaign. The World Bank is certainly correct that both learning and equality are essential for accelerated growth and development in the world's poorest countries. Why, then, does an institution that directly and indirectly employs a great deal of education expertise and that by its count has more than 1,000 publications on education promulgate a strategy that, notwithstanding its title and its enthusiasm, offers a narrow construction of learning, has little to say about equality and how to achieve it, and proposes to leave largely intact a schooling model structurally incapable of providing mass education?

Of course, the World Bank notes that managing schooling is a national responsibility and that the World Bank and other external agencies should defer to national leadership on education policy and practice. That cannot be a persuasive explanation, however, since whenever it deems it important to do so, the World

Bank is explicitly instructive, regularly using aid conditions to indicate, sometimes in fine detail, what governments should be doing. We need to look elsewhere to understand the World Bank's education strategy.

One approach to that puzzle emerges from an analysis of the World Bank's global role in managing the integration of poor countries into the international political economy (Samoff, 2009). From that perspective, the World Bank is structurally concerned with managing the mass, not empowering the mass. Accordingly, while it may use terms like empowerment, its deep concern is to support education systems that prepare workers for the global political economy's evolving labor needs, that detach citizenship from militant democratic activism, and that include a welcoming terrain for foreign and local private investors. Like national governments, it is often apprehensive about the political assertiveness of a more educated populace and regularly allies with those governments in containing activism based in education institutions.[x]

An explanation at that level, however, is necessary but not sufficient. How does a structural role become practical action? Why, for example, are well meaning, competent, and experienced educators within the World Bank so persistently inattentive to education as a process?

With infrequent exceptions, the World Bank finds a focus on process intolerably messy. Process has to do with interactions in which cause and effect are often not readily distinguishable, in which even before and after may be cloudy, and in which people keep changing both ground rules and meanings. The analysis of process is difficult to accommodate in an understanding of research that insists that independent and dependent variables be specified unambiguously and shorn of interaction effects, that only readily quantified results are worth noting, and that the researcher and the researched be different people. Studies that seek to situate-in rather than dissect-out the phenomena of interest, that regard claims of fact as socially located narratives, and that insist that meanings are contextual are unpersuasive to decision makers who regard economics as the modal social science.

Consequently, the World Bank's research strategies, proudly proffered as standards to be emulated, are often blinders, not horizon-expanders. A careful reading of the World Bank's education research publications finds many variants of the quasi-experiment. For example, to compare the educational effectiveness of, say, increasing textbooks and reducing class size, a researcher locates three schools that are similar in most characteristics, except that one has a higher ratio of textbooks per pupil and a second has smaller classes. Then, the researcher compares scores on a national examination across the three schools (more textbooks, smaller classes, average textbooks and classes) to determine whether textbooks or smaller classes are associated with higher scores. That research finding can then be used to calculate which initiative is most cost effective, which then becomes the recommended course of action. For many years the utility of scores on national examinations as a measure of desired education outcomes— "learning" is an inappropriate term here—was commonly assumed rather than critically examined. Perhaps recognizing the sharp limitations of those examinations, *WBES 2020* proposes to rely more heavily on the cross-national assessments conducted by outsiders. As this simplified example makes clear, there is no need to pay attention to the learning process, that is, to how, exactly, teachers and learners have changed their behavior as a result of increased textbooks or smaller classes, or how, exactly, instructional materials and class size have affected examination scores. The preferred research method compares inputs by measuring outputs without paying much attention to what goes on in between. Learning as process is obscured in education's black box.

The World Bank's effort to function as a development advisory service also turns attention away from the learning process. The World Bank seeks to improve education by identifying and replicating global education best practices (the terminology has varied). In practice, however, education and at its core the learning process are fundamentally local, interactive, contextually contingent, negotiated, and continually changing. That search for near-universal truths and decontextualised recommendations reinforces the inclination to retain unchanged, rather than look inside, the education black box (Samoff, 2007).

Research thus sits at a critical juncture between the World Bank's structural role in the global political economy and its understanding of and recommendations for improving education in poor countries. Its constrained and constraining construction of research sharply limits the sorts of explanations that are deemed reasonable and credible. Focused largely on inputs and outputs but not the learning process, its recommendations leave intact Africa's inherited schooling model. More of the same schooling becomes a major objective rather than a lament about the difficulties of transforming what is fundamentally problematic.

## LITTLE LEARNING, LESS ALL

Let us take stock. What is new here, or not? What is new here includes the recognition that education must be understood as far more than schooling and that therefore reform and improvement efforts must address interests and institutions outside the education ministry and the education sector. Also invigorated in *WBES 2020* are the recognition that the education community is, well, everyone, and the significantly increased role for cross-national assessments, which suggests less reliance on national examinations and even less on teacher-set tests. Though presented as new, much of the World Bank's 2020 education strategy emphasizes and reinvigorates analytic perspectives and recommendations that have been common over the past two decades (see, for example, World Bank, 1995). *WBES 2020* calls for greater attention to a system approach, with continued attention to inputs and increased attention to outputs. It calls for expanded data collection, referring largely to detailed school information. A boxed note proudly reports the volume of World Bank publications on education, though it neither notes nor explains the inattention to others' research. In short, once again we find the education black box, the banking model of education, and a very narrow conception of learning.

Most dramatic, *Learning for All* has little to say about learning and even less about all. Rather, we find an enthusiastic and upbeat effort to refine and update an approach to education in poor countries that is more an impediment to than a stimulus for change. The World Bank's failure to address the assumptions and structure of education systems reinforces and entrenches their conservative charter. The World Bank's inattention to the priorities and organization of the education systems that are to be improved, reinforced by its uncritical acceptance of patterns of schooling common across Africa, embed a model of education that is itself a major obstacle to achieving learning for all. Schools designed to educate a small elite do not attempt to provide effective mass education, and when they do, they reinforce inequality and demoralize most learners. More of the same simply will not do.

Achieving education for all requires deep and critical rethinking about the objectives and organization of education systems and schooling. An education system that everyone understands is intended to educate elites generates discontent and anger at every choke point. Perhaps that is the best hope for change.

## NOTES

[i] Here and throughout this chapter I focus on Africa, the continent with the most countries deemed least likely to achieve education for all by 2015 and the focus of most funding and technical assistance agencies' support to education.

[ii] On the conflation of knowledge and information, see Samoff and Stromquist, 2001.

[iii] A continent that includes many of the world's poorest countries and those least likely to achieve the 2015 education for all goals, Africa is an essential proving ground for *Learning for All*. For an overview of education in Africa, see Samoff, 2007a.

[iv] Criticized and subsequently refined and elaborated, Bowles and Gintis' notion of correspondence remains insightful (1976, 1981).

[v] It is both folly and essential to talk about more than fifty countries in the singular. The diversity across Africa is enormous, rich, and productive. Divergences in experience and policies are striking. Equally striking, however, are powerful commonalities, including the widespread and generally uncritical retention of a common schooling model. The analytic challenge is to draw insights from what is common while respecting the individual variations and innovations.

[vi] I draw here on Samoff, 2007a.

[vii] On ability grouping, Oakes provides an overview of relevant research for the U.S. (1985, 1992). Chisaka and Vakalisa found that teachers spent lest time preparing for lower ability groups, reducing overall learning and increasing disruptive behavior (2003). Ventkatakrishnan and William found no advantage to ability grouping in mathematics classes in South Africa (2003). In an international comparison, Entorf and Lauk concluded that ability groups magnified existing education inequalities (2006).

[viii] In practice, examinations commonly measure language competence (ability to understand the instructions and questions), memorization, and ability to recall under pressure, and perhaps not even that very well. Though important, exploring whether or not examinations measure what they claim to measure and whether or not examinations results are useful indicators of learning is beyond the scope of this discussion of the World Bank's education strategy.

[ix] Confusing here is the World Bank's tendency to treat as synonyms *equality* (sameness: treating people with different attributes and backgrounds in the same way) and *equity* (fairness: achieving fairness or justice for people with different attributes and experiences). For example, though titled

"Progress toward Gender Equity," Figure 3 provides information on gender [in]equality. In that confusion of the two constructs, there is no discussion of equity or of the circumstances in which achieving equity may require, at least for a time, treating groups differently (for example, paying or waiving girls' school fees).

x    For higher education examples in Africa, see Samoff and Carrol, 2004.


## REFERENCES

Bowles, S. & Gintis, H. (1976). *Schooling in capitalist America*. New York: Basic Books.

Bowles, S. & Gintis, H. (1981). Education as a site of contradictions in the reproduction of the capital-labor relationship: Second thoughts on the "correspondence principle." *Economic and Industrial Democracy, 2*(2), 223-242.

Chisaka, B. C. & Vakalisa, N. G. (2003). Some effects of ability grouping in Harare secondary schools: A case study, *South African Journal of Education, 23*(3), 176-180. http://www.ajol.info/index.php/saje/article/viewFile/24930/20617 (2011.08.17).

Entorf, H. & Lauk, M. (2006). *Peer effects, social multipliers and migrants at school: An international comparison*. IZA Discussion Paper, 2182. Bonn: Forschungsinstitut zur Zukunft der Arbeit. http://ftp.iza.org/dp2182.pdf (2011.08.17).

Freire, P. (1970). *Pedagogy of the oppressed*. New York: Herder and Herder.

Oakes, J. (1985). *Keeping track: How schools structure inequality*. New Haven: Yale University Press.

Oakes, J. (1992). Can tracking research inform practice? Technical, normative, and political considerations. *Educational Researcher, 21*(4), 12-21.

Samoff, J. (2007a). Education for all in Africa: Still a distant dream (with Bidemi Carrol). In R. F. Arnove & C. A. Torres (Eds.), *Comparative education: The dialectic of the global and the local*, 3rd ed. (pp. 357-388). Boulder: Rowman & Littlefield.

Samoff, Joel. (2007b). Education quality: The disabilities of aid. *International Review of Education, 53*(5-6), 485-507.

Samoff, J. (2009, July). The fast track to planned dependence: Education aid to Africa. Paper presented at the International Political Science Association XXI World Congress, Santiago, Chile.

Samoff, J. & Carrol, B. (2004). *From manpower planning to the knowledge era: World Bank policies on higher education in Africa* (Paris: UNESCO Forum on Higher Education, Research and Knowledge). [http://unesdoc.unesco.org/images/0013/001347/134782eo.pdf (2011.07.19)]

Samoff, J. & Stromquist, N. P. (2001). Managing knowledge and storing wisdom? New forms of foreign aid? *Development and Change, 32*(4), 631-656.

Ventkatakrishnan, H. & William, D. (2003). Tracking and mixed grouping in secondary mathematics classrooms: A case study. *British Educational Research Journal, 29*(2), 189-204.

World Bank. (1995). *Priorities and strategies for education: A World Bank review*. Washington, D.C.: World Bank.

World Bank. (2011). *Learning for all: Investing in people's knowledge and skills to promote development. World Bank Group Education Strategy 2020*. Washington, D.C.: World Bank. http://siteresources.worldbank.org/EDUCATION/Resources/ESSU/Education_Strategy_4_12_2011.pdf (2011.07.19).

*Joel Samoff*
*Center for African Studies*
*Stanford University, U.S.A.*

# PART III

# RESEARCH AND POLICY

## CHAPTER 9

ANTONI VERGER AND XAVIER BONAL

# "ALL THINGS BEING EQUAL?"

*Policy Options, Shortfalls, and Absences in the World Bank
Education Strategy 2020*

## INTRODUCTION

The World Bank's new education sector strategy (*World Bank Education Strategy
2020*, hereafter referred to as *WBES 2020*) establishes the guidelines for new
education priorities in low-income contexts for the coming decade. *WBES 2020*
attempts to move the focus of education reforms further away from an inputs
rationale to a reform agenda with outputs, governance, and managerial solutions at
its core. More specifically, it advocates: (a) the adoption of a *systemic* approach to
education reform that strengthens the role of non-government players and
incentives in education, (b) a more discernible focus on learning outcomes, which
implies measuring school results in order to generate a knowledge base with which
to inform policy-makers and families, and (c) the dissemination of innovative
approaches and demand-side interventions that can contribute to improving
learning outcomes effectively.

*WBES 2020* deserves our attention due to its enormous impact on the field of
education for development. The World Bank's Education Strategies, which are
carefully distributed all around the world, have a great capacity for establishing
education agendas globally. They are perceived, and to a great extent used, as a
policy guide by many stakeholders operating in the field of education for
development, including donors, NGOs, and ministries of education in less-
developed countries. The education sector strategies are probably the most
outstanding policy document contributing to positioning the Bank as the
intellectual leader of education reform in the field of development aid.

The explicit title of *WBES 2020*, *Learning for All*, is a clear recognition that
something else must be done, beyond policies focusing on access, to ensure that
schooling involves positive learning experiences. This could be perceived as a step
forward in the World Bank commitment to education for development. However,
as this paper argues, the Bank's explicit and underlying policy options in *WBES
2020* reflect more continuities than breaks when compared to previous strategies,
and moreover these policy options might not be adequate to achieve the "learning
for all" goal.

*S.J. Klees et al. (eds.), The World Bank and Education*, 125–142.

To develop this argument, this chapter is structured into two main sections. In the first section, we briefly review the development of the World Bank agenda in the educational field, as a way of putting the *WBES 2020* and its content and priorities into historical perspective. As we shall see, this agenda has broadened and become more ambitious with the passage of time. The current strategy involves telling developing countries worldwide why they should introduce complex changes in the governance of their education systems to enhance the learning opportunities for all students. However, when it comes to the *WBES 2020* defining specific prescriptions, all things seem to remain quite equal in the World Bank's education policy toolbox.

In the second section of this paper we identify and explore the main weaknesses of the policy ideas included in *WBES 2020*. We develop three sets of arguments in this respect. The first one refers to the Bank's strong attachment to a disciplinary and methodological approach that is incapable of understanding what children learn and do not learn at school and why. The second group of arguments refers to the pro-market ideological bias of the Strategy with regard to public sector reform and new forms of educational provision. In third place the article points out the main shortfalls of the Strategy, with special reference to those omissions related to the complexity of the relationship between education and poverty.

## *WBES 2020* IN PERSPECTIVE

The World Bank does not have an official mandate on education due to the fact that UNESCO is formally the United Nation's institution specializing in education. Nevertheless, paradoxically, the Bank has become one of the most influential international organizations in the field of education for development (Mundy, 2002). In fact, after reading *WBES 2020*, which has the approval of the organization's Executive Board of Directors, it might well be considered that the Bank has an implicit and broad mandate on education. This mandate could be summarized as the improvement of learning outcomes globally as a means of reducing poverty and integrating countries into the global economy.

The World Bank's first projects, when it was established in 1945, focused on infrastructure development and had no connection whatsoever with education. In the nineteen sixties however, the Bank began to involve itself in education affairs, although often indirectly. The first education initiatives were subordinated to major infrastructure projects (e.g., they consisted of training programs designed to provide local workers with the skills they required in the construction and maintenance of new infrastructures) or consisted of education infrastructures themselves. Thus the first education projects that the Bank was involved in were very much restricted to the material aspects of education systems: the building of schools or the transfer of material assets for laboratories, workshops or libraries (Jones, 1997). Over the years the Bank moved from the hardware to the software of education systems, hired more staff specializing in education and adopted an agenda that was much more oriented towards "education policy" and not only to manpower demands (Human Development Network, 2002; Mundy, 2002).[1]

The 1980 Education Policy Paper encourages the Bank staff, for the first time, to use rates of return in its analytic and projects lending work. As a consequence of the adoption of the rate of return analysis, the Bank's education policy agenda was condensed into the so-called "short menu" of education policy (Heyneman, 2003). This menu, which clearly crystallized in 1986 into the Bank's policy note "Financing Education in Developing Countries," advocated: (a) concentrating public investment in primary education, encouraging the privatization of higher education levels, (b) increasing the private cost for attending secondary and higher education, and (c) installing cost-recovery measures (loan schemes and taxes on graduates) in higher education (Jones, 1997).

The "short menu" prevailed for years in the Bank's discourse and practice regarding education, and was reinforced in the 1995 World Bank policy review *Priorities and Strategies for Education*. This document was given the status of a "policy review," although in reality it is highly prescriptive in nature.[ii] In addition to funding options similar to those included in the short menu, the review pledged its commitment to policies such as the decentralization of education systems, school autonomy, and the measurement of education outcomes. It also expressed an interest in the area of curriculum planning, highlighting the importance of subjects such as mathematics and language for economic development, and recommended establishing clear performance indicators to monitor the extent to which learning standards were being attained (Lauglo, 1996; World Bank, 1995). The 1995 Policy Review represented an expansion of the short education menu, which was very much focused on education financing, and a move towards a more comprehensive approach to education reform, including recommendations concerning curricula and the regulation and provision of education.

The first official education sector strategy was published in 1999.[iii] This strategy set out the following priorities: promoting quality education for all in order to address the huge gaps in learning among and within countries (with a focus on girls and on the poorest), early child development (ECD), innovative delivery (i.e., education services provided via ICTs) and systemic reform. The systemic reform focused on three areas that had already been formulated in a very similar way in the 1995 Policy Review: (a) standards, curriculum and achievement assessment, (b) governance and decentralization, and (c) encouraging investment in education by the private sector (World Bank, 1999).

The 1999 Strategy was updated in 2005. The most significant innovation included in this update is an apparent loss of centrality of the rates of return analysis due to a renewed emphasis on public investment in higher education. This shift was justified by the strategic contribution of universities to the building of "knowledge economies" (World Bank, 2005). The "knowledge economy" idea became a very powerful economic imaginary in the last decade, and most countries on the planet, those from both the developed and the developing world, expressed and still express their ambition to become such a type of economy (Robertson, 2005). However, it should be also considered that, since the World Education Conference held in Dakar in 2000, the donor community, and in particular the Education for All Fast Track Initiative, headquartered in the World Bank, has concentrated more efforts on the funding of basic education. Consequently, financial resources have been freed for the Bank to lend in other levels of education.

In 2011, after a long and unprecedented consultation process that included dozens of meetings in 53 different countries, *WBES 2020* was published. Despite the input received from hundreds of stakeholders during these consultations, the new Education Sector Strategy reflects more than anything continuity within the World Bank's education policy agenda. The focus on systemic reform, learning outcomes, evaluation and measurement (both at the national and cross-national levels), the key role of the private sector, the positive effects of ECD, and the importance of education as a key tool for tackling poverty and reinforcing employment markets is formulated in a similar way in all the Strategies (including the 1995 Policy Review). The last two Strategies emphasize the importance of generating a knowledge base for education systems, and put forward initiatives aimed at achieving this (EKMS in the 1999 Strategy, and SABER in the 2020 Strategy).[iv] The first education strategy documents use human capital theory to justify investment in education (and the involvement of the World Bank in education), whereas the most recent strategy uses a revised version of this theory devised by the Bank's current education champion, Eric Hanushek, who replaces "years of schooling" with "learning achievement" as the independent variable for economic growth. Lastly, the Bank's desire to collaborate in bilateral and multilateral aid delivery partnerships with other aid agencies has been expressed since the 1995 policy review, although it is more broadly developed in the subsequent Sector Strategies.

Naturally, some differences can also be identified. In terms of systemic reform, the current Strategy displays less interest in decentralization and curriculum policies than that expressed in the 1995 and 1999 documents, and gives more importance to governance changes based on accountability and incentives schemes, and also to the role of the private sector. Despite reservations, the 1999 Strategy acknowledged the importance of teachers' organizations in formulating and implementing reforms, yet in *WBES 2020* there is not a single reference to them. The current Strategy lacks the technological optimism of the 1999 document, and attributes a much more secondary role to ICT education. Lastly, it is significant that, for the first time, *WBES 2020* acknowledges that there is no trade-off between equity and quality, and that more equitable systems in fact achieve better results.

The continuity in the themes, priorities and policy options of the Bank's education strategies over time, and also the different levels of emphasis given to certain topics at different moments, can be clearly seen in the following charts (see Figure 1).[v]

**1995**

**1999**

**2011**

*Figure 9. Keywords Clouds in Past and Current Education Strategies*
*(1995, 1999 and 2020)*

EXAMINING THE BANK'S "LEARNING FOR ALL" STRATEGY

The explicit title of the new strategy, *Learning for All*, carries an implicit recognition of the limits of past education strategies, which have failed to transform educational investment into sufficient learning, especially for the poor (Bonal, 2007; Jones, 2006). Far from introducing self-criticism, the *WBES 2020* interprets the history of the Bank's strategic policies as an accumulative process of learning "what works best" in education. In this section, we point out the main problems and shortcomings that prevail in the causal ideas and methodological strategies that support the World Bank's current education agenda. Specifically, we problematize three main aspects: the predominant economic approach to education analysis and reform; the emphasis placed on education markets and the role of the private sector; and the shortfalls in the complex relationship between poverty and education.

*Captured by the Method: Learning within the System Approach*

The World Bank's main policy recommendations in the field of education included in this and in previous Strategies are shaped by an economic rationale and spring from an economics-based view of education problems. In fact, as the World Bank itself admits, one of the implicit objectives of the Education Strategies is to inform outsiders about things that insiders take for granted, such as "the value of an economics-based approach to education development" (HDN, 2002, p. 430). However, this disciplinary bias also has its limitations, and contributes to constraints by the analytical methods it uses for studying educational systems and policies. The goal of developing a universal and irrefutable scientific knowledge base and methodology for evaluating educational reforms, together with a strong belief in market solutions for such development, leads the Bank into dismissing other more context-sensitive approaches for assessing educational policies. The inclusion of such approaches would make the Bank more cautious about any pretension of universality.

One of the main features of *WBES 2020* is its desire to overcome input-driven reforms and place learning outcomes as the central goal. Learning for all, and not simply access for all, is set up as the main priority. As stated in the Strategy: "improving systems also requires ensuring that inputs are used more effectively to accelerate learning. While past strategies have recognized this goal, the new strategy gives it more emphasis, setting it in a context of education system assessment and reform" (p. ix).

However, what does moving beyond input-driven policies mean for the Bank? The Bank interprets this as changing the governance and management of schools and teachers and aligning financing rules and incentive mechanisms with the goal of learning for all (p. x). Beyond a widespread support for the introduction of market rules and demand-side interventions into education systems, it is not possible to distinguish in the Strategy which specific forms of governance and management are the ones that would ensure learning, as it is not possible to identify which specific causal relations explain learning better. The Bank is extremely vague about how to introduce reforms in these areas: "The mechanisms that connect the various parts of the system need to be reformed so that functions, authority, and relationships of accountability within the system are clear and aligned with national educational goals" (p. 18).

Here lies one of the main contradictions of the Strategy. The Bank defends evidence-based policies, but is unable to provide convincing evidence about what really works to ensure that children do learn at school. Actually, the Bank defines the Strategy in terms of two main approaches: strengthening education systems and building a high-quality knowledge base. Interestingly enough, the nature of these two approaches is significantly different. Both of them carry a substantial level of generality, but while the first approach can be translated into specific measures that would potentially improve learning, the second approach can only be understood as providing the necessary means for knowledge and not as a strategic action that would improve learning. In other words, it is possible to establish a relationship between better education systems and better learning, but not between knowing more about the education system and better learning (and thus it is of course possible to have an extensive knowledge about an education system and have a high rate of low performers). Acquiring knowledge about the education system is of course necessary, but one would expect a strategic paper to reveal which knowledge and for what specific purposes.

The nature of the knowledge about education systems that the Bank expects to obtain reflects a systemic view of education systems, which can be defined as the chain between input-processes-outcomes of different integrated education factors. For the Bank, better knowledge about education systems means obtaining more information about each of these phases. Applying a systemic approach to policy making is a difficult task, since policy-makers cannot control all the factors that may potentially improve education systems. Thus, "the key to implementing the system approach is to recognize that it does not imply *acting* on all parts of the system at once, but being aware of them and analyzing how they affect each other" (p. 42). This fact, for the Bank, can be translated into the principle "analyze globally, act locally" (p. 6).

The priorities established by the *WBES 2020* are a good example of how the Bank aims to lever its capacity to lead the global analyses of education systems. Among other applications, this makes it possible to run cross-country regression analyses with numerous observations, which can respond to the expressed aim of generalizing results. "All things being equal," the Bank should then be able to deduce what works better universally to improve learning. The Bank's implicit message to national governments seems to be: "improve your data collection capacity so that we can run more reliable cross-country analysis and regressions."

Due to the territorial scope of the World Bank, its methods of study and policy recommendations must necessarily be applicable to different social contexts and different education systems. However, at the same time, the World Bank is increasingly defending the importance of context-based policies and strategies. Despite this intention, the Bank is constrained by a method that intrinsically ignores the context. While learning processes are by their very nature contextually based on the living conditions and cultural experiences of individuals, the World Bank confines the Strategy within the limits of education systems. The Strategy "redefines" the term education system as a network of relationships, including all potential players intervening in the learning opportunities offered by a society, i.e., within and outside of formal education institutions (p. 16). However, the methods for providing evidence are restricted to techniques (such as regression analysis or production functions)[vi] that reveal the inability of the Bank to grasp those factors that are not easily measurable or observable. According to Weaver (2007): "[Within the Bank] considerable weight is given to economic and technical factors that are easy to identify and measure, whereas complex political and social risk assessments that involve soft qualitative indicators are usually neglected or distrusted as 'unscientific'" (p. 507).

The system approach defended by the World Bank is in fact a sign of the power of the method. The best example of this can be found in Point 20 of the executive summary, where the Strategy states that "careful system analysis will allow for clearer differentiation of countries by level of educational system, rather than by overall development alone" (p. xi). This is actually a declaration of principles: the performance of education systems, rather than their development, is the main goal. Why the good performance of education systems is not translated into more development, or why good educational performance is unable to reduce poverty and inequality, are questions that are omitted in *WBES 2020*.

A final observation about the power of the method has to do with the possible reasons that motivate the inclusion of learning as a priority goal of the strategy. There is of course evidence showing the limits to the extent that educational expansion can be converted into learning. Other strategic declarations, such as the recent *Metas Educativas 2021* (Educational Goals) for Latin America, stress the fact that Latin American countries have been able to expand primary and secondary education over the past decade, but unable to achieve high educational performance. However, over the past decade we have witnessed the widespread application of performance evaluation systems and especially the consolidation of PISA as the main reference of skill acquisition in educational systems. PISA is, as *WBES 2020* acknowledges, a powerful instrument for assessing educational performance, but it is in no way a context-based instrument for discovering how and why children learn in different educational systems. The main asset of PISA is that it is a measurable instrument that facilitates comparisons. The temptation to reduce learning measurement to performance in international standardized tests (such as PISA, TIMSS or PIRLS) is too strong to be avoided. Nonetheless, useful learning for social and labor inclusion goes far beyond merely performing well in standardized tests.

Reducing the analysis of learning factors to variables that are measurable and quantifiable, as well as internationally comparable, is actually a clear sign of the power of the method. In *WBES 2020*, the World Bank proclaims itself as the global leader and promoter of a paradigm of educational research that incorporates a pretension of universality and irrefutability that cannot easily cope with the goal of contextually based learning.

*Overrating Market Solutions*

The World Bank has been backing private sector participation in education for decades. However, in this regard the 2020 Strategy goes a step further than previous policy papers. The current Strategy puts stronger emphasis on the importance of the private sector for meeting the EFA goals, it is openly supportive of "for-profit" private education providers[vii], it raises the educational lending profile of the International Finance Corporation (IFC)—the World Bank Group agency that deals directly with the private sector, and it considers that the private sector can be of direct benefit to the poor.[viii] In relation to the latter, it should be acknowledged that the 1999 Strategy rather established an indirect relationship between private schooling and poverty, the rationale being that those families that can afford it should attend private schools, because by doing so they release government resources that can be invested in improving the public schools attended by the poor. By contrast, *WBES 2020* states that: "Although it is often assumed that the private sector serves mainly students who can afford to pay, private entities are important providers of education services to even the poorest communities, especially in areas that governments do not reach" (p. 20).

Implicit in *WBES 2020* is the fact that private institutions are inherently better than state schools, and that poor students will benefit from attending private schools—by means of a voucher system, for example (p. 6). However, the Strategy provides no evidence of the supposed better performance of private schools, though it should be acknowledged that evidence on the topic is very mixed. In fact, it is not possible to reach universal conclusions on this topic because research results are highly contingent on the different types of private schools, the socio-economic composition of schools and the education regulations prevailing in different countries (Calero & Escardíbul, 2007; Vandenberghe & Robin, 2004). Interestingly enough, recent analyses of PISA data tell us that, "all else being equal" (especially when controlling for the socio-economic status of students), the type of ownership of the school, whether it is a private or a state school, has only modest effects on students achievements or none at all (Fertig, 2003; OECD, 2005; Corten & Dronkers, 2006).

*WBES 2020* strongly advocates that governments establish partnerships with the private sector and regulate this sector in a way that encourages the emergence of private providers and controls the quality of the services they provide. In line with the categories suggested by Ball and Youdell (2007), we might consider that the World Bank supports two types of privatization: on the one hand, the privatization *of* education, and on the other, privatization *in* education. The privatization *of* education consists of encouraging the increase of private provision and the number of private schools within education systems. The Strategy suggests that this can be done by means of contract schools or subsidies to the private sector. The main objective of the privatization of education is to expand the schooling resources available in a particular territory.

For its part, privatization *in* education consists of encouraging state schools to behave and be run like private providers, with the aim of making them more competitive and raising their quality standards. According to *WBES 2020*, these

133

objectives can be achieved by introducing incentives schemes and competitive funding formulas (vouchers, results-oriented financing, etc.). Influenced by economic theory and by a rationalistic conception of humans as benefit-maximizers, competition and school choice are two core policy principles in the 2020 Strategy. Both principles are expected to be important elements in the "results chain that lies between inputs and learning outcomes" (p. x) that the 2020 Strategy attempts to identify: "Power of greater autonomy at the provider level and of competition for resources (such as through the use of performance incentives or vouchers) [will contribute] to generate a strong motivation among providers for better service delivery" (p. 15). At the same time, the Strategy assumes that choice and competition will contribute to low-quality schools losing enrollment and consequently disappearing from the market.

Applying market metaphors such as choice or competition to education systems sounds persuasive. However, such metaphors are very difficult to translate successfully into practical policies. Optimum school choice requires conditions, such as perfect information or sufficient offer, which are hardly ever met in low-income contexts. Even when the right to choose is guaranteed by the state, most families, especially those affected by poverty, fail to exercise this right as the Bank would expect (i.e., by choosing the better school). Rather than choosing based on school quality, families usually choose a school accordingly to criteria such as proximity, cost, social relations, pre-conceptions of the different types of schools, religious preferences or discipline in class (Nieuwenhuys, 1993; Härmä, 2009; Fennel, 2012). Moreover, in poor, rural, or under-populated areas families may not have enough providers to be able to choose.

Regardless of whether they are desirable or not, markets in education may not be feasible in many countries where the World Bank intervenes, because they are very costly and technically demanding. In order to work properly, markets in education require a very complex and often expensive set of support services and procedures (transportation, quality assurance, information systems, dispute settlement systems, bidding processes, etc.) the implementation of which might be too challenging in low-income countries (Verger, 2011). Not surprisingly, the 2011 Independent Evaluation Group report finds quite uneven results in the World Bank portfolio of education projects due to "design and implementation weaknesses" including "overly complex designs relative to local capacities" (IEG, 2011, p. 13). Furthermore, if the for-profit sector is to be included in the provision of public education, as *WBES 2020* suggests, the economic incentives that the state would have to provide them to deliver their services in poor areas could make the proposal even more expensive (Rosenau, 2000).

In many low-income countries, the amount of private education on offer is very low. Thus, instead of expecting state regulation to encourage the flourishing of private education entrepreneurs, states would reach the EFA targets in a quicker and more sustainable way by enlarging and strengthening the public sector. At least, this is the conclusion of Lewin (2007) in a cross-country research on this topic in Sub-Saharan Africa. As Lewin warns, markets-in-education policies are too often inspired by experiences and models drawn from well-developed, professionalized, regulated, and (already) partly marketized education systems. These policies are not easily transferable to partly developed, poorly professionalized, largely unregulated systems such as those existing in the countries where the World Bank operates.

Moving Lewin's argument on a little further, it should be acknowledged that even in rich countries, the evidence for the positive effects of markets in education is still not conclusive. After reviewing hundreds of pieces of research on school choice and competition between schools, a recent OECD Education Paper concludes that, "if any effects are found at all, they are small" (Waslander et al., 2010, p. 64). However, the World Bank misrepresents an important part of the literature on the topic and, very selectively, overestimates the results of its own impact evaluations and the research of like-minded scholars. Its policy recommendations contradict research that points out to the neutral or even negative effects of education markets in dimensions such as achievement (see Rouse & Barrow, 2009; McEwan & Carnoy, 2000), efficiency (Levin, 1999), and especially equity (Reay, 2004; Fiske & Ladd, 2000; Alegre & Ferrer, 2010).

*WBES 2020* is very optimistic about the potential role of the IFC in benefiting the poor through private education. Among other factors, the Strategy supports the IFC due to its capacity for providing financing for "larger network providers who have the ability to invest across borders and go down-market to reach poorer populations" and "small and medium enterprises which typically target poor populations" (p. 32). However, as recent research shows, the IFC is not reaching the poorest countries and the poorest populations. Between 2006 and 2010, only 4.8 percent of IFC education investments were made in low-income countries, and 67 percent of the current projects are at the tertiary education level (Mundy & Menashy 2012). Furthermore, as the same study shows, equity investments in education are considered risky within the IFC. In 2010, an internal rate of return of -32 percent was reported in educational projects.

To conclude, it is a very positive fact that the Bank, via *WBES 2020*, is moving away from a too simplistic focus on inputs when it comes to education reform. However, the current focus on managerial solutions, private education, and education markets should not detract from the fact that most education systems in low-income contexts still have strong dependence on increasing levels of public investment in schools building, books, teacher training and salaries (Glewwe, 2002).[ix]

*Closing the Learning Gap: A Goal without Means*

One of the salient features of *WBES 2020* is the importance given to the relationship between equity and learning. This is certainly a new strategic direction that is absent in previous strategies. The 1995 Policy Review was clearly dependent on an economic policy that almost despised social and educational inequalities as factors preventing development. There, the goal of economic growth was the main, and almost exclusive, priority for the World Bank.

In contrast, the current Strategy aligns the objective of Learning for All with the equity goals that underlie the education MDGs. This assertion is repeated in several sections of the Strategy, and it is based on the evidence provided by the PISA results. Thus, the Bank highlights that "the latest (2009) PISA results reinforce the lesson that the countries that are most successful overall in promoting learning are those with the narrowest gaps in learning achievement among students" (p. viii). When reading this, one would expect that recognizing the centrality of equity would be translated into a set of policy recommendations to address the inequalities in education systems effectively. However, the "equity matters" discourse does not lead to any redistributive orientation of education policies. The Bank's emphasis on evidence-based policy is absolutely partial here. While the Strategy recognizes the importance of equity, it ignores those forms of evidence that explain why education systems remain unequal. Evidence related to education system regulations, school segregation, differences in school quality or the "peer effect" on learning is completely ignored.[x]

Interestingly enough, the Strategy draws a narrow equivalence between equity and targeting population groups that experience specific barriers to learning. It states: "A well-functioning education system will therefore have policies or programs that specifically address the disadvantages faced by some population groups ... and will target special resources to assist those disadvantaged groups" (p. 21). The reduction of equity to targeting resources means also avoiding possible universal policy strategies that could potentially reduce educational privileges and redistribute educational opportunities among the most disadvantaged groups.

Within the notion of targeting, the Bank includes "demand-side interventions, such as the abolition of school fees and targeted scholarships, cash transfers that compensate families for the opportunity cost of children's school attendance, and vouchers that enable poor students to attend private educational institutions" (p. 6). This quote shows that the Bank includes demand-side interventions of a very different nature within the same set of policy instruments. However, abolishing school fees, arranging conditional cash transfers (CCTs), or giving vouchers to poor students to attend private institutions are policies that respond to very different conceptions of educational equity. Moreover, the evidence regarding the effects of some of the proposed policies is not at all conclusive, and as a consequence it is questionable whether they can be taken as best practices for achieving learning for all.

CCT evaluations, for instance, offer a picture of different effects at different levels, depending very much on program design (Bonal et al., 2012). Impacts on school access are normally positive (because of conditionality) but are less definite in learning processes and educational performance (Reimers et al., 2006). The educational quality of the schools attended by the program's beneficiaries and the living conditions of poor children are decisive factors preventing the expected effects of the transfer on learning (Tarabini, 2008; Bonal & Tarabini, 2010).

For its part, the impact of voucher programs on educational equity also presents mixed evidence, but the scale tips in favor of studies that show that vouchers increase segmentation of the education system according to the socioeconomic status of students (UNESCO, 2009; Waslander, 2010). In this sense, it is paradoxical that the Bank on the one hand defends the importance of equity for learning achievement, while on the other it advocates for voucher schemes and other market policies in education that most evidence shows as increasing education inequalities and school segregation. In any case, as occurs with CCTs, considering vouchers as a policy instrument that "works" or "does not work" is misleading, since their effects depend to a great extent on how these programs are designed and how the beneficiaries are selected (Levin, 2002). Instead of formulating over-simplistic bi-variable relations between policy interventions and outcomes, the Bank would benefit from formulating their impact evaluation questions in a more nuanced manner (i.e., what works for whom in what circumstances and how) (Pawson & Tilley, 1997), as well as from embracing qualitative methodological approaches to capture the importance of local regulations, preferences and social norms when it comes to understanding and evaluating the schooling experience of children (Fennell & Arnot, 2008; Klees, 2008).

*WBES 2020* is also clear about the need for targeting policies to be inclusive enough to reach the poorest. The policy paper recognizes the need to look beyond the educational experience of children for the factors that prevent learning.

> Learning is not only about schooling. Investments in the nutritional and health status of very young children and the quality of their interaction with parents and caregivers determine the readiness of children to learn. Likewise, programs that address hunger, malnutrition, and disease among schoolchildren significantly improve their academic performance .... Indeed, learning is not simply the business of education agencies; it should also involve social welfare and/or social protection and health agencies in the design and implementation of policies across sectors that ensure young children have the foundational skills to succeed in school. (pp. 12-13)

The above statement acknowledges the importance of the effects of poverty on education. Actually, this relationship is powerful enough to reduce the potential positive effects of education to a fight against poverty (Bonal, 2007; Jones, 2006). However, the educational policy paradigm that has sustained the World Bank education policy over recent decades has in fact explicitly disregarded the effects of poverty on education. The reason for this is that human capital theory incorporates a view of education as a *cause* of development, and never as an effect of social and economic policies. For the Bank, conceptions of educational development have always been equivalent to educational investments, as a form of capital investment. This understanding of the role of education for development has not left room for other approaches that could question the universality of the principles of human capital theory. Consequently, if the Bank took the above assertion seriously, it would mean a real paradigm change in its educational policy strategy. It would mean also putting development before education, and understanding that education development is not only a cause of development, but also a consequence of development processes in multiple areas (economy, health, etc.). And that would mean connecting education to policies and outcomes in other areas of development with determination.

Educational development needs the adoption of a multi-sectorial approach that acknowledges that there are non-educational factors preventing learning. *WBES 2020* performs an interesting exercise by including all possible links between the education strategy and other Bank sector strategies (see Annex 3 of the Strategy). For each strategy the Bank tries to identify the education contributions to the sector in question and, vice versa, how other sectors contribute to education. But linking all sectors with education is not exactly developing a multi-sectorial approach. A real multi-sectorial approach should actually be included in the core of the policy paper and not in the appendix, and should be necessarily integrative. It should address aspects related to conditions governing the educability of children (López & Tedesco, 2002), i.e., identifying the minimum social requirements needed for a child to learn at school. If closing the learning gap requires poor children to learn, as the Bank states in several parts of the policy paper, the Strategy should concentrate on those social, psychological, material, or cultural factors that prevent poor children from taking advantage of their school experience. *WBES 2020* emphasizes mainly nutritional and health aspects as non-educational variables related to learning. But this is a reductionist interpretation of the multiple dimensions of poverty impacting on the learning conditions of children. Looking at the conditions of educability involves both a multifaceted understanding of poverty and the use of qualitative methods able to grasp the living experiences of children in diverse social spaces. It will be difficult to capture these elements using the quantitative cross-national studies or positivistic impact evaluations usually undertaken by the Bank.

## CONCLUSIONS

*WBES 2020* does not introduce significant policy innovations compared to the previous World Bank education strategies. In this document, the focus on systemic reform, learning outcomes, evaluation, and measurement, the key role of the private sector, and the importance of education as a key tool for tackling poverty and for reinforcing employment markets is formulated in a way very similar to previous Strategies.

Continuity would not be a problem if there were not serious limitations in some of the key analytical ideas behind the Strategy and in the policies it prescribes. The expression "all things being equal" in the title of this chapter refers not only to whether or not the World Bank is presenting substantial changes in *WBES 2020*. "All things being equal" is also a common expression used by the Bank economists to illustrate empirical evidence in education. As we have argued in this paper, the system approach defended by the Bank reflects its attachment to a disciplinary knowledge and to empirical methods that attempt to explain how variables behave in hypothetical contexts of "other things remaining equal." Yet, since learning is a highly contextually-based phenomenon, this form of empirical evidence is not the most appropriate way of explaining policies about how children learn at school and why.

Once again, the latest Education Sector Strategy reveals a strong faith in the superior efficiency and quality of market solutions and private schooling, which are causal beliefs that are not supported sufficiently by evidence. In fact, evidence rather shows that market solutions affect education equity purposes negatively. The latter observation precisely undermines the most significant conceptual innovation in *WBES 2020,* which is that of acknowledging education equity as a means of education quality and learning. We have also shown that *WBES 2020* fails to capture the complexity of the education and poverty relationship accurately, since it does not contemplate the multiple dimensions of poverty influencing the learning conditions of children.

In *WBES 2020,* the World Bank accurately considers that an inputs approach to education reform is too simplistic and insufficient, and that policy-makers need to pay more attention to the governance of education systems. However, this message should not be misunderstood as disregarding inputs, since education systems in most developing contexts are in need of increasing resources, sometimes urgently so. Furthermore, the emphasis on demand-side and managerial interventions could obscure variables (such as the peer effect, the educability conditions of children, or local education rules and norms) that are key to an understanding of student learning, and that are unfortunately absent in the 2020 Strategy "Learning for all."

## NOTES

[i] The adjustment in lending generated the conditions for this to happen. SAPs meant that countries would have fewer resources available from public budgets for social services such as education. Consequently, they had to borrow from the Bank to cover their often-expanding education needs (Mundy, 2002).

[ii] In fact, the World Bank itself considers it to be de facto a primary sector strategy. See "Previous Education Strategies" in: http://go.worldbank.org/208ECTQCC0

[iii] The Sector Strategies were promoted with Wolfensonh's deep organizational reform of the World Bank (1996-2000). Before this reform, the Bank was organized accordingly to territorial criteria. As a consequence, the Country Assistance Strategies (CAS) were the organization's main strategic documents. Wolfensonh's reform introduced a thematic focus in the organization (via the strengthening of thematic research and thematic networks), and consequently the Thematic or Sector Strategies became an important political product within the Bank, at a CAS level (HDN, 2002; Nielson et al., 2006).

[iv] EKMS stands for Education Knowledge Management System and SABER for System Assessment and Benchmarking for Education Results.

[v] Word clouds have been created using the on-line application "Wordle." To strengthen the comparative power of the charts, we have not included words like World Bank, schools, countries or education.

[vi] See examples of how these techniques can be problematic to guide policy when used uncritically, in Glewwe (2002) or Klees (2008).

[vii] Interestingly, the 1995 Policy Review states that, in order to license a private school in Nigeria, "the proprietor must meet many ostensibly reasonable requirements (for example, showing that the school will be non-profit)" (World Bank, 1995, p. 123).

viii Interestingly, Figure 1 also shows how, with the passage of time, the "private" concept has gained terrain (to the detriment of the "public" one) in the World Bank policy discourse.
ix This affirmation is also valid for richer countries such as Argentina (see Santos 2007).
x See for instance Dupriez et al. (2008) and Hanushek et al. (2003) for evidence of the importance of some of these factors in explaining differences in student performance.

## REFERENCES

Alegre, M. À. & Ferrer, G. (2010). School regimes and education equity: some insights based on PISA 2006. *British Educational Research Journal, 36*(3), 433–461.

Ball, S. J. & Youdell, D. (2007). *Hidden privatisation in public education.* Brussels: Education International.

Bonal, X. (2007). On global absences: Reflections on the failings in the education and poverty relationship in Latin America. *International Journal of Educational Development, 27*(1), 86–100.

Bonal, X., Tarabini, A., & Rambla, X. (2012). Conditional cash transfers in education for development: Emergence, policy dilemmas and diversity of impacts. In A. Verger, M. Novelli, & H. Kosar-Altinyelken (Eds.), *Global education policy and international development: New agendas, issues and programmes.* New York: Continuum.

Bonal, X. & Tarabini, A. (2010). *Ser pobre en la escuela. Hábitus de pobreza y condiciones de educabilidad.* Buenos Aires: Miño y Dávila.

Calero, J. & Escardíbul, O. (2007). Evaluación de servicios educativos: El rendimiento en los centros públicos y privados medido en PISA-2003. *Hacienda Pública Española/Revista de Economía Pública,* 183(4), 33-66.

Corten, R. & Dronkers, J. (2006). School achievement of pupils from the lower strata in public, private government-eependent and private government-independent schools: A cross-national test of the Coleman-Hoffer thesis. *Educational Research and Evaluation, 2,* 179-208.

Dupriez, V., Dumay, X., & Vause, A. (2008). How do school systems manage pupils' heterogeneity? A reanalysis of PISA 2003. *Comparative Education Review, 52*(2), 245-273.

Fennell, S. & Arnot, M. (2008). Decentring hegemonic gender theory: The implications for educational research. *Compare, 38*(5), 525–538.

Fennell, S. (2012). Why girls' education rather than gender equality? The strange political economy of PPPs in Pakistan. In S. Robertson, A. Verger, K. Mundy, & F. Menashy (Eds.), *Public private partnerships in education: New actors and modes of governance in a globalising world.* London: Edward Elgar.

Fertig, M. (2003). Who's to blame? The determinants of German students' achievement in the PISA 2000 study. IZA Discussion Paper Series, 739.

Fiske, E. B. & Ladd, H. (2000). *When schools compete: A cautionary tale.* Washington D.C.: Brookings Institution Press.

Glewwe, P. (2002). Schools and skills in developing countries: Education policies and socioeconomic outcomes. *Journal of Economic Literature, 40*(2), 436-482.

Hanushek, E. A., Kain, J. F., Markman, J. M., & Rivkin, S. G. (2003). Does peer ability affect student achievement? *Journal of Applied Econometrics, 18*(5), 527-544.

Härmä, J. (2009). Can choice promote Education for All? Evidence from growth in private primary schooling in India. *Compare: A Journal of Comparative and International Education, 39*(2), 151-165.

Heyneman, S. P. (2003). The history and problems in the making of education policy at the World Bank 1960-2000. *International Journal of Educational Development, 23,* 315-337.

HDN (Human Development Network). (2002). World Bank strategy in the education sector: Process, product and progress. *International Journal of Educational Development, 22,* 429-437.

IEG. (2011). *IEG Annual Report 2011: Results and performance of the World Bank Group.* Washington D.C.: World Bank.

Jones, P. W. (1997). On World Bank Education financing. *Comparative Education, 33*(1), 117-130.

Jones, P. W. (2006). *Education, poverty and the World Bank*. Rotterdam: Sense.

Klees, S. J. (2008). Reflections on theory, method, and practice in comparative and international education. *Comparative Education Review, 52*(3), 301-328.

Lauglo, J. 1996. Banking on education and the uses of research. A critique of: World Bank priorities and strategies for education. *International Journal of Educational Development, 16*(3), 221-233.

Levin, H. M. (1999). The public-private nexus in education. *American Behavioral Scientist, 43*(1), 124.

Levin, H. M. (2002). A comprehensive framework for evaluating educational vouchers. *Educational Evaluation and Policy Analysis, 24*(3), 159-174.

Lewin, K. M. (2007). The limits to growth of non-government: Private schooling in sub-Saharan Africa. In P. Srivastava & G. Walford (Eds.), *Private schooling in less economically developed countries: Asian and African perspectives*. Oxford: Symposium.

López, N. & Tedesco, J. C. (2002). Las condiciones de educabilidad de los niños y adolescentes en América Latina, *Documentos del IIPE*. Buenos Aires: IIPE-UNESCO

McEwan, P. J. & Carnoy, M. (2000). The effectiveness and efficiency of private schools in Chile's voucher system. *Educational Evaluation and Policy Analysis, 22*(3), 213-219.

Mundy, K. (2002). Retrospect and prospect: Education in a reforming World Bank. *International Journal of Educational Development, 22*(5), 483-508.

Mundy, K. & Menashy, F. (2012). The role of the IFC in the promotion of public-private partnerships for educational development. In S. Robertson, A. Verger, K. Mundy, & F. Menashy (Eds.), *Public-private partnerships and the global governance of education*. London: Edward Elgar.

Nielson, D. L., Tierney, M. J., & Weaver, C. E. (2006). Bridging the rationalist–constructivist divide: Re-engineering the culture of the World Bank. *Journal of International Relations and Development, 9*(2), 107-139.

Nieuwenhuys, O. (1993). To read and not to eat: South Indian children between secondary school and work. *Childhood, 1*(2), 100-109.

OECD. (2005). *School factors related to quality and equity. Results from PISA 2000*. Paris: OECD.

Pawson, R. & Tilley, N. (1997). *Realistic Evaluation*. London: Sage.

Reimers, F., Silva, C. S., & Trevino, E. (2006). Where is the "education" in Conditional Cash Transfers in Education? *UIS Working Papers, 4*, 1-80.

Robertson, S. L. (2005). Re-imagining and rescripting the future of education: Global knowledge economy discourses and the challenge to education systems. *Comparative Education, 41*(2), 151-170.

Santos, M. E. (2007). Calidad de la educación en Argentina: determinantes y distribución utilizando los resultados de PISA 2000. *Revista Bienestar y Política Social, 3*(1), 79-109.

Tarabini, A. (2008). Educational targeting in the fight against poverty: Limits, omissions and opportunities. *Globalisation, Societies and Education, 6*(4), 415-429.

Reay, D. (2004). Exclusivity, exclusion, and social class in urban education markets in the United Kingdom. *Urban education, 39*(5), 537-560.

Rosenau, P. V. (2000). *Public-private policy partnerships*. Boston: MIT Press.

Rouse, C. E. & Barrow, L. (2009). School vouchers and student achievement: Recent evidence and remaining questions. *Annual Review of Economics, 1*(1), 17-42.

UNESCO. (2009). *EFA Global Monitoring Report 2009. Overcoming inequality: Why governance matters*. Paris: UNESCO.

Vandenberghe, V. & Robin, S. (2004). Evaluating the effectiveness of private education across countries: A comparison of methods. *Labour Economics, 11*(4), 487-506.

Verger, A. (2011). Framing and selling global education policy: The promotion of PPPs in education in low-income countries. *Journal of Education Policy*. DOI:10.1080/02680939.2011.623242

Waslander, S., Pater, C., & van der Weide, M. (2010). Markets in education: An analytical review of empirical research on market mechanisms in education. *OECD EDU Working Paper* 52.

Weaver, C. (2007). The world's bank and the bank's world. *Global Governance: A Review of Multilateralism and International Organizations, 13*(4), 493-512.

World Bank. (1995). *Priorities and strategies for education*. Washington, D.C.: World Bank.

World Bank. (1999). *Education sector strategy*. Washington, D.C.: World Bank.

World Bank. (2005). *Education sector strategy update: Achieving education for all, broadening our perspective, maximizing our effectiveness*. Washington, D.C.: World Bank.

World Bank. (2011). *Learning for all: Investing in people's knowledge and skills to promote development*. Washington, D.C.: World Bank.

*Antoni Verger*
*Department of Sociology*
*Universitat Autònoma de Barcelona, Spain*

*Xavier Bonal*
*Department of Sociology*
*Universitat Autònoma de Barcelona, Spain*

## CHAPTER 10

JOEL SAMOFF

# "RESEARCH SHOWS THAT ...": CREATING THE KNOWLEDGE ENVIRONMENT FOR LEARNING FOR ALL

In its Education Strategy 2020 (World Bank 2011), and indeed across its development activities, the World Bank insists on evidence-based policy, evidence-based decisions, evidence-based management, and evidence-based assessment. Excellent, we can all agree. Research, rather than personal, institutional, or political agendas should inform and guide decisions about what is likely the most important development activity and the most contested of public policies. Both practitioners and academics will applaud the reduced role for whim, caprice, political opportunism, and chance. Yet, on closer inspection that clearly desirable insistence on evidence obscures contested meanings—what exactly is evidence?—and functions to impose a conceptual and methodological orthodoxy that may undermine education reform and marginalize innovation. How can the emphasis on research and evidence turn out to be so problematic?

The insistence on finding and defining what can be disseminated as the *correct* development model, rather than critically exploring alternative development strategies, is accompanied by a similarly unrelenting insistence on specifying the *correct* methodology. With occasional exceptions, the strategies for developing the needed evidence are assumed to be widely understood and broadly accepted. Science becomes agreed conventions rather than a fiercely contested terrain. As gatekeeper for development assistance, the World Bank has become an arbiter of quality in education research. That effort to specify the research and research methods that are legitimate sharply limits the development knowledge on which the World Bank draws and impedes rather than advances the development of new knowledge. What is offered as solution is fundamentally problematic.

To explore these issues, we must review three major problematic consequences of the World Bank's insistence on its narrow notion of what constitutes research and science. First, that methodological orthodoxy validates as fact observations and inferences that require critical attention. Second, the World Bank's unhesitatingly self-referential approach to evidence precludes the development of knowledge through the confrontation of alternative ideas and perspectives. Third, the widespread conversion of independent research into contract consulting regularly risks transforming critical inquiry into dependent confirmation of previously asserted certainties. Then, it will be fruitful to outline the role the World

*S.J. Klees et al. (eds.), The World Bank and Education, 143–157.*

Bank could play in creating the knowledge environment for learning for all. We must also consider how the World Bank's aspirations to foster knowledge production are impeded by and perhaps incompatible with its global role and its structural and institutional imperatives. Ultimately, it seems clear, even for its own institutional agenda—managing the integration of poor countries into the global political economy—the World Bank's approach to research on education is both near-sighted and short-sighted.[i]

## METHODOLOGICAL ORTHODOXY

In its most recent education strategy,[ii] the World Bank seeks to shift the emphasis from education for all to learning for all. Having gathered broad support and very substantial funding since its 1990 inaugural conference in Thailand, the Education for All campaign has largely focused on expanded access to primary school. Enrollment is the key indicator. As enrollment rates increased, attention shifted to disadvantaged and difficult-to-reach groups. While concerns about education quality have been expressed throughout the campaign, they are increasingly the center of policy attention. Reflecting that shift, *WBES 2020* announces that "The centerpiece of the new education strategy is learning for all" (p. 29). Welcome progress: it is learning, rather than schooling, that matters.

Over several decades, the World Bank and most other external assistance agencies have focused very little attention on what happens inside classrooms. Largely concerned with inputs (for example, school buildings, teacher education, textbooks) and sometimes with outputs (understood as students' successful entry into the labor market) the external attention only rarely addressed what has commonly been termed the education black box.

*WBES 2020* largely continues that trajectory. How is learning for all to be achieved? "Not only through more investment in inputs (for example, more trained teachers or university professors, a better curriculum, more learning materials), but also through greater attention to institutional changes in the education system" (p. 29). What sorts of changes are envisioned? The emphasis is to be on governance, finance, accountability, and management. The education black box remains obscure. What teachers actually do, how learners interact, the use of strategies to encourage student inquiry, whether the classroom walls have posters and pictures that capture attention or student work that reinforces achievement and pride, and more are neither noted nor addressed.

If not through direct attention to the learning process, how to improve learning? Strengthening the education system (Priority 1) requires "building a high-quality knowledge base for education reform" (Priority 2). "At the global level, the World Bank's priority will be to support the development of a knowledge base on education systems" (p. 21). Here we encounter a major dimension of the methodological orthodoxy. How to build a sound education knowledge base? What should that knowledge base include? What constitutes relevant evidence? The entire discussion of this priority focuses on improved education statistics and quantitative performance evaluations (pp. 21-24). The exclusions are dramatic.

Teachers' narratives cannot provide evidence of learning. Nor can students' essays, or learners' achievement portfolios. Missing too are the reflections and assessments of those most involved in education, as well as the observations and evaluations of parents, communities, and local organizations.

The model for research is the laboratory experiment, with carefully specified independent and dependent variables and controls for everything else, modestly adapted to field settings (since no one seeks to deprive learners of instructional materials, the challenge is to find comparable schools with more and fewer books per student). Learning becomes a measured outcome, for which the usual tool is a national examination. Both international assessments and locally developed tests have come to play greater roles. That concern with assessing learning is not in principle problematic. But the exclusion of other explanatory strategies and learning indicators surely is.

Evidence is to undergird policy and practice. But only a particular sort of evidence, gathered in approved ways, will do. That approach continues to do poorly in understanding learning as an interactive process, in assessing curiosity, concept development, problem solving, and applying information to unfamiliar settings. Alternative notions of evidence, of knowledge, and of the research process are not simply ignored but commonly rejected as non-scientific. As well, focused on a very limited notion of cognitive achievement, that approach generally ignores the broader expectations for education systems, for example, developing competence and self-confidence, encouraging cooperation, promoting national integration, nurturing democratic practice, and reducing inequality. The World Bank's required methodology vitiates learning as an interactive and regularly non-linear process.

## FINANCIAL-INTELLECTUAL COMPLEX

Integrating research and development assistance—a combination that the World Bank proudly proclaims is its compelling advantage—creates a powerful financial-intellectual complex whose influence on research and the research process reaches far beyond the settings where it has a direct role. The problematic consequences of the resulting methodological orthodoxy and of the World Bank's role as the global external examiner of research quality are significant and persisting. Since I have discussed them elsewhere (Samoff, 1996a, 1996b, 1996c, 2007c) I shall summarize the major themes here.

(1) Circumscribed or tenuous propositions are converted into certainties that are then promulgated as guides to action. Research findings in disparate sites are summarized, simplified, and combined. Weak propositions acquire official sanction. Stripped of their situational specificity and of the limitations and ambiguities inherent in the original research, they become the pathways to be followed.

(2) Embedded in the ways that issues are framed, fundamental misunderstandings are entrenched. Directly (by commissioning and funding research) and indirectly (by specifying which research and which sorts of research can be used to

justify funding requests and development strategies) the World Bank frames both the issues that are worthy of research attention and how they are to be addressed. What is problematic in education in Africa? Frame the question and look for answers within Africa itself. Ignore the ways in which the external environment influences and constrains outcomes within Africa. Ignore the ways in which globally dominant ideologies are expressed as ostensibly value-free analytic constructs and then internalized and institutionalized within African education systems. Study the poor to explain poverty. Study the characteristics and behaviors of those who operate and participate in poorly performing education systems to explain poorly performing education systems. Specifying the research frame is often more consequential than specifying the research topic.

(3) Generally unaddressed, the links between power relations and knowledge are mystified. The World Bank's role in setting the research agenda and framing the issues to be studied is rarely noticed and hardly ever the focus of critical examination. Where the funders determine the selection of topics, methods, and researchers, limit access to source materials, and manage the dissemination of findings, the process of knowledge creation itself is obscured. The power relations embedded in that process become simply the way things are, not arrangements that require systematic scrutiny and assessment. Power relations that might be regarded as profoundly problematic if they were seen clearly are so enmeshed in everyday practices that they pass unnoticed and unchallenged.

(4) Development fads become certified wisdom. That the development advisory service is also the funding source and the research manager creates pressure to find prime solutions to what are deemed to be pressing problems. At one moment a particular approach is regarded as unimpeachably correct, even though a longer view shows a succession of strategies, each presented as *the* solution and each subsequently displaced by another prime solution. Allocate resources to textbooks, not reducing class size. No, class size affects time on task and matters more than thought earlier. Vocationalized education is essential for reducing unemployment among those who finish school. No, the costs of vocationalized education far exceed the benefits gained. No, vocationalized education really is essential, now with a different curriculum. Reduce spending on higher education to increase the resources for basic education. No, starving higher education weakens teacher education and thus undermines the basic education that was to have benefitted. Centralized education leadership is necessary for setting directions, specifying policy, and managing resources. No, decentralization is essential for promoting transparency, accountability, effective management, and ownership of education reform. No, decentralization diffuses authority and responsibility, facilitates wide regional variations, and reinforces inequalities. A methodology that seeks prime solutions, success in short time horizons, and results rendered unambiguous by counting fosters the succession of prime solutions, each queen for a day or two.

The continuities over several decades are striking. Notwithstanding the broad and inclusive discussions during the development of *WBES 2020* and not-withstanding occasional sharp challenges and more or less organized resistance, the World Bank's assumptions, standard operating procedures, style, and language continue to structure the education and development discourse, specify the legitimate participants in discussions of education policy, entrench flawed understandings by according them official status, seed and fertilize theoretical and analytic fads, and largely ignore learning by treating education primarily as a mix of techniques and managerial and administrative tasks.

## WHICH RESEARCH WARRANTS ATTENTION?

Evidence based policy and evidence based practice of course depend on evidence, that is, reliable information about settings, participants, initiatives, and outcomes. The World Bank invests energy and resources in developing a storehouse of information derived from many sources and with pride characterizes itself as a knowledge bank.[iii] Several World Bank policy documents and chief executives have asserted that its role as a depository of knowledge is far more important than the funds it provides:

> the World Bank's main contribution must be advice, designed to help governments develop education policies suitable for the circumstances of their countries. (World Bank, 1995, p. 14)

For most of its life, the World Bank was very clear that valid knowledge was produced in the North:

> developing countries will remain importers rather than principal producers of technical knowledge for some time. (World Bank, 1999, p. 24)

> For developing countries, acquiring knowledge from abroad is the best way to enlarge the knowledge base. ... Developing countries, whatever their institutional disadvantages, have access to one great asset: the technological knowledge accumulated in industrial countries. (p. 27)

The characterization of the World Bank as a knowledge bank in the mid 1990s was apparently accompanied by a recognition of the importance of what was termed local knowledge and the creation of an indigenous knowledge initiative. Yet the World Bank retained responsibility for collecting, filtering, managing, and vetting local knowledge (Samoff & Stromquist, 2001). The primary source for the knowledge that mattered continued to be the World Bank itself.

In its public persona, the World Bank has strongly supported the widely accepted notion of scientific knowledge as the result of the cumulation and integration of many studies and of the confrontation of diverse perspectives. With different conceptions, assumptions, values, and starting points scholars study particular education systems and experiences. With different guiding ideas and methodologies they report findings, propose interpretations, and develop meanings. Though periodically cacophonous, conflicted, and unruly, that process produces understandings that reach beyond the initial research setting and that secure support from other researchers, policy makers, and practitioners. We must not be naïve about how that occurs. Though it is often unstructured, that process is not ungoverned. What comes to be termed knowledge certainly reflects disparities and

147

relationships of power. The uneven distribution of influence and power is also reflected in the selection and protection of the authorities and gatekeepers of the knowledge generation process. Still, even through the sifting and winnowing is politically constrained, the credibility and legitimacy of knowledge require diversity of sources, orientations, and methods.

What, then, is the evidence base for *Learning for All*? The document's authors are certainly familiar with recent research on education and development and have access to a very wide range of published and unpublished sources. Notwithstanding that familiarity and access, a careful reading of *WBES 2020* finds that for most of the major issues and themes addressed, its authors have relied on research undertaken and commissioned by the World Bank. A review of the listed sources is instructive.

*Learning for All* lists 15 Background Notes, apparently explicitly commissioned for its preparation. It identifies 117 references. Of those, most are from the World Bank itself (Table 1). Nearly three-quarters of the listed sources are by or from funding and technical assistance agencies. Even that understates the overwhelming reliance on in-house sources. Of the quarter of the research that appeared in scholarly journals or books, several were written by World Bank staff or consultants. While authors' names are difficult clues to decipher, few suggest Third World origins, and Africa remains invisible. Here, then, the World Bank continues a long-standing self-referential practice. The evidence that warrants attention, it tells us, is the evidence that its own or its commissioned research has generated. Research undertaken in the Third World or developed by Third World researchers outside the World Bank's research framework, we find, has nothing to contribute. The evidence-based analysis and recommendations in the World Bank's education strategy, it turns out, rest on a very shallow and insubstantial foundation. Equally problematic, the World Bank sees that reliance on its own research as a great success, not a profoundly disabling practice.

*Table 1. World Bank Group Education Strategy 2020: References*

| Reference Type | N | % |
|---|---|---|
| World Bank sources (all types)[a] | 64 | 55% |
| Other Funding and Technical Assistance Agencies | 20 | 17% |
| Published and unpublished papers and books | 30 | 26% |
| Independent evaluations | 2 | 2% |
| International laws and conventions | 1 | 1% |
| *Total* | 117 | 101% |

[a]Includes World Bank reports, papers, books, documents, databases, and World Bank (IEG) evaluations, as well as references that identify the World Bank as the publisher or source.

What about failure? Research on education transformation and reform initiatives provides evidence of failure as well as success. In an evidence-based approach that can draw on a massive collection of research on education and development, what do we learn about and from unsuccessful World Bank projects, programs, and recommendations? Very little. The self-referential sourcing is strikingly uncritical, notwithstanding extensive evidence from the World Bank's own evaluators and from a more and less friendly critical literature.[iv] We find no systematic exploration of, or effort to learn from, what has not worked, or not worked well, or not worked as well as anticipated, or not worked as well as hoped.

A very limited commentary in *WBES 2020* on critical assessments of earlier World Bank education activities focuses on a portfolio note prepared by the Independent Evaluation Group (pp. 32-33). The discussion is general and cast in terms of managing risks. Overall, *WBES 2020* reports, education's outcome rating, with some ups and downs, is about the same as the overall World Bank average (three-quarters of education projects in 2001-2009 received an IEG rating of satisfactory or higher). Several cautions raised by the IEG (for example, earlier efforts focused on learning outcomes have been among the "less well-performing" World Bank projects) are dismissed as mis-directed or characterized as risks to be addressed by improved monitoring.

Missing is systematic attention to what did not work and why. Missing is the analysis of what led earlier World Bank education specialists to make recommendations that proved to be more problems than solutions. Missing is evidence on the consequences of flawed policy and practice and the discussion of how the new strategy will address those consequences. Missing is a sense of fallibility and humility. A lost opportunity. Rather than using available research to develop a strategy that accommodates the contingent and the unexpected and that incorporates a strong thread of critical self-reflection and the need to adapt and adjust, we find unqualified assertions about the correct objectives and means: "*Learning for All* is the *right* goal" (p. 32); improving project outcomes by "selecting the *right* operational instruments" (p. 10); employing "a multisectoral approach to educational development that provides the *right* incentives, tools, and skills" (p. 61, emphasis added).

## WHEN RESEARCH BECOMES CONSULTING

A major casualty of the pressure to shift resources from higher to basic education has been research. Where funding for core instructional activities is sorely limited, funding for research hardly exists. The deterioration of research capacity is especially clear in Africa (Saint 1992; Samoff and Carrol 2004). In many countries, with salaries insufficient to feed their families, education researchers look to external funding to make research possible. Unencumbered research grants are few and difficult to obtain, especially for scholars whose libraries do not permit a comprehensive review of relevant research and for whom there is little time or support to develop effective proposals. More readily available are commissions and contracts from the World Bank and other funding and technical assistance agencies. The scholars most successful in that arena secure support not only for their research projects but also for attending conferences, purchasing computers and mobile telephones, and acquiring new vehicles. Education research becomes part of the aid relationship. Research becomes consulting.

In some respects, that is a very positive outcome. Where there are few national and institutional resources to support systematic inquiry, this arrangement enables some research to be undertaken. Senior scholars can provide fieldwork opportunities and experience with data interpretation and analysis for younger colleagues and selected students. Without that funding, African participation in international conferences, collaboration with overseas partners, and publication in the most respected journals would be even more limited.

Yet, the conversion of research into consulting has several problematic consequences. (1) The range of topics and methods narrows. With rare exceptions, the funders specify the issues to be studied and the approaches deemed appropriate. As personnel change and political directions shift, research priorities can change rapidly, with more fad and caprice than sustained agendas. Uncommon are research initiatives that emerge organically from high priority issues specified by the national or local education community. (2) The reports that result from commissioned research generally have restricted circulation. Most often, they are considered proprietary rather than public. Rarely are their findings and interpretations subjected to scrutiny by other scholars with relevant expertise and experience at open debates or discussions. In the absence of the ordinary confrontation of ideas and perspectives that increases the credibility of research, untested observations become authoritative conclusions. (3) This strategy for funding research undermines the academic reward system. Active researchers with external support focus on satisfying their funders, with far less concern for the incentives and rewards of the institutional promotion and tenure system. University leaders find it difficult to develop a coherent research strategy, to link research projects to the instructional program, and even to assure that researchers-as-consultants show up for class and read their students' assignments. (4) In practice, research capacity may be undermined rather than strengthened. The effective privatization of research funding leads scholars to seek individual funding and to create consulting firms entirely dependent on foreign patrons. While doing so may make more research possible, at the same time that privatization functions to undermine the institutional capacities and autonomy essential for high quality research programs.

## A MORE PRODUCTIVE RESEARCH STRATEGY

The World Bank's 2020 education strategy is clear that effective education policy and practice require evidence, that is, credible research about education systems and education communities in all their complexities. Its own preparation suggests that the needed research will come largely from the World Bank and its fellow funding and technical assistance agencies or from the research contracting and commissioning that they manage. Surely that will not do. To meet the standards of validity and reliability, education research must have a much broader base and much more diverse sources. To be credible, education research must rely on data-gatherers, interpreters, and analysts who are at home in the environments that are the primary focus of support efforts. To be relevant education research must reflect the aspirations, efforts, and frustrations of education communities in a very large number of local settings. However competent the World Bank's researchers and consultants, the needed global research on education and development cannot be undertaken and managed by Washington and the other capitals of the North and those who depend on their funding.

Recognizing the importance of knowledge generation, *WBES 2020* presents the World Bank's view of what needs to be done (system approach, learning assessments, impact assessments)—generally a continuation of the black box approach with limited attention to content and interactions in learning settings— but says little about who is to do that. The education strategy intended to promote learning for all in the world's least affluent countries includes no explicit strategy for developing research capacity and knowledge production in those countries. Learning's settings are local, interactive, and worldwide. Achieving education for all and learning for all requires imaginative and energetic attention to education research, which in turn requires and innovative and critical efforts to foster high quality locally based research on learning and learning institutions.

To address that strategy gap it is useful to outline here several conceptual and practical elements of a global research development strategy. I shall focus specifically on orientations and initiatives relevant to the World Bank's articulated education mission and objectives. Four themes stand out.

*Local Roots*

Like effective education, high quality education research must have strong local roots. A global research development strategy must incorporate the recognition that much or most of the most promising innovation in education will emerge and be refined at sites scattered around the world. Notwithstanding the World Bank's and others' relentless efforts to identify and disseminate international "best practices," at its core learning is an interactive process and therefore essentially and necessarily local (Samoff, 2007b). Sustainable education innovation and reform are driven by local needs rather than by a centralized group of education innovators.

This recognition requires supporting the development of innovation and experimentation at multiple dispersed sites. That in turn requires a corresponding development of research capacity. That recognition also carries an immediate implication for the World Bank. Broadening and strengthening its knowledge foundation, including analysis and methodology, requires that the World Bank rely less on in-house studies and publications and much more on research undertaken outside its research corral. To facilitate these developments it is long overdue to create an innovation fund designed to support new education research, unencumbered by the priorities, agendas, and methodological strictures of the aid agencies. An overarching challenge is to reduce the prospect that education for all results in admitting many more learners to schools where there is little effective learning.

Helpful in supporting the innovation and outreach in education research will be periodic systematic and state of the art reviews of research on education, understood in its broadest terms. For this too the World Bank must be willing to detach funding from control. That is, to serve its own objectives, the World Bank needs a research monitoring process that is genuinely managed by others.

## Institutional Research Capacity

Second, a global education research development strategy requires recognizing the global interest in competent, indeed outstanding, research capabilities in poor countries. To date, developing research capacity has largely taken the form of providing funding to scholars for specific projects. Of course individual researchers can and do provide important information on and insights into education issues. With very rare exceptions, their accomplishments reflect significant institutional support, often in the form of research assistance, released time, access to libraries and data analysis facilities, as well as support for collegial communication, participation in national and international conferences, and other travel. Earlier in their careers they drew on institutional support as students and apprentice researchers. If achieving learning for all requires high quality research, generating and managing that research requires effective, imaginative, and energetic research institutions. Accordingly, developing research capacity requires moving far beyond grants to individual researchers and their projects.

Institutional support for education research has nearly always been based in the North.[v] While funded northern education research programs have increasingly recruited partners in the South, notwithstanding the institutional labels of those links, in practice the associated resources are largely directed to individual researchers and students with little or no explicit support to their institutions. That is insufficient. Achieving learning for all requires outstanding education research institutions in the countries where education for all remains a future goal. Allocating resources to education research is not in competition with funding for basic education but rather required for it.

An education strategy for the next decade must include an institutional research capacity development component. At a minimum, global support to education must include base funding to establish and maintain Third World research institutions, centers, and programs that can become sufficiently skilled and respected to attract scholars, students, and support. Funding for those institutions must provide for advanced and continuing education for their staff. Most important, a global education strategy must envision using the research generated by those institutions and integrating them into international efforts to study learning and schooling.

## It Takes a Community

Third, a global education research development strategy requires recognizing that notwithstanding the inclination to focus on solo research stars, high quality research requires an inter-related set of activities and a research community. What is needed?

As I have noted, at the base must be research institutes, centers, and programs of varying size and complexity in the Third World. Funding for higher education must be sufficient to establish research, not only classroom teaching, as a core activity of academic staff and students and to develop and sustain the research infrastructure. To be sustainable, that funding must be largely locally generated, but for the poorest countries, achieving learning for all will require significant external support for research as well as for classes, teachers, and institutional materials. Since research requires the exchange and confrontation of ideas—a necessity, not a luxury—the research community depends on effective, reliable, and affordable communications channels among scholars that carry data as well as voices. Essential too are periodic symposia, conferences, seminars, and other scholarly exchanges, at regional, national, continental, and internal levels. The exchange and clash of ideas requires publication outlets at multiple levels, some serving less experienced scholars and the smaller scale, others reaching more broadly and ultimately assuming some of the gatekeeping role currently dominated by education journals based in the North.

*Practitioners as Researchers*

It is common to think of research and teaching as two very distinct activities. In some respects they are, even though most education researchers are also university instructors. Emphasizing that separation, however, overlooks the important ways in which competent teachers are continually engaged in research activities. More or less systematically they compare alternative learning and teaching strategies, instructional materials, and assessment tools. They monitor and gather information about progress and then use that information to inform and revise their pedagogy. They are also critical observers of the operation of the education system, including power relations and personal and institutional alliances and dependencies within and across schools. While teachers generally do not use this terminology to describe their everyday practices, they are in fact engaged in data gathering and analysis, systematic comparisons, semi-controlled experiments, and hypothesis testing. Some education systems have recognized the importance of this role of practitioner as researcher and incorporated it into their teacher education programs. Namibia is an outstanding example (Zeichner & Dahlström, 1999; Zeichner et al., 1998).

A fourth component of an education research development strategy, then, recognizes that important research findings and insights will come from practitioners, not only from specialized institutions or people formally responsible for research. That in turn requires that the international community support the incorporation of, exposure to, and participation in education research into professional pre-service and in-service education programs for teachers and other educators, as well as practitioners' participation in discussions and assessments of research findings and analyses.

153

## THE KNOWLEDGE ENVIRONMENT FOR LEARNING FOR ALL

Achieving learning for all, the World Bank's 2020 education strategy insists, requires an evidence-based approach. Yet, its conception of evidence, and of the research that generates that evidence is so narrow and so flawed that it undermines the effort to base policy and action on evidence. Fulfilling the commitment to learning for all requires more critical attention to the research process, recognition of the debilitating limitations of the World Bank's narrowly construed social science mainstream, and active support for the development of research and research capacity in Africa.

## THE WORLD BANK'S ROLE

There remains an unresolved puzzle. My concern here has been to highlight a major gap in the World Bank's 2020 education strategy and to outline what is needed to address it. I have argued that achieving learning for all requires supporting the development of a vibrant community of education researchers in the Third World and the institutions necessary to sustain it. Why, though, is *WBES 2020* so inattentive to what seems so clearly a requisite for making progress toward its stated objectives? The answer does not lie in insufficient competence, commitment, or concern. My experience over several decades confirms the deep and perceptive involvement of many World Bank colleagues in education and development. The explanation is not personal. Rather, the explanation must be sought in the structural role of the World Bank and its institutional imperatives. Since developing that explanation is beyond the scope of this chapter, I note here simply a schematic overview of important elements in that analysis.[vi]

Remedying the major omission I have addressed here with critical attention to and support for strengthening institutional and community research capacity in the Third World faces major impediments in the World Bank. Proceeding down that path would require ceding control in two essential domains.

First, giving up or even sharing control over the specification of what are acceptable research and research methods would put at risk the management of the way education and development are framed in poor countries. Repetition, for example, might be understood in some circumstances as good education policy rather than sharply criticized as inefficiency. Rate of return analysis might be discarded as both incalculable and irrelevant. Impact assessments might be shown to be far too clumsy and imprecise to identify the features of the learning environment that are the most consequential for learning outcomes. International assessments could be exposed as strategies for imposing and internalizing particular notions of learning and knowledge, which in turn embed inequalities of power.

Second, giving up the self-referential reliance on in-house and more generally affluent-country research to rely more heavily on research and research institutions in the Third Would could put at risk the World Bank's ability to fulfill its structural role of managing the integration of poor countries into the global political economy. Others' research might show that World Bank recommendations, with associated incentives, conditions, and sanctions, not only in education but the entire Washington Consensus and its sequels, are wrong, to be discarded rather than accepted as the basic development framework.

Especially powerful here is the near invisibility of this dimension of the global political economy. The reliance on in-house research and contracted researchers, the dramatic inattention to Third World research capacity, and the assertion of a bank's role as the overseer of good social science and knowledge production seem so, well, normal, hardly worthy of comment. The failure to provide strong support for developing Third World research capacity is both a major omission from a serious strategy for achieving learning for all and at the same time, though often unnoticed, even by those within its walls, a requisite for the maintenance of the World Bank's contemporary global role. Achieving learning for all requires challenging that role.

## NOTES

i   My starting point is the World Bank Group Education Strategy (World Bank, 2011, hereafter *WBES 2020*). The analysis of the role of research in developing and implementing that strategy necessarily requires attention to the World Bank and its roles more generally. For that, it is essential to distinguish between the occasional vibrant debates and clash of ideas among World Bank staff on the one hand and on the other, the policies, strategies, and recommendations that the World Bank presents to the world and especially to poor countries that depend heavily on support provided and influenced by the World Bank. For an analysis of the complexities of World Bank education policies and their consequences in Africa, see Samoff and Carrol, 2004. For an overview of the multiple layers of the aid relationship, see Samoff, 2009. My research and the examples here are drawn largely from education in Africa; for an overview, see Samoff, 2007a.

ii  Over several decades the World Bank has issued a series of documents that combine an analysis of what the World Bank deems most problematic in education and an announcement of what the World Bank thinks should be done and proposes to do. While their designations differ—some are formally policy documents (World Bank, 1980, some are labeled reviews (World Bank, 1995), and the most recent is a strategy—they serve as a reference on agenda and priorities for the World Bank staff and others.

iii The assertion of that role—managing the world's accumulated development information and understandings—is not without controversy. Nelly Stromquist and I have addressed issues and consequences in Samoff and Stromquist, 2001.

iv  Several sorts of reviews, often very probing and at times sharply critical, by the World Bank's evaluators, the Independent Evaluation Group and its predecessor, the Operations Evaluation Department, are available on the IEG web site: ieg.worldbankgroup.org [2011.07.25]. Systematic critiques of World Bank policy and practice, including detailed research, are available on several web sites; among the most comprehensive are www.brettonwoodsproject.org [2011.07.25] and www.actionaid.org [2011.07.25].

v   Recent examples are the three education Research Programme Consortia supported by the Department for International Development, hosted at the Universities of Bristol, Cambridge, and Sussex. My point here is to note the model, which does not devalue the thorough and insightful research they have undertaken.

vi  Critical analysis of the World Bank and its role has mushroomed, including informed commentaries by former World Bank staff. Starting points include *Alternatives Sud* (2006); Amin (2009); Browne (2006); Easterly (2006, 2008); Ellerman (2005); Jones (2006); Joseph and Gillies (2009); Moyo (2009); Mundy (2007); Riddell (2007); and Stiglitz (2006). Note that the literature is bifurcated. While some authors seek to remedy the problems they identify, others conclude that the World Bank itself is more problem than solution and that, at a minimum, its development research and advisory roles should be relocated elsewhere. My own overview of a strategy for exploring the aid relationship more broadly is developed in Samoff (2009).

## REFERENCES

*Alternatives Sud.* (2006). Objectifs du millénaire pour le céveloppement. Points de vue critiques du Sud. *Alternatives Sud,* 13(1).

Amin, S. (2009). Aid for Development. In H. Abbas & Y. Niyiragira. (Eds.), *Aid to Africa: Redeemer or coloniser?* (pp. 59-75). Oxford: Fahamu Books.

Browne, S. (2006). *Aid and influence: Do donors help or hinder?* London; Sterling, VA : Earthscan.

Easterly, W. R. (2006). *The white man's burden: Why the West's efforts to aid the rest have done so much ill and so little good.* New York: Penguin Press.

Easterly, W. R. (2008). *Reinventing foreign aid.* Cambridge, MA: MIT Press.

Ellerman, D. (2005). *Helping people help themselves: From the World Bank to an alternative philosophy of development assistance. Evolving values for a capitalist world.* Ann Arbor: University of Michigan Press.

Jones, P. W. (2006). *Education, poverty and the World Bank.* Rotterdam: Sense Publishers.

Joseph, R. & Gillies, A. (Eds.). (2009). *Smart aid for African development.* Boulder: Lynne Rienner.

Moyo, D. (2009). *Dead aid: Why aid is not working and how there is a better way for Africa.* New York: Farrar, Straus and Giroux.

Mundy, K. (2007). Global governance, Educational change. *Comparative Education,* 43(3), 339-357. www.informaworld.com/10.1080/03050060701556281.

Riddell, R. (2007). *Does foreign aid really work?* New York: Oxford University Press.

Saint, W. S. (1992). *Universities in Africa: Strategies for stabilization and revitalization.* Washington, D.C.: World Bank.

Samoff, J. (1996a). *Analyses, agendas, and priorities in African education: A review of externally initiated, commissioned, and supported studies of education in Africa, 1990-1994* (with N'Dri Thérèse Assié-Lumumba). Paris: UNESCO.

Samoff, J. (1996b). Chaos and certainty in development. *World Development,* 24(4), 611-633.

Samoff, J. (1996c). Which priorities and strategies for education? *International Journal of Educational Development,* 16(3), 249-271.

Samoff, J. (2007a). Education for all in Africa: Still a distant dream (with Bidemi Carrol). In R. F. Arnove & C. A. Torres (Eds.), *Comparative education: The dialectic of the global and the local,* 3rd ed. (pp. 357-388), Boulder: Rowman & Littlefield.

Samoff, J. (2007b). Education quality: The disabilities of aid. *International Review of Education,* 53(5-6), 485-507.

Samoff, J. (2007c). Institutionalizing international influence. In R. F. Arnove & C. A. Torres (Eds.), *Comparative education: The dialectic of the global and the local,* 3rd ed. (pp. 47-77). Boulder: Rowman & Littlefield.

Samoff, J. (2009, July). The fast track to planned dependence: Education aid to Africa. Paper presented at the International Political Science Association XXI World Congress, Santiago, Chile.

Samoff, J. & Carrol, B. (2004). *From manpower planning to the knowledge era: World Bank policies on higher education in Africa.* Paris: UNESCO Forum on Higher Education, Research and Knowledge). http://unesdoc.unesco.org/images/0013/001347/134782eo.pdf (2011.07.19).

Samoff, J. & Stromquist, N. P. (2001). Managing knowledge and storing wisdom? New forms of foreign aid? *Development and Change,* 32(4), 631-656.

Stiglitz, J. E. (2006). *Stability with growth: Macroeconomics, liberalization and development.* Oxford: Oxford University Press.

World Bank. (1980). *Education sector policy paper.* Washington, D.C.: World Bank.

World Bank. (1995). *Priorities and strategies for education: A World Bank review.* Washington, D.C.: World Bank.

World Bank. (1999). *World Development report 1998/99: Knowledge for development* (Washington, D.C.: Oxford University Press for the World Bank). http://go.worldbank.org/UF2JZG2IN0 (2011.07.25).

World Bank. (2011). *Learning for all: Investing in people's knowledge and skills to promote development. World Bank Group Education Strategy 2020.* Washington, D.C.: World Bank. http://siteresources.worldbank.org/EDUCATION/Resources/ESSU/Education_Strategy_4_12_ 2011.pdf (2011.07.19).

Zeichner, K., Amukushu, A., Muukenga, K., & Shilamba, P. (1998). Critical practitioner inquiry and the transformation of teacher education in Namibia. *Educational Action Research, 6,* 183-203.

Zeichner, K. & Dahlström, L. (Eds.). (1999). *Democratic teacher education reform in Africa: The case of Namibia.* Boulder: Westview.

*Joel Samoff*
*Center for African Studies*
*Stanford University, U.S.A.*

## CHAPTER 11

NELLY P. STROMQUIST

# THE GENDER DIMENSION IN THE WORLD BANK'S EDUCATION STRATEGY

*Assertions in Need of a Theory*

## INTRODUCTION

For more than two decades the World Bank has declared itself a supporter of women's issues. It is legitimate then to treat it as an institution whose understanding of gender should be both mature and refined. Not only does the World Bank have an official commitment to treating gender issues but this institution has by now commandeered the global agenda in this and other pertinent areas as well. It has replaced the World Health Organization as the major donor in the health field (Petchesky, 2003) and the UN Educational, Scientific, and Cultural Organization in the area of education (World Bank, 2002). The fall of the Soviet regime led newly independent countries of Eastern Europe to seek international assistance, adding to the rolls of existing developing countries and thus to the number of potential World Bank clients. The Bank's latest iteration on education and its role in development, *World Bank Education Strategy 2020* (*WBES 2020*, hereafter), presents a terrain from which to examine its views and proposals on gender and development.

This chapter focuses on the framing of gender in education as presented in *WBES 2020*'s discourse. To do so, it moves into five parts: a presentation of the analytical methodology used in the chapter, a discussion of what gender in education implies, the World Bank's use of decentralization and privatization to implement its efficiency principle, and general implications for gender transformation derived from the *WBES 2020* document.

## ANALYTICAL APPROACH

This study examines the form and content of the World Bank's educational policy, with a special emphasis on its *WBES 2020*, but it complements that analysis with other Bank documents that also address gender issues. Critical content analysis is used as the main methodological tool. This approach implies deconstruction of text so that oppositions, inconsistencies, and contradictions in language can be detected; moreover, it examines presuppositions in the arguments made (Derrida,

*S.J. Klees et al. (eds.), The World Bank and Education,* 159–172.

1976; Rosenau, 1992). Augmenting this idea, Gough (2002) states that deconstruction involves demystifying a text, so that its internal hierarchies and its presuppositions are exposed. Applying critical content analysis to the *WBES 2020* we pay attention to the presence and absence of certain terms. We consider how certain concepts are defined, what claims are made about them, and what evidence is offered for such claims. We also pay attention to the way the discourse is formulated: what is mentioned, what is absent, and what is glossed over. The concept of "slipping in" is useful to see how in a list of innocuous or relevant terms, another concept—with a much different meaning and degree of consensus— is brought in to include it in the same argument.

The documents the World Bank uses in its education strategy are mostly self-referential. Three possibilities may account for this: (1) World Bank knowledge is so superior that other studies are of little use, (2) the Bank disrespects any discipline that does not rely exclusively on quantitative research methods, and (3) the Bank chooses to ignore scholars and other institutions whose findings counter its own. The first reason would be unacceptable in academic circles, as no researcher can really claim such a monopoly on knowledge; acting otherwise would be tantamount to arrogance. The second reason has some explanatory grounds as most of the studies produced and cited by the Bank rely on survey methods and multiple regressions and are conducted by economists. The third reason looks to be a strong possibility because the discourse of the Bank is always devoid of controversy. It gives the appearance that all the findings it reports have been observed persistently, with no significant deviations or contradictions.

## FRAMING GENDER

In the fields of feminist, racial/ethnic, cultural, and area studies, gender studies have been identified as the "source of most of the intellectual innovations in the academy since the 70s" (Dugger, 2001, p. 128). Munck argues that feminist research methods have "caused a conceptual overhaul of the social sciences (1999). Gender studies is a multidisciplinary field with contributions that include philosophy, anthropology, sociology, political science, history, education, and economics. Economics is crucial, yet only one facet of gender.

As is amply recognized, gender refers not only to the conditions of women and men but to a structural relationship between the sexes which is linked to the state, the economy, and other macro- and micro-processes and institutions (Moghadam, 1990). But, what are the implications of such intellectual awareness? First, a complete analysis of gender has to be done at multiple societal levels while attentive to the interaction between these levels as well as to intersectionality, or the compounding effects of gender and factors such as social class, rural/urban residence, ethnicity and race, and sexual orientation—to mention some of the most important social markers. Second, efforts to decrease gender effects in society have likewise to involve multiple institutions and actors, not only the state but diverse elements of civil society.

A basic content analysis, in terms of frequency of key terms, reveals that *WBES 2020* mentions gender 23 times, women 10, equality 21, and equity 12. However, these terms are never defined or examined in relation to each other. Femininity and masculinity, key concepts in the understanding of the construction of gender in society, are mentioned 0 times. Empowerment—a construct that is widely accepted in feminist theory as fundamental to the process of social change—is mentioned 3 times, none of which refers to dynamics of individual and collective gender transformation. Today, as women's issues are seen as intrinsically linked to human rights, such a referent is crucial to frame demands for women's access to multiple rights. *WBES 2020* mentions human rights 3 times, in all cases in reference to the UN Universal Declaration of Human Rights—but never to the notion of women's advancement as a human right. Moreover, social justice is mentioned 0 times. Patriarchy, considered in many gender theories as the key ideological architecture that sustains gender, is mentioned 0 times.

In *WBES 2020*, gender according to the World Bank is one more element is a list of *disadvantaged populations*, which include groups by income levels, ethnolinguistic groups, rural residents, and persons with disabilities. This classification is deficient in that: (1) it misses the fact that women constitute half of the population, (2) gender is a deep cultural construction with substantial manifestation in society, (3) many of the people who speak minority languages, live in rural areas, or experience physical disability are *also* women, and (4) the powerful interlocking effects of gender on other social markers are not problematized. Including gender in such a list can be considered an instance of "slipping in," namely adding gender to others with differential value and meaning such as disability, geographic location, income levels, thus making all equal by association. Analytically speaking, it is erroneous and superficial to refer to various disadvantaged people in society by simply merging them into a single list, without giving attention to each of the groups involved. Such enumeration does not acknowledge that the discrimination against these populations have different causes (see Table 1) as well as very different consequences.

As can be observed, in the case of gender, powerful cultural factors combine with economic (the sexual division of labor) and political (the still limited access of women to public decision-making) to make it a much more complex "disadvantage" to correct than would seem at first sight. Treating girls as a disadvantaged group in education—without further elaboration—transforms a phenomenon that involves the structure, content, and processes of schooling into technical task that can be addressed without reforming the educational system.

Table 1. Major Causes of Disadvantage by Social Marker

| | Cultural/ Ideological | Economic | Political | Percent of population most affected |
|---|---|---|---|---|
| Gender | ✓ | ✓ | ✓ | Women—who comprise 50% or more of any given national population |
| Sexual orientation | ✓ | | | Between 2 and 13%[1] |
| Poverty | | ✓ | ✓ | Varies by country. World average: 80%[2] |
| Race | ✓ | ✓ | ✓ | Varies by country |
| Ethnicity | ✓ | ✓ | ✓ | Varies by country |
| Rural residence | | ✓ | ✓ | Varies by country. World average: 44%[3] |
| Disability | ✓ | | | Varies by country. World average: 17%[4] |

[1] Based on estimated numbers of homosexual persons in Western countries; multiple studies.
[2] Poverty defined as living on less than $10/day (Chen & Ravallion, *The developing world is poorer than we thought, but no less successful in the fight against poverty*, World Bank, August 2008).
[3] UN Population Division, *World Urbanization Prospects: The 2003 Revision*.
[4] Estimate for adult population 18 years old and over (WHO & the World Bank, *World Report on Disability*, 2011).

## GENDER AND EDUCATION

The World Bank positions itself as a major knowledge institution. *WBES 2020* states that the Bank has produced since 2001 over 280 pieces of "research and other analytical work that examines critical education issues," "over 900 analytical works that include the dimension of education topics," and "more journal articles than the 14 top universities and only Harvard University comes close" (p. 36). In spite of its work on gender and education it chooses to ignore copious evidence showing that schools are *gendered institutions* and fails to take into account the need to work on the educational content and the educational experience that reproduce gender ideologies and hierarchies. In other words, the World Bank's analysis of gender and education continues to be focused exclusively on school access. In so doing, it fails to recognize that, while it is true Africa and South Asia indeed evince very serious inequalities in access to the detriment of girls and women at all levels of education, this is not the situation in Latin America, East Asia, and Central Europe. Access is only one facet of schooling; further, access to primary education in these latter regions has been long resolved, as well as has access to secondary and even to tertiary education as a way to advance women's conditions. What has not been problematized in the Bank's analysis are the content of learning and the schooling experience, both of which contain powerful messages that account for the reproduction and maintenance of gender ideologies and hierarchies.

Let us explore what is missing regarding the treatment of gender in *WBES 2020.*

## Schools as Gendered Institutions

There is a vast amount of literature demonstrating that women's education makes multiple contributions to society via the increased nutrition and health of children, tangible family planning, and increased children's education (King & Hill, 1991; Patrinos, 2008; Gakidou et al., 2010; among many others). Benefits for the women themselves have also been detected such as greater employment, political participation, and community involvement. And yet, gender asymmetries in crucial social dimensions persist.

A key explanation for the enduring disadvantages women experience is that the educational content and experience that girls and boys have within education system do not challenge explicitly the gender regime of their respective societies. Through interactions with teachers and peers, individuals develop subjectivities that reflect, rather than refract, social norms and expectations regarding dominant female and male identities. Unless the school system openly challenges received knowledge and norms, it will foster and reproduce prevailing understandings of what is "normal." This includes acceptance of the sexual division of labor and the belief that men and women represent different natures and are to fulfill differential missions in life.

Connell (1993), a perceptive analyst of school environments, observes that we need to engage in "curricular justice," meaning knowledge that empowers the disadvantaged students by recognizing their knowledge and identities. In her view, the hegemonic curriculum of today privileges the history, culture, and language of dominant classes, including that of one gender over another. Connell and other scholars remind us that it is crucial to go beyond compensatory education and seek the reorganization of the cultural content of education as a whole. At a minimum, work must be conducted in the schools to modify the curriculum to make it much more gender-sensitive and to provide training to teachers and administrators, both those in service and those undergoing formation. A common response to these proposals has been that the content of education is a national arena, not subject to international advice. This argument crumbles in light of the influence by international organizations regarding the improvement of math and science, more recently reading, and the expansion of vocational educational subjects. Besides, working with women-led NGOs and other progressive institutions of civil society in any particular country would enable these groups to express their own positions on the question of gender.

A recent measure of gender progress, namely the gender gap index, provides strong evidence of the limits of education in producing substantial changes in women's empowerment. This index, developed by Hausmann et al. (2010), looks at outcomes enjoyed by women and men along four dimensions: economic participation and opportunity, educational attainment, health and survival, and political empowerment. This index, based on data for 134 countries, shows that the gender gap has been successfully closed in health outcomes (in 96 percent of the countries) and in educational access (in 90 percent of the countries). However, gender gaps remain sizable in economic outcomes (closed in 59 percent of the countries) and even greater in political outcomes (closed only in 18 percent of the countries). These differential outcomes must be taken as evidence that access to education at present does not produce assertive women who question the social relations of gender and who therefore seek changes in the way gender functions in society. In other words, the ideologies of femininity and masculinity are so deeply engrained that challenging them requires explicit targeting rather than assuming they will become part of people's reflection as their levels of education increase.

*The Role of Parents.* Research on ways to break the vicious circle of the intergenerational maintenance of low levels of education has identified the crucial importance of working with adults and thus parents (Mayo, 1999; Foley, 1999). But having parental participation is not sufficient. Parents need to receive new knowledge about rights of women and men and the need to see women as citizens in their own right, not as key agents for having and socializing children. Indeed, the increased use of social mobilization campaigns is based on the principle of changing the mentalities of parents and working at the household and community levels. It is mainly the parents who must be made to understand how schooling can help their children, including daughters, move into more independent and successful lives.

*WBES 2020* notes that the Bank has invested less than 1 percent on *adult literacy*—0.7 percent to be exact (p. 49). The reference is to adult literacy, not adult *education*—which is a much broader area. From gender analytical perspectives, this is seriously insufficient; the lack of attention to adult education signals a limited understanding of the need to work at the household level, a level indispensable to the altering of gender relations and their reproduction over time. The perennial low attention to adult education must be considered a major flaw in attempts to modify the ideology and practice of gender. Working with adults with families cannot be substituted just by paying greater attention to basic education in the formal schooling system.

*The Role of Women-led Social Movements.* *WBES 2020* repeatedly refers to the need to be inclusive and to integrate all stakeholders in education. Yet, at no point does it identify as potential partners the large and growing number of women-led NGOs nor does it seem aware of the existence of powerful transnational networks active in women's issues, such the International Council on Adult Education at the global level and the Women's Popular Education Network (REPEM) in Latin America. The document does acknowledge that "people learn throughout life" (p. 25), but this point is not developed. As a multinational institution, the Bank deals primarily with nation-states. The contradictions and tensions in working with an institution (the state) that plays an active role in the domination and subordination of women are not problematized. It should be added that the Bank emphasizes attention to social capital in the form of networks but disregards role of history and institutions, and the importance of distributional considerations (Hoff & Stiglitz, 1999). On the other hand, another World Bank document, *Integrating Gender into the World Bank's Work: A Strategy for Action* (World Bank, 2002), advises the establishment of partnerships "with active women's advocacy groups or women's and gender studies units in research or educational institutions" (p. 33). The lack of reference in *WBES 2020* to this recommendation may suggest either that (1) at higher levels of decision-making gender issues fade, or (2) there is disagreement within Bank staff on how to proceed regarding gender issues.

New social actors have become increasingly recognized in politics as well as in the academic literature on social change. Although not successful with the World Bank, feminists have attained greater political participation in debates and discourses in multilateral organizations regarding world economic governance. They want greater gender mainstreaming in all policies as well as accountability; they pursue views of women as autonomous citizens. Several global and regional networks addressing gender and education have been in existence for some time. Some of them are: Development Alternatives with Women for a New Era (DAWN), Association of African Women for Research and Development (AAWORD), Women's Environment and Development Organization (WEDO), Asia South Pacific Association for Basic and Adult Education (ASPBAE), and the Latin American REPEM. In fairness to the World Bank it must be acknowledged that many other international bodies are not characterized by the inclusion of women's voices. In fact, the MDGs, one of the most powerful global policies, were drafted without the participation of civil society, including women's and human rights groups (Petchesky, 2003).

Without doubt, the major accomplishment of the feminist movement has been the establishment of a single organization to deal with women's and gender issues at the global level. This organization, established in 2010, is the UN Entity for Gender Equality and the Empowerment of Women (commonly known as UN Women). It is currently led by the former president of Chile, Michelle Bachelet. As a woman and a person with strong commitment to social justice, Bachelet is resolved to including civil society institutions in many of UN Women's deliberations. This inclusion specifically refers to women-led and feminist NGOs throughout the world and represents a major turn in global gender politics. Its five priority areas are: (1) women's economic empowerment, (2) women's political participation and leadership, (3) ending violence against women and girls, (4) engaging women and women's rights fully in peace and post-conflict processes, and (5) engaging women in national development planning and budgeting (UN

Women, 2011). Reading *WBES 2020*, nothing of this surfaces; the gender world that is depicted is a static one, anchored in a blind—but not very real—commitment to educational access.

## THE EFFICIENCY PRINCIPLE

A persistent message in World Bank messages is the notion that the fundamental challenge facing education is not financial resources but efficiency. This is categorically spelled out in the assertion that "a root cause of low-quality and inequitable public services—not only in education—is the weak accountability of providers to both their supervisors and their clients" (World Bank, 2003). Consequently, the Bank advocates three kinds of reforms: information reforms, school-based management reforms, and performance-linked teacher pay measures. Among school-based management reforms, two are salient: decentralization and privatization (Bruns et al., 2011). How do they link to gender? Let us examine the evidence below.

### Privatization and Gender

The core assumption underlying privatization is that individual choice enables competition among service providers and thus schools of high quality will be preferred by parents. This assumption makes no distinction between poor and rich families, implying that all of them will engage in similar responses. *WBES 2020* asserts that "private entities are important providers of education, even to the poorest communities" (p. 23). But, as Jones (1997) observes, it is an unexamined assumption to believe that all parents can pay for the education of their children. It should be noted that at no point does *WBES 2020* consider that calling for fees goes against the Universal Declaration of Human Rights, which explicitly requires that "education shall be free, at least in the elementary and fundamental stages." Within this context, it must be noted that *within* public education, fees are now being charged. A 2005 World Bank survey reported that 83 percent of 95 countries charged some form of user fees and that since 1994 only 15 countries have eliminated user fees (Barrera-Osorio, 2008). This major contradiction—between calling for an education that is based on fees (as privatization and cost-sharing are) and the universal acknowledgment that basic education should be free—appears to challenge an important human right, a challenge that merits attention on jurisprudence grounds since the Universal Declaration of Human Rights, although not a convention, has acquired semi-legal status.

Privatization brings up another instance of slipping in. Here the *WBES 2020* observes, "Demand-side interventions, such as the abolition of school fees and scholarships, cash transfers to compensate for the opportunity costs of school attendance, and *vouchers* that enable poor students to use also privately provided services, have also helped to raise enrollment rates" (p. 6, emphasis added). This phrase seamlessly moves from referring to the public school system to the private one.

Contrasting the belief that even poor parents can pay for the education of their children with accumulated knowledge about the intersection of gender and poverty leads to a much weaker endorsement of privatization. Poor families, especially those existing in areas where basic infrastructure regarding water and fuel is minimal—as in the case of several African and Asian countries, particularly in their rural areas—systematically rely on girls to procure water and wood. With this considerable contribution, the opportunity costs of girls is high and likely to be increased by having to pay additional fees to attend public school. We know that tuition fees and user charges affect the poor and especially girls. Precisely because of this, social programs offering scholarships or stipends for girls, such as those in Mexico and Bangladesh, have been established.

Educational privatization does not unleash any dynamics that facilitate the enrollment and successful completion of female students. Research from Ghana (Subrahmanian, 2002) shows an interesting connection between privatization and gender; it found that as privatization creates a dual school system, increases in girls' access to schooling tend to be concentrated in low-quality private schools. Regarding costs, a common response of privatization regarding its negative impact on poor families is that private schools will be asked to offer scholarships to disadvantaged students. Such a strategy, by its very nature, covers a small number of beneficiaries; consequently, scholarships reduce the burden of privatization only on a few poor families.

From a national development point of view, privatization has come under attack. Hoff and Stiglitz (2005, p. 3) argue that, "Privatization without institutions to enforce good corporate governance may vitiate property rights and give those with control rights an interest in the persistence of a weak, corrupt state that would not interfere with their theft." Little in *WBES 2020* recognizes this downside of privatization, whether in general or in education.

*Decentralization and Gender*

Decentralization is considered one of the most important forms of policy reform and institutional redesign in the past decades. Through various forms of policy borrowing, today the majority of developing countries are engaged in some form of decentralization. It is advocated for greater economic efficiency of the public sector and for a greater participation and representation in institutions, increasing thus their democratization.

In subtle ways, while not mentioning education *decentralization* explicitly, the World Bank continues to push this as a strategy that will secure better achieving schools. *WBES 2020* states that school-based management "aims [note the disclaimer] to empower stakeholders at the local level" (p. 33) and "Research around the world has found that these policies change the dynamics within schools because parents become more involved or because teacher behaviors change" (pp. 18-19). However, the conclusions presented by *WBES 2020* on privatization and decentralization are not based on a comprehensive review of the literature. In fact, there are several scholarly investigations, from Nepal (Carney, 2009) to South

Africa (Sayed & Soudien, 2005) to Mexico (Buenfil, 2000) that evince the strong disparity between the Bank's assumptions and realities about democratization through decentralization. Moreover, a recent review of World Bank policies on decentralization found that in several county cases, such policies did not make a provision for mandatory gender-sensitive implementation (Global Campaign for Education and RESULTS, 2011). Decentralization may favor regressive policies and practices concerning girls. For instance, in rural villages of Africa and South Asia (India and Bangladesh) traditional local authorities are male dominated. Moreover, strong cultural traditions built on patrilineal principles, which means that girls are seen as contributors to their husband's family, operate to preserve the gender status quo; namely, the belief that a girl's education does not result in future benefits for her family of origin. Decentralization does not acknowledge the negative consequences of local traditional authorities on education. The views of community elders and local elites are often based on a dichotomous world, in which men lead and women take care of household and children, which results in conservative positions vis-à-vis women's capacities to choose autonomous careers. How do we make sure that decentralized bodies are attentive to distributive justice and equity? To what extent do the new structures created by decentralization provide opportunities for introducing gender concerns in education? As David (2010, n.p.) notes in the context of increasing privatization in the UK, "the type of laissez-faire, free-for-all scenario called for by school autonomy" makes it difficult to attend to gender and race equality issues.

Limited research has inquired into the gender consequences of decentralization. We do know that democratic processes call for participation and that participation by women in the public sphere, even at the local level, is not always easy. EDUCO, highly vaunted as a successful reform in democratization of schooling in El Salvador, has a majority of men in its school management committees. Consequently, we cannot claim that decentralization is positive on gender redressing efforts and practices.

## WORLD BANK'S GENDER POLICY

The World Bank policy on gender is still guided by a policy document produced in 1994, *Enhancing Women's Participation in Economic Development. A World Bank Policy Paper*, which is complemented by another document called Operational Guidelines 4.20 (also adopted in 1994 and updated in 2002 and 2004). The policy paper calls for investing proportionally more in women than in men and asks for a systematic treatment of gender issues in country assistance strategies. It highlights the importance of the "package approach" to schooling interventions to improve the condition of girls' schooling. The package approach is defined as the deployment of multiple interventions—from the provision of latrine and washing facilities, to the removing of sex stereotypes in educational materials, to the building of fences around school to provide a safe environment for students, to the training of teachers in gender issues, and to the increased recruitment of women teachers. Nothing of this is recalled in *WBES 2020*. While there is explicit reference to training, it appears only in reference to the Education Management and Information System, which the World Bank is now proposing as one of the core strategies to improve education systems, the other being its intention to become a knowledge powerhouse by building a knowledge base at the global level.

An important point, observed by Zuckerman (2007) is that OP 4.20—a major enforceable operational guide—"contains a critical footnote excluding 'development policy loans' from OP 4.20 stated objectives to address gender disparities and inequalities in bank loans" (p. 2). Such loans accounted for 40 percent of total Bank commitments in 2009. Others have observed that low-inflation and tight spending policies advocated by the Work Bank counter official objectives of achieving the MDGs, particularly universal primary education. It is also the case that the "Bank" includes IBRD and IDA credits but not programs financed under the International Finance Corporation (IFC) (Work Bank, 2011). IFC provides loans to the private sector and it provided close to $6 billion in 2010 (IFC, 2010). The relevance of IFC to education is that it has become a major provider of loans for private entrepreneurs seeking to establish community schools. At present, these loans are given in 11 African countries and IFC has expressed its intention to cover all countries in the African region by 2020. The amounts given to individual entrepreneurs are small (most are less than $10,000) but they foster the creation of for-profit schools providing basic education. On the basis of 2009 data, if we put together the $47 billion given through development policy loans with the $6 billion given through IFC, $53 billion going into development through World Bank institutions are not bound by any consideration of gender issues.

## CONCLUSIONS

*WBES 2020* offers some improvement compared to previous strategies. Among the positive features of the document are the following: (1) Recognition that learning should be promoted beyond school provision to include nutrition and health. (2) Attention to learning outcomes, as opposed to school access alone. While positive, the document always links this strategy to testing, which makes the promotion of learning less related to the enhancement of teacher competence than to the development of nationwide systems of standardized testing. (3) Acknowledgment that a system-wide perspective could be useful. Yet, this objective is also tempered by the assertion that all loan disbursements will be conditional upon pre-defined results attained and verified. On the contrary, it should be argued that a system-wide perspective should call for significant instances of flexibility as different factors and actors are taken into account. (4) Recognition that different geographic regions, given their variance in average level of development, require different educational strategies. However, upon closer reading, it becomes clear that privatization will be emphasized in all regions, with IFC more active in African countries and the provision of conditional cash transfers (including those for girls) in low-income countries.

Regarding gender, however, the new education strategy of the World Bank contains little change. It continues a steadfast endorsement of education as a neutral institution and does not attach to it the development of subjectivity that occurs within it to the persistent enactment of rigid and stale forms of femininity and masculinity. *WBES 2020* frames the key education problem facing the construction and maintenance of gender differences exclusively as one of access. In this respect, the most current document of the World Bank, though entitled "Learning for All," does not seem to include the Bank itself as an institution that has more to learn.

Its two major forms of administrative reform, which center on privatization and decentralization, are not analyzed through a gender lens. Yet, given the increased burden for families that is to come through privatization and the potential role of local elites in governance through decentralization, there is a strong probability—detected already in several studies—that girls will be negatively affected by those two measures.

While the decentralization and privatization reforms recognize new social actors, *WBES 2020* recognizes only private entrepreneurs and parents, thus failing to recognize the most committed stakeholders on gender, namely women-led and feminist organizations. But perhaps a more important part of the problem is the Bank's unwavering commitment to the field of economics as the main discipline to understand social structures and practices.

The World Bank's reluctance to use the substantial evidence produced by feminist scholars—evidence that invalidates many of its unexamined assumptions—and its lack of a theoretical framework explain to some extent its inability to achieve any progress in its understanding of how gender functions in society and through institutions such as the school system. The World Bank continues to cite itself for most intellectual work. *WBES 2020* contains easily identifiable World Bank authors for 69 of 117 references; in other words, 59 percent of the citations are in-house, not including Bank consultant and Bank-funded research. Such an amount of self-reference is simply not acceptable in academic circles and makes doubtful the Bank's capacity to self-correct, an essential ingredient of academic inquiry. Under those conditions, to position oneself as a provider of technical assistance is dangerous, as it is clear that the World Bank's analysis of gender in education is not only hopelessly anchored in access issues but in addition chooses to dismiss the considerable progress in gender theory in multiple academic settings, an intellectual progress that has demonstrated the impact of ideology as well as the compounding effects of multiple social markers in shaping disadvantages for girls and women. One wonders why an institution that seeks to be a knowledge institution does not recognize research with findings that contradict its own cherished beliefs. In this context, *WBES 2020* contains a significant negative feature in my opinion. This regards the World Bank's official intention to become not only a knowledge diffuser but also a knowledge generator (pp. 60-64), and subsequently to become a major actor in the provision of technical support (pp. 64-69). Given the practices above described, it is doubtful that the World Bank may perform as an impartial institution.

Those who conduct research on gender fully recognize the importance of working simultaneously on redistribution and recognition issues if gender as a social marker is to be minimized in society (Fraser, 1995). The World Bank, by pursuing an economistic approach to gender (Bergeron, 2003; Subrahmanian, 2002), considers only the potentially redistributive aspects of schooling (and in so doing emphasizes merely the basic level of education) and does not acknowledge the need to alter social perceptions of women's inferiority and their frequent subordination in multiple social arenas. The World Bank still has to design a *gender-based approach to national development* that considers the circumstance in which formal education can indeed play a transformative role.

## REFERENCES

Barrera-Osorio, F. (2008). The effect of a reduction in user fees on school enrollment: Evidence from Colombia. In M. Tembon & L. Fort (Eds.), *Girls' education in the 21st century. Gender equality, empowerment and economic growth*. Washington, D.C.: World Bank, pp. 201-208.

Bergeron, S. (2003). The post-Washington consensus and economic representations of women in development at the World Bank. *International Feminist Journal of Politics, 5*(3), 397-419.

Bruns, B., Filmer, D., & Patrinos, H. (2011). *Making schools work. New evidence on accountability reforms*. Washington, D.C.: The World Bank.

Buenfil, R. (2002). Globalization and education policies in Mexico, 1988-1994: A meeting of the universal and the particular. In N. P. Stromquist & K. Monkman (Eds.), *Globalization and education. Integration and contestation across cultures* (pp. 275-297). Lanham, MD: Rowman & Littlefield.

Carney, S. (2009). Negotiating policy in an age of globalization: Exploring educational "policyscapes" in Denmark, Nepal, and China. *Comparative Education Review, 53*(1), 63-88.

Connell, R. W. (1993). Poverty and education. *Harvard Educational Review, 64*(2), 125-147.

David, M. with Ringrose, J. & Showunmi, V. (2010). Browne Report + the White Paper = A murkey outlook for educational equality. *GEA Policy Report*, October-December.

Derrida, J. (1976). *Grammatology*. Baltimore: The Johns Hopkins Press.

Dugger, K. (2001). Women in higher education in the United States: 1. Has there been progress? *International Journal of Sociology and Social Policy, 21*(1-2), 118-130.

Foley, G. (1999). *Learning in social action. A contribution to understanding informal education*. London: Zed Books.

Fraser, N. (1995). From distribution to recognition? Dilemmas of justice in a "post socialist" age. *New Left Review, 218*, 68-93.

Gakidou, E., Cowling, K., Lozano, R., & Murray, C. (2010). Increased educational attainment and its effect on child mortality in 175 countries between 1970 and 2009; A systematic analysis. *The Lancet, 276*(9745), 959-974.

Global Campaign for Education & RESULTS. (2011). *Making education right. Ending the crisis in girls; Education*. Johannesburg and Washington, D.C.: Global Campaign for Education & RESULTS

Gough, N. (2000). Globalization and curriculum inquiry: locating, representing, and performing a transnational imaginary. In N. P. Stromquist & K. Monkman (Eds.), *Globalization and education. Integration and contestation across cultures* (pp. 77-98). Lanham, MD: Rowman & Littlefield.

Hausmann, R., Tyson, L., & Zahidi, S. (2010). *The global gender gap Report 2010*. Geneva: World Economic Forum.

Hoff, K. & Stiglitz, J. (1999, November). Modern economic theory and development. Washington, D.C.: World Bank, draft.

Hoff, K. & Stiglitz, J. (2005). The creation of the rule of law and the legitimacy of property rights: The political and economic consequences of a corrupt privatization. Policy Research Working Paper 3779. Washington, D.C.: The World Bank.

IFC. (2010). *IFC Annual Report 2010. Where innnovations meets impact.* Washington, D.C.: International Finance Corporation.

King, E. & Hill, A. (Eds.). (1991). *Women's education in developing countries: Barriers, benefits and policies.* Washington, D.C.: World Bank.

Mayo, P. (1999). *Gramsci, Freire and adult education. Possibilities for transformative action.* London: Zed Books.

Moghadam, V. (1990). *Gender, development, and policy: Toward equity and empowerment.* Helsinki: World Institute for Development Economics Research of the United Nations University.

Munck, R. & O'Hearn, D. (Eds.). (1999). *Critical development theory: Contributions to a new paradigm.* London: Zed.

Patrinos, H. (2008). Returns to education: The gender perspective. In M. Tembon & L. Fort (Eds.), *Girls' education in the 21st century. Gender equality, empowerment and economic growth.* Washington, D.C.: World Bank, pp. 53-66.

Petchesky, R. (2003). *Global prescriptions. Gendering health and human rights.* London and Geneva: Zed and UNRISD.

Rosenau, P. (1992). *Post-modernism and the social sciences: Insights, inroads, and intrusions.* Princeton: Princeton University Press.

Sayed, Y. & Soudien, C. (2005). Decentralisation and the construction of inclusion education policy in South Africa. *Compare,* 35(2), 115-125.

Sen, G. (2000). Gender Mainstreaming in Finance Ministries. *World Development,* 28(7), 1379-1390.

Subrahmanian, R. (2002, April). *Gender and education. A review of issues for social policy.* Social Policy and Development Program No. 9. Geneva: UN Research Institute for Social Development.

UN Women. (2011, 18 May). Michelle Bachelet outlines UN women priorities at an event in the UK Parliament. New York: UN Women.

World Bank. (1995). *Enhancing women's participation in economic development. A World Bank policy paper.* Washington, D.C.: World Bank.

World Bank. (2002, January). *Integrating gender into the World Bank's Work: A Strategy for action.* Washington, D.C.: World Bank.

World Bank. (2003). *World Development Report 2004: Making services work for poor people.* Washington, D.C.: The World Bank.

World Bank. (2011, January). Guidelines. Procurement of goods, works, and non-consulting services under IBRD loans and IDA credits and grants by World Bank borrowers. Washington, D.C.: World Bank.

World Bank. (2011). *Learning for all: Investing in people's knowledge and skills to promote development. World Bank Education Strategy 2020.* Washington, D.C: World Bank.

Zuckerman, E. (2007, January). Critique: Gender equality as smart economics. A World Bank Group Gender Action Plan (GAP) (Fiscal Years 2007-2010). Washington, D.C.: Gender Action. http://www.genderaction.org/images/04.22.08_EZ-GAPlan Critique.pdf

*Nelly P. Stromquist*
*College of Education*
*University of Maryland, U.S.A.*

## CHAPTER 12

SALIM VALLY AND CAROL ANNE SPREEN

# HUMAN RIGHTS IN THE WORLD BANK 2020 EDUCATION STRATEGY

## DICHOTOMIZING DEVELOPMENT AND RIGHTS

At the outset of the World Bank's new *Education Strategy 2020. Learning for All* (hereafter, *WBES 2020)*, the right of all children to access education is proclaimed together with a ringing endorsement of the Universal Declaration of Human Rights and the Convention on the Rights of the Child. Yet, human rights do not feature again in the document. Our critique concerning the rhetoric behind the World Bank strategy as an attempt to colonize the human rights discourse, embraces Uvin's sardonic sentiment "like Moliere's character who discovered that he had always been speaking prose, that human rights is what these development agencies were doing all along. Case closed; high moral ground safely established" (Uvin, 2010, p. 165).

We argue that an explicit human rights focus and evidence of an understanding of the right to, in, and through education is absent throughout the Strategy. The Bank continues in fact to eschew a rights-based approach to education promoting instead a "system approach" (which will be discussed in detail later). Conceptually, *WBES 2020* remains firmly ensconced in market dynamics, privatization, and modernization theory, all of which actually undermine the right to education specifically, and human rights generally. There is no indication that human rights considerations inform any facet of the education system, including policy, budgeting, curriculum, management, assessment, teaching, and learning. In contrast, embracing a human rights framework would impose obligations on duty bearers to promote, respect, protect, and fulfill the right to education across these areas. Yet, the document ignores these vital political aspects, favoring instead a narrow economically defined, skills-oriented interpretation of education.

The "new" education strategy continues to be imbued with the "old" platitudes and deficit arguments quite familiar to critics of the Bank, showing once again that portmanteau notions of development and rights as employed in the Strategy are of rhetorical value only, and they obfuscate rather than clarify rights in education. This "new" Bank strategy still views education as a means of accumulating human capital to increase economic growth, labor productivity, competitiveness, and technological skills for the labor market. *WBES 2020* continues to employ a "template" and formulaic approach to education and development, categorizing

*S.J. Klees et al. (eds.), The World Bank and Education*, 173–187.

countries into low- and middle-income countries and fragile states. The Bank then identifies a focus area for its support. Higher education for low-income countries, for instance, is not seen as a priority. In this way, country-driven priorities, because of the template approach, are undermined. Furthermore, the ostensibly direct and functionalist relationship assumed to exist between education and economic growth, or "economic success," while ignoring unequal trade, inequalities within countries, climate change-induced environmental disasters, famine, military occupation, global structural unemployment, and financial crises should be contested. Nor can the resort to the mantra of "market imperfections" by the development economists sustain the often spectacular failure of technicist and economistic analyses in education today, given the current global financial crisis. We suggest this an ahistorical promotion of "development" primarily through economic goals presented in the Strategy is seriously flawed and remains hostage to conceptual conservatism, and argue that development and human rights are not incompatible—they must be linked.

Furthermore, we argue that given the resources at the disposal of the World Bank, its influence and "advice" have a pervasive and profound effect on the policy and practice of education systems globally, including the ever-present specter of its sanction or at the very least disapproval. This conservatism and underlying overt economic assumptions, despite claims by the World Bank of "political neutrality," are essentially ideological. The effects of this ideological position are manifest in:

– How and *what* questions are examined for the purposes of education policy-making and practice.
– The ascendancy of *technical solutions* uninformed and deliberately obfuscatory of contextual and historical analysis.
– The reliance on *"experts"* who provide such technical advice to the exclusion of other expertise, especially since the criteria by which they are chosen is rarely defined or agreed by those who are directly affected by the nature of their advice.
– The socially divisive and privileging effects of the "solutions" that are provided by such advice and its deleterious consequences for socially and economically disadvantaged social classes (Motala et al., 2010, p. 250).

While we clearly recognize that education has undoubted value in relation to economic development and the potential for employment and meaningful work, we believe that is not the sole or primary purpose of schooling. Motala and Chaka (2005, p. 2) write, "The benefits of education (like the requirements of development) are predicated on specific contexts, and the value of education is largely dependent on its socially-defined purposes constituted by reference to history and context." In countries evincing high levels of poverty, unemployment, and social inequality, schooling, technological acumen, and other learning attributes are important. That importance is derived, however, not only from their uses in the labor market, productivity, and competitiveness but in their social, political, and cultural uses, and in enhancing the ability of the citizenry to participate in democratic processes (Motala & Chaka, 2005). In this way, education acts as a multiplier, enabling access to and increased opportunities for fuller participation in all aspects of society.

The framework introduced by the late UN special rapporteur on the right to education, Katarina Tomasevski (2001), resting on the Four As, or availability, acceptability, accessibility, and adaptability, with further subsequent refinements, provides a conceptual and pragmatic basis for human rights in education and development. In addition, the writers of the World Bank document seem to disregard the seminal work by Sen whose key proposition is that development must be judged by the expansion of substantive freedoms—not just by economic growth or technical progress. While Sen is concerned with economic development, it is not regarded as "merely the expansion in the production of inanimate objects of convenience—the goods and services" (Dreze & Sen, 2002, p. 3). Much like education rights, these goods and services are important in relation to their role in enhancing "social opportunities and freedoms of people" in their social, class, and gendered locations. We suggest that Sen's conception of capabilities can be useful in extending beyond the World Bank's narrowly based purposes of education to include substantive freedoms and personal capabilities that are tied to more humanistic goals of well-being and not exclusively to economic opportunities.

The remainder of this chapter expands on the issues raised in this introductory section. It is divided into the following sections: what's in a strategy; human capital versus human rights; the right to education; and rethinking rights, education, and development.

## WHAT'S IN A STRATEGY?

For most of its history the Bank has claimed it had a purely economic mandate and its Articles of Agreement proscribed it from playing a political role. The provision in the Agreement prohibiting the Bank from "political activity" states, "The Bank and its officers shall not interfere in the political affairs of any member; nor shall they be influenced in their decisions by the political character of the member or members concerned. Only economic considerations shall be relevant to their decisions ..." (International Bank for Reconstruction and Development, 1989). Through various iterations of policy documents in recent years, the Bank has begun to acknowledge human rights but has continued to profess that it cannot explicitly support "a human rights agenda" because of the overtly political nature of "rights." Yet, this ambiguity is disingenuous, and critics of the Bank have suggested that taking an apolitical or neutral stance is a canard. We argue along with others that the application of "free market solutions" to issues of development is a "political objective masquerading as an economic one" (Graaff, 2003, p. 25). Rather than supporting and enhancing rights in public education, the Strategy lauds a "system approach" in "leveraging the private sector" (p. 26). Limbani Nsapato from the Africa Network Campaign on Education for All, argues significantly that

the manner of this call seems to dilute and unburden the state of responsibility in providing education as a human right. This actually is a fast track towards the privatization of education. While addressing the global economic crisis, it is more likely that poor countries could be forced to reduce public spending in education to achieve certain macroeconomic targets, and become compelled to push the responsibility to the private sector as conditions for accessing financial support from the bank. (2011, p. 2)

For those like Nsapato familiar with the devastating effect of the cost of education on poor communities, a truism, seemingly still lost on bank executives, is stated: "Privatizing education should be rejected...," for besides its negative consequences for poor families, "It could also contribute to the dwindling of education quality due to lacking monitoring and regulatory frameworks" (Nsapato, 2011, pp. 2-3).

After all its "consultative" forums, policy discussions, and all the wide-ranging criticism of its own work, the new World Bank Strategy shows no departure from its past paradigm or an honest appraisal of the harm that previous policies have caused. Ironically, evidence-based data on the use of their funds is what the Bank requires of their aid recipients while exempting itself from any rigorous reappraisal. In a section titled "Why a new strategy?" (executive summary, p. 1) the document unreflectively suggests in bold type that the "Bank Group has made substantial contributions to education over the past 49 years ...." Yet, most observers are aware that the World Bank has attracted a fair share of critics over its scorecard, particularly its human rights violations in relation to economic, social, and cultural rights. Major critiques have focused on those egregious instances of rights violations such as the support for coal mining and thermal power plants; the building of dams; the rights of indigenous people; and suppression of labor rights under its structural adjustment programs (see Bradlow, 1996; Danaher, 1994). In this chapter, though, we specifically focus on human rights as they relate to education. We argue that the history of the Bank's involvement in education overall has been a negative one. The structural adjustment policies pursued by the Bank in the 1980s resulted in reducing the public expenditure on education (particularly when the need for and access to education was expanding) and diminishing the role of the state through the Bank's private sector arm, the International Finance Corporation (IFC). Furthermore, its loan policies encouraged the introduction and expansion of private education and promoted education as a tradable commodity through pushing various trade agreements. Private education, encouraged globally by the Bank, now perversely finds expression in the following way in the new Strategy document: "And it [the Bank Group] recognized the growing role of the private sector in education by creating a health and education department at IFC" (executive summary, p. 3).

Tomasevski's global report in 2006, providing an overview of the right to education in 170 countries, was unequivocal in its critique of the World Bank (Tomasevski, 2006a). In a summary of her global report she writes, "It [the global report] focuses on the conversion of education from free to for-fee and on the World Bank as the key architect of this model" (Tomasevski, 2006b). The user fee model promoted by the World Bank at that time (and now abandoned) had a dramatic impact on access to schooling and the retention rate as the cost of schooling became too onerous for families to sustain. Continuing policies supporting privatization and decentralization (that are found throughout *WBES 2020*) are not politically "neutral"; they are lodged within a particular ideological paradigm and policy agenda within an explicitly political neoliberal framework. Importantly, these policies and practices have significantly undermined educational efforts and human rights in many countries around the world.

Much like the rights rhetoric, "education quality" too becomes a buzzword usurped by the document framers (this notion is taken up in greater detail in Crain Soudien's chapter in this volume). Notions of quality and rights in education started in Jomtien and Dakar's Education For All (EFA) Declarations and over time have narrowed to the current meaning of numeric measures of outcomes and accountability. *WBES 2020* provides the evidence that *Learning for All* at the Bank really means "learning for growth," which has largely replaced the rights and equity-based approaches which characterized the EFA discussions in Dakar and Jomtien. We argue that quality and rights should not be exclusively conflated with accountability measures as they appear to have been in the *WBES 2020* document.

*WBES 2020* is also revealing because it begins to recognize the global context around education has changed dramatically over the last few decades and calls for rethinking education approaches. The second line of the strategy "Education has many development benefits: more rapid growth and poverty reduction, as well as better health, reduced fertility, improved resilience to economic shocks, and greater civic participation" (box insert, p.12). This provides a clue to what the Bank privileges in terms of the role and purposes of education in a "dynamic and changing world." For instance, in the production-driven and mechanistic way *WBES 2020* approaches youth and world demographics: "If these youth are equipped with appropriate skills and know-how when they enter the workforce, the 'youth bulge' (see figure 6) could translate into remarkable economic dividends for these countries" (p. 21). Again, its view of education is seen through the rate-of-return prism of educational investments and, most importantly, is not borne out by the reality of massive (and increasing) youth unemployment or at best precarious short-term youth employment that is not commensurate with the high levels of skills many of these young people possess.

As evidenced throughout the *WBES 2020* document, the "new" Strategy still views education as a means of accumulating human capital to increase economic growth, labor productivity, competitiveness, and technological skills for the labor market. The numerous references to competition and the market reflect the Strategy's unchanging and instrumental vision for education. (See for instance the Growth Commission insert, p. 11, "education—which makes it easier to pick up new skills—and a strong rate of job creation, which makes it easy to find new employment.") Competition and relative advantage gained through education has been widely perceived as the engine that powers national prosperity and individual worth. Yet, the reality is that this heightened competition has often undermined equity. It also emerges from a very real and quite substantial pressure that global capitalism is placing on the economy to reduce the cost of labor and shrink investment in the public sector.

Lodged in this human capital framework, *WBES 2020* continues to treat vital pedagogical processes and classroom interactions as a "black box." While the emphasis on primary education in the document is evident, this is also problematic because it is essentially silent on significant issues such as the retention rate or "push out" factors for pupils in secondary education—core target areas of skill development and employment training. Subjects and learning areas not seen to have a purchase in the global marketplace also receive less attention and funding because they are viewed as merely "ornamental." In contrast, a human rights-based approach would be attentive to rights in and through education (and not just access to education, which is the Bank's primary focus). Rights in education include attention to factors that push out learners; learner-centered, participatory, and democratic school processes; issues of redistributive funding and equity-based policies; addressing teachers' working conditions; as well as issues of discrimination along lines of "race," gender, class, ability, and citizenship.

The latest World Bank document is once again "old wine in new bottles." For as long as the World Bank's prescriptions on education are predicated on human capital theory, where education is seen as a marketable commodity and human rights conveniently confined to a mere declaration, we will continue to have "more of the same." Those serious about education should rather focus their praxis on the broader humanizing purpose of education.

## HUMAN CAPITAL VS. HUMAN RIGHTS

While the document carefully avoids mentioning human capital theory, it remains the theoretical basis underpinning *WBES 2020*. Human capital theory is based on the fundamental belief that there is a direct link between education and economic growth. Under human capital theory, the value of education is reduced to its economic pay-off for the individual, and for the economy as a whole. Human capital theory (which was popular in the 1960s, and fell into disfavor after being heavily criticized by Marxists and dependency theorists in the 1970s and 1980s) experienced a revival in the 1990s. Knowledge becomes a commodity, which individuals may exchange for a qualification or credentials that may be of value within a competitive market.

Education and training is transformed into a panacea for economic performance as it is assumed that investment in human capital and technology will automatically increase productivity and skills. *WBES 2020* promotes the need for an "agile" workforce—a current preoccupation of transnational corporations that require mobile productive workers to be distributed at short notice to temporary employment without the burden on the employers to carry the cost of training. In the concept note (World Bank, 2010, p. 2), we read that globalization and new information technologies "are pressuring countries to become more productive and competitive, a challenge that translates into a call for a more highly skilled and more agile workforce. As a result, education systems face increased challenges to equip post-basic graduates with knowledge and skills relevant to a rapidly changing context...." Ironic, since millions of exploited workers throughout the world have, in any case, become "agile and flexible"—forced to traverse borders, swim across rivers, and climb walls in order to be more "productive members" of an iniquitous world economy.

Under the resurgence of neoliberal macro-economic perspectives, education is viewed as an economic investment in which students and workers are both a value-added product and a means by which the economy is to be improved. The first line of the concept note for instance, reads, "A country's prospects for development depend on the quality of its people—the skill and creativity of its work force, the capability of its leaders to govern and to manage its resources, and the ability of its adult generation to raise healthy and educated children." There are numerous references throughout the document that speak to an instrumental and economistic vision defining education for the development of workforce skills and efficient management of resources. Also, *WBES 2020* conveniently transfers the responsibility for unemployment to individual deficiencies, implying that lack of employment is a reflection of a person's skills level and abilities instead of an intrinsic weakness of the economic structure and how employment is distributed. In this sense it remains an ideological hoax that ends up blaming the victims. For Marginson (1999, p. 29):

> ... the hopes of national governments that education will usher in a new wave of economic prosperity and success are bound to be disappointed, just as the hopes of 1960s human capital reformers were disappointed. Education cannot in itself generate capital movements or create wealth, except to the extent that it becomes a fully fledged market commodity in its own right. The inevitable economic "failure" of education, associated with credentialism and the demands of educators for more resources to fulfill their multiplying tasks, sustains the recurring policy cycle of illusion/disillusion, and its partner cycle of spending/cuts, that has dominated educational politics since the 1950s.

He adds, that the difference between the cycle in the high modernization period and in the global era is that "while governmental illusions about education are as large as they ever were, government capacity to pay is not" (Marginson, 1999, p. 29).

Today the proponents of human capital theory, despite a seemingly broader understanding of capital, continue to advocate market-led neo-liberal policies as a basis for reform. There are many criticisms that can be leveled at the human capital approach assumed in *WBES 2020*. First, education is perceived as a panacea for problems that have their root causes elsewhere in the wider economy and society. There are many factors involved in employment: schooling plays a role but it is more about how the economy is structured and how decisions are made. For us, this raises a concern over the false assumptions about education and the workforce, particularly in the context of massive job loss in the global financial crisis. Watkins mentions for example that "education's role as a motor for development is often deceitful" (2011, p. 12). He refers to the socio-economic background of children, which largely militate against what schools can do.

179

Watkins is also useful in understanding how *WBES 2020* and its preoccupation with quality learning is actually about meeting the labor market requirement of the global economy:

> As far as market needs are concerned, an abundant and cheap work force isn't so much of a problem anymore. However quality concerns remain, as firms are also dependent on skilled workers to develop their delocalized national productive bases. Indeed, transnational corporations are increasingly engaged in short term strategies relying on workers who will be productive at short notice and with low training costs. To be effective, this global strategy is therefore highly dependent upon the existence of a system enabling the international comparison of educational "skills" in order to assess the relative advantages of each national job market. (2011, p. 16)

When *WBES 2020* focuses on issues of "quality" learning, this is clearly coupled to the Bank's notions of the global "knowledge economy" and economic growth. Watkins (2011, p. 16) explains, "This new concern has again been fundamental in reshaping the private sector's agenda for public education. There is now growing interest in the private sector in influencing the assessment of learning outcomes, to test the skills they prioritize and smooth the way for an easy selection of optimally 'productive employees'." Within this view, the key to social creativity and productivity lie in private competition, deregulation, and policies that create the right incentives (rewards and sanctions) for individuals to work hard and use their capabilities to the fullest. It often leads to pronouncements that "money doesn't matter" (i.e., teacher preparation and salaries, class size, and classroom resources) for education quality, and to policies that hold schools accountable only for test score performance.

*WBES 2020* continues with the Rostowian hierarchy of development that holds that nations pass through particular phases in their development and that these could be reproduced to varying degrees by others intent on "catching up" with "developed" countries (Rostow, 1960). Although giving the impression that differentiating countries by "development levels" stated as "...developmental groupings based on whether a country is middle-income, low-income, or fragile, and sets out distinct priorities for each of these groups ...." (executive summary, p. 7) is benignly done in order to facilitate assistance and knowledge sharing, the mark of modernization theory is obvious. The significance of such a perspective for education in general is support for schooling based on the idea of human capital growth as intrinsic to the growth of the economic abilities of countries. Theodore Schultz (1963) is one of the leading exponents of this approach in the field of education, arguing influentially that education is a productive investment indispensable to rapid economic growth.

A trenchant critique that wielded considerable influence in the 1970s was that of "dependency theory," powerfully argued in the writings of theorists like Frank (1969), Amin (1973, 1974), Baran (1973), and Rodney (1972). From this perspective, the generation of structural underdevelopment was, therefore, a function of the penetration of the "peripheral" underdeveloped economy by the structure and fundamental characteristics of capitalist economies with the purpose of draining the surplus generated within such dependent economies. In a famous essay entitled "The Development of Underdevelopment," Frank (1966, p. 3) wrote:

> Even a modest acquaintance with history shows that underdevelopment is not original or traditional and that neither the past nor the present of the underdeveloped countries resembles in any important respect the past of the now developed countries. The now developed countries were never underdeveloped though they may have been undeveloped.

Simmons, too, comments on the false "promise of schooling" and a human capital approach to development. For instance, he argues that while the ostensible goal relates to income distribution and raising living standards of the poor majority, educational investment as presently understood is more likely to enhance the power and privilege of those who are already socially advantaged "far more than it enhances the power or position of those who [are] not" (1986, pp. 7-8). This means, in his view, that the real cause of unemployment is not attributable to the educational system but to the economic system, in which unemployment benefits employers because it reduces the costs of labor. How and why education continues to privilege the economically advantaged underscores why "rights through education" need to be manifest in any understanding of the purposes of schooling.

External factors play an important role in the responsiveness of education systems to labor markets and economic growth. Yet despite these external factors in linking education and development, the document continues to privilege technological and skills development, which it believes would lead to greater productivity and the alleviation of poverty. For commentators like Easton and Klees (1992), too, the problem of development cannot be resolved through neoclassical theories about the development of human capital, or through forecasting and the supply and demand analyses that characterized manpower planning. Nor can it be dealt with through a strategy for education and training alone. Meaningful strategies would require a better understanding of the problems of how labor markets are shaped and segmented through a variety of social, political, environmental, cultural, and economic forces and a better understanding of the interventions needed to deal with the problems of such segmentation.

## THE RIGHT TO EDUCATION

In contrast to the human capital approach described above, the human rights approach is interested in rights to education, rights in education and rights through education. Whereas in human capital approaches economic growth is the object of development, in rights based approaches it is the realization of fundamental human rights. These include the enactment of negative rights such as protection from abuse, as well as positive rights, for example celebration and nurturing of learner creativity, use of local languages in schools, pupil participation in democratic structures and debate (Tikly, 2011).

Throughout this chapter we have argued that the right to education has to do with access to schooling but also about rights in education and rights through education. Although there is mention of access to education, rights "through and in" are not recognized in World Bank thinking. From a human rights perspective, education has an intrinsic rather than instrumental value. The latter is commonly manifest in concerns for human capital development, cost-effectiveness, and efficiency. Our understanding of a rights-based approach to education builds from and is situated in the Four As developed by the late Katarina Tomasevski, which states that education should be: Available: education should be free and government-funded with adequate infrastructure and teachers; Accessible: systems should not discriminate and positive steps should be taken to reach the most marginalized; Acceptable: the content of education should be relevant, culturally appropriate, and of quality; Adaptable: education should respond to changing needs of society and to different contexts (Tomasevski, 2001).The right–to-education framework has multiple dimensions: first, education is a fundamental right, meaning that governments are obliged to ensure some education for all children. At the same time, the framework urges for rights *in and through* education, requiring curricula and pedagogy that are meaningful and responsive to the needs of all learners.

Through this framework human rights considerations should inform every facet of the education system. Legislation gives effect to the right to basic education and defines some of the corresponding duties and duty-bearers. But in the absence of clear norms and standards, many governmental obligations remain loosely specified (Lake & Pendlebury, 2008). Under a rights-based approach, government has an obligation to respect, protect, promote, and fulfill these rights through policy and legislation; yet many of these obligations are imperfect and the precise content and meaning of the right to education remain open to debate. In many ways rights are political resources that can be used to extend and deepen meaningful access to education, and mobilizing public action for its full realization is imperative.

Important, too, is the view of Sen that a theory of human rights "cannot sensibly be confined within the juridical model within which it is so frequently incarcerated" (Sen, 2004, p. 315). Elsewhere we have warned against "constitutional romanticism," or proceeding as if rights exist for everyone instead of recognizing circumstances where people's rights on paper do not translate to rights on the ground (Spreen & Vally, 2006). It is therefore vital that the concerns and needs of those who are most vulnerable are key to defining rights in and the purposes of schooling, and what is meant by education quality. Lake and Pendlebury (2008, p. 23) make the point that, while "legislation and litigation can get results, enduring respect for human rights is sustained not just by a country's constitution, government and legal system." Quoting Pogge (2002), they argue that rights are secured by "a vigilant public that is willing to work towards the political realization of the right"(Lake & Pendlebury, 2008, p. 23). So, too, is "an active and responsible citizenship who understand the law and its limitations and are willing to insist on their rights and mobilize when these are not forthcoming" (Vally, 2007,

p. 5). This suggests why the Bank's symbolic rhetoric and policies explicitly undermining rights must be addressed.

## RETHINKING RIGHTS, EDUCATION, AND DEVELOPMENT

The recurrence of the themes of economic growth and modernization pose grave dangers for developing countries if these themes are not mediated by recognition of the limits of such growth in relation to the broader humanizing objectives of education (Motala et al., 2010). Economic growth reflects only a partial reality while it disguises—even while it is useful—the reality of inequality and poverty usually associated with high levels of unemployment and social fragmentation. As we have argued, conceptions of development have come a long way from Rostow's model of growth or indeed from the paradigm of modernization. Development is now seen as a complex process encompassing a broad matrix of objectives, which include political, social, economic, environmental, and cultural considerations. Indeed, questions about the ownership of the development process and its indigenization are intrinsic to its goals.

Similarly, the broader role of education is essential to realize the potential of education in expanding the humanist, long-term, socially important, and sustaining goals of what development should be about; only then will the human rights enshrined in international declarations begin to have substantive value, and only then can education assume a role in dealing with the social cleavages that exist globally (Motala et al., 2010).

We turn again to our previous examination of the relationship between education rights, capabilities, and development. At present, even a cursory reading of the mainstream media makes it impossible to avoid the conclusion that most commentators about education see the relationship as being primarily about reinforcing the economic, labor market, rates of return, productivity, and international competitiveness goals of development. In part, the idea that education is key to development is attributable to agencies like the World Bank and a raft of educational economists who argue the justification for high levels of social investment in human capital as critical to the development of nations. They suggest that although development requires capital investment and technical processes, capital and technology are inert without human knowledge and effort. In this sense, human learning is central to development. Some, though, have now grown increasingly skeptical about conceptions of education limited to its role in economic development. We argue that the overstatement of the ostensible benefits of education relative to economic growth is not harmless or inaccurate. It has definite consequences for education policy because it is misleading about the actual value and purposes of education—which it limits to augmenting "human capital"—and because it holds out a promise about the value of education to economic growth that is largely unproven. By implication, we argue that the qualitative value of education is greatly undervalued because of the extraordinary emphasis placed on development construed as economic growth.

In the same vein, while we recognize that knowledge, skills, and competencies are important for all societies—critically important even, for the well-being of nations—reducing the discussion about knowledge and skills to its use for employment in a market-dominated economic system is a serious limitation on how the question of skills can and must be understood. This is because, in the first place, no capitalist economy in the world or in any period of its history, (outside the periods of worldwide war), has been able to provide full employment in the economy. In fact, the reality for most developing countries is high levels of unemployment as a structural condition of the economy—as an inevitable and crucial condition necessary to its reproduction (Motala et al., 2010). We therefore agree with the skepticism expressed by Ohiorhenuan (2002, p. 3), who argues that trying to eradicate poverty is futile where (presumably as in the case of the Bank) the focus is on the symptoms of poverty rather than its causes—that is, "target[ing] the shadow rather than the substance."

## CONCLUSIONS

The aim of this section is to set out a rights-based alternative to understanding education and to use this to assess the extent to which *WBES 2020* advances social justice principles and concerns. A recent article by Tikly (2011) argues that capabilities have been posited by Sen as an alternative to a focus on economic wealth as a measure of development and are described by Nussbaum as "a species of a human rights approach" (2006, p. 78), and thus have the potential to bridge and extend the human capital and rights-based approaches to education quality mentioned above. Simply put, capabilities are the opportunities that individuals and groups have to realize different "functionings" that they may have reason to value and that contribute to well-being (Sen, 1999).

Capabilities thus imply more than simply skills in a narrow sense. "Education quality" may be defined in terms of the opportunities to develop the greater capability sets that are afforded to different individuals and groups through the processes of teaching and learning (Tikly, 2011). For Sen, what counts as a capability, however, is context-dependent and needs to be arrived at through processes of agency. The attempt to assert a broader conception of education reflective of a humanizing discourse and genuine development—not one that largely meets the labor market needs of big business—exemplify the contradictory nature and the contestation over how education is to be interpreted, and what social outcomes, for whom, and at what cost these are to be achieved.

Discussions about the skills needs of society rarely transgress the bounds of these economic-determinist approaches despite the strong and seemingly instructive legislative injunctions about the broader humanizing and citizenship-related role of education and training systems. This, despite the occasional genuflections by political leaders and the leaders of education institutions to the idea that knowledge is essential to the development of a citizenry, for the fullest expression of civic rights and responsibilities, for such elementary rights as numeracy and literacy, accessing public goods, making choices, understanding the complexities of the market and, importantly, for ensuring greater levels of democratic accountability of public representatives and organizations. An alternative to the World Bank's educational strategy would recognize, too, that the role of education involves understanding the many cultures, values, and belief systems in society and rebutting "race," gender, ethnic, and other stereotypes. An alternative education strategy would be based on a realization that in developing countries in particular there are a wide range of socially useful activities which members of society can be engaged in, such as in the case of health and the general welfare of working class and poor communities in particular, and that a wide range of educational activities and purposes are possible to support the lives of working class families, from childcare and the processes of early childhood development to care for the aged, frail, and disabled.

Alternative educational practices and approaches would urge that communities can and must be supported in these endeavors since they have limited resources to do so themselves and that there are a wide range of community projects which can be supported relating to areas like primary health, the local economy, housing development, service infrastructure, land usage, recreation and cultural activities, and support for schools. Indeed, there are examples of communities that support the unemployed through funding useful activities such as childcare, community and school meals services, school renovation, maintenance of public spaces, etc. And these activities are undertaken collectively often leading, as in the case of the Argentinean factory occupations, to co-operative forms of production and distribution. We know, too, that much more has to be done to exemplify the potential for co-operative forms of production and distribution, and to understand the educational requirements of such forms of production because there is a valuable history of worker co-operatives in many countries which provide the evidence and the potential for humanizing and creative approaches to the formation of skills and competencies in developing societies (Motala et al., 2010).

Despite the glossy rhetoric about rights, quality, and participation in education, limiting the purposes of education in *WBES 2020* to developing skills for the "economy" is fundamentally flawed because its effect is to place the blame for the lack of capacity and knowledge on the poor themselves or on the government alone, the poor being answerable for their predicament since they have "no one to blame but themselves."

We suggest that all education must pay serious attention to the broader humanizing goals of learning, lodged in a human rights framework, whether as early childhood development, further education, higher education, or adult education, even if some of these arenas might conceivably be more directly related to employability and economic function. The broader humanizing goals of education remain incontrovertibly important in all education because of the rapid changes to economic and social systems and the dynamic it imposes on all learning. Even in periods of unprecedented economic growth and great competitiveness, another way is possible. No society can ignore the broader purposes of education and its role as the pre-eminent engine for the achievement of such purposes, which are not limited to economic outcomes alone.

185

## NOTE

[i] For a discussion of rights "to, in and through" education, see Katarina Tomesevski's *Manual on Rights Based Education: global human rights requirements made simple* (UNESCO, 2004).

## REFERENCES

Amin, S. (1973). *Unequal development*. Sussex: Harvester.
Amin, S. (1974). *Accumulation on a world scale: A critique of the theory of underdevelopment*. New York: Monthly Review Press.
Baran, P. A. (1973). *The political economy of growth*. London: Penguin.
Bradlow, D. (1996). The World Bank, the IMF and human rights. *Transnational Law and Contemporary Problems, 6*(1), 48-89.
Danaher, K. (Ed.). (1994). *50 years is enough: The case against the World Bank and the International Monetary Fund*. London: South End Press.
Dreze, J. & Sen, A. (2002). *India: Development and participation*. New Delhi: Oxford University Press.
Easton, P. & Klees, S. (1992). Conceptualizing the role of education in the economy. In R. Arnove, P. G. Altbach, & G. P. Kelly (Eds.), *Emergent issues in education: Comparative perspectives* (pp. 13-24). New York: State University of New York Press.
Frank, A. G. (1966). The development of underdevelopment. *Monthly Review, 18*(4), 17-31.
Frank, A. G. (1969). *Capitalism and underdevelopment in Latin America*. London: Penguin.
Graaff, J. (2003). *Poverty and development*. Oxford: Oxford University Press.
International Bank for Reconstruction and Development. (19890. Articles of Agreement (as amended effective 16 February 1989), Article IV, Section 10, http://www.worldbank.org/html/extdr/backgrd/ibrd/arttoc.htm
Lake, L. & Pendlebury, S. (2008). Children's right to basic education. In S. Pendlebury, L. Lake, & C. Smith (Eds.), *South African child gauge 2008/2009*. Cape Town: Children's Institute, University of Cape Town, pp. 19-23.
Marginson, S. (1999). After globalization: Emerging politics of education. *Journal of Education Policy, 14*(1), 19-31.
Motala, E. & Chaka, T. (2005). The case for basic education. CEPD Occasional Paper No. 4. Braamfontein: Centre for Education Policy Development.
Motala, E., Vally, S., & Spreen, C.A. (2010). Reconstituting power and privilege or transforming education and training? In P. Bond, B. Maharaj, & A. Desai (Eds.), *Zuma's own goal: Losing South Africa's war on poverty* (pp. 241-259). Asmara: Africa World Press and South Africa Netherlands Research Programme on Alternatives in Development.
Nussbaum, M. C. (2006). *Frontiers of justice: Disability, nationality, species membership*. Cambridge, MA: Belknap Press.
Nsapato, L. E. (2011, January 22). What good will new World Bank education strategy bring to Malawi? *Nyasa Times*.
Ohiorhenuan, J. (2002, September 25). The poverty of development: Prolegomenon to a critique of development policy in Africa. Sixth Professor Ojetunji Aboyade Memorial Lecture. Pretoria: United Nations Development Programme.
Pogge, T. (2002). *World poverty and human rights*. Cambridge: Polity Press.
Spreen, C. A. & Vally, S. (2006). Education rights, education policies and inequality in South Africa. *International Journal of Educational Development, 26*(4), 352-362.
Rodney, W. (1972). *How Europe underdeveloped Africa*. London: Bogle-L'Ouverture Publications.
Rostow, W. W. (1960). *The stages of economic growth*. Cambridge: Cambridge University Press.
Schultz, T. (1963). *The economic value of education*. New York: Columbia University Press.
Sen, A. (1999). *Development as freedom*. Oxford: Oxford University Press.

Sen, A. (2003, October 28). The importance of basic education speech to the Commonwealth Education Conference, Edinburgh.

Sen, A. (2004). Elements of a theory of human rights. *Philosophy and Public Affairs, 32*(4), 315-356.

Simmons, J. (Ed.). (1986). *The education dilemma: Policy issues for developing countries in the 1980s.* New York: The World Bank and Pergamon.

Tikly, L. (2011). A roadblock to social justice? An analysis and critique of the South African education Roadmap. *International Journal of Educational Development, 31*(1), 86-94.

Tomasevski, K. (2001). *Right to education primer No. 3. Human rights obligations: Making education available, accessible, acceptable and adaptable.* Gothenburg: NovumGrafiska.

Tomasevski, K. (2006a). The state of the right to education worldwide. Free or fee: 2006 Report, Copenhagen: Right to Education Project, http://www.katarinatomasevski.com/images/Global_Report.pdf

Tomasevski, K. (2006b). Six reasons why the World Bank should be debarred from education. http://www.foro-latino.org/flape/boletines/boletin_referencias/boletin_20/Doc_Referencias20/katarina_tomasevski/Lecturas/3.pdf.

Uvin, P. (2010). From the right to development to the rights-based approach: How "human rights" entered development. In A. Cornwall & D. Eade (Eds.), *Deconstructing development discourse: buzzwords and fuzzwords* (pp. 163-174). Warwickshire, UK: Practical Action Publishing and Oxfam.

Vally, S. (2007). Rights and responsibilities in education. *The star series—Education in South Africa today* (pp. 3-5). Johannesburg: Wits School of Education/The Star.

Watkins, P. (2011). *The quality debate.* Rosebank, South Africa: Global Campaign for Education, Rosebank.

World Bank. (2010, February). Concept note for the World Bank Education Strategy 2020. Washington, D.C.: World Bank.

World Bank. (2011). *Learning for all: Investing in people's knowledge and skills to promote development. World Bank Group education strategy 2020.* Washington, D.C.: World Bank.

*Salim Vally*
*School of Education*
*University of Johannesburg, South Africa*

*Carol Anne Spreen*
*Curry School of Education*
*University of Virginia, U.S.A.*

## CHAPTER 13

SUSAN L. ROBERTSON

# THE STRANGE NON-DEATH OF NEOLIBERAL PRIVATIZATION IN THE WORLD BANK'S *EDUCATION STRATEGY 2020*

## INTRODUCTION

In 2012, the World Bank Group will celebrate half a century of engagement in the field of education development (Jones, 2007). And, while "… arguably the most prestigious and … most powerful producer … of international development knowledge" (Berger & Beeson, 1998, p. 487), to many observers, the Bank's pro-poor achievements, especially over the past quarter of a century, have been way too few. Instead, since the 1980s and the turn to "neoliberalism" as the ideological paradigm guiding development, World Bank policy has had detrimental outcomes for economic growth and global social equality. The education sector was not exempted from this paradigm shift, or its effects. Klees describes the Bank's neoliberal policies in education as a "Great Experiment" (2008, p. 312) involving "user-fees, the privatization of more educational activities, and the direct connection of management and financing of education to measurable output."

This mix of policy—widely referred to as the Washington Consensus—"derived its appeal from a simple narrative about the power of globalization to lift nations out of poverty" (Rodrik, 2011, pp. 164-165). By the mid-1990s, however, the Washington Consensus was widely regarded as a "damaged brand," not only because of the ideological opposition it had engendered, but because of growing evidence that two decades of neoliberal development policies had reinforced, rather than mitigated, global poverty and inequality (Wade, 2004; ILO, 2004; Klees, 2008; Rodrik, 2011). The attempt to find a path forward through promoting "good governance"—known as the post-Washington Consensus—was not sufficient to stave off the crisis that was the inevitable outcome of financial deregulation. By 2008, when the world was facing its worst global financial crisis since the 1930s, neoliberalism as a development paradigm was again called into question. Indeed, some intellectuals went so far as to talk about a new "post-neoliberal" world order while the Bank, for its part, promised the modernization of the multilateral system and a "New World Bank Group." Had the Bank finally changed its mind on neoliberalism, and instead sought to lay out a new development trajectory for the next decade?

*S.J. Klees et al. (eds.), The World Bank and Education,* 189–205.

According to Harrison (2005), shifts in direction are not new for the World Bank. In looking back over the Bank's post-war history, Harrison (2001, 2005) argues that what is most striking about the Bank is that it has trouble sticking to its own convictions. He notes a constant set of forward and backward movements, declaring war on those states it had previously funded with optimism, to be followed by tactical retreats from policies it had promoted with great zeal. Harrison goes on to argue: "In reviewing all of these changes in direction—often unexplained by the Bank—one gets the impression of an inconsistent and reactionary institution, unsure of how to represent itself to the outside world, yet at the same time deploying considerable resources to rebut or partially assimilate the criticisms of others" (Harrison, 2001, p. 530).

Given this history, one might be encouraged to think the Bank would, at last, engage in a tactical retreat from neoliberalism. Yet, despite the crisis that has engulfed the heartlands of neoliberal ideology, the United States of America and the United Kingdom, if we look critically at the *World Bank Education Strategy 2020 (WBES 2020*, hereafter)—the focus for this chapter—free-market economics is alive and well. In the World Bank's *New World, New World Bank Group: (I) Post Crisis Directions* report (2010) that framed the priorities for *WBES 2020*, while regulatory and supervisory failures are recognized as lying at the heart of the crisis (World Bank, 2010, p. 4), the Bank nevertheless goes on to argue for a bigger role for itself in global governance, and for an expanded role for the private sector in development. Paradoxically, rather than a *retreat* from these policies, as Harrison suggests, it is clear that the Bank proposes to deal with the failures of neoliberalism by *reinventing* further rounds of neoliberal intervention (Peck, 2010).

This chapter explores this strange "non-death of neoliberalism" (Crouch, 2011) in the Bank's education sector policy priorities, and its implications for education as a societal good and human right. A key point of entry will be the two education sector strategy reports, *Education Sector Strategy 1999* (World Bank, 1999) and *WBES 2020* (World Bank, 2011), used to guide the Bank's education operations. In order to locate these reports in wider political and economic developments, I begin with some opening remarks on neoliberalism as a political project. Second, I then focus on the *Education Sector Strategy 1999* Report, focusing particularly on the ways in which an expanded private sector, together with the International Finance Corporation (IFC, the Bank's private sector investment arm), are promoted as having the knowledge and capacity to play a more central role in education as "an emerging market." Third, I show the ways in which a small group of global education policy entrepreneurs advanced, and sought to materialize, this agenda for education under the rubric of public-private partnerships (PPPs). I examine the evidence these policy entrepreneurs create and use to advance their arguments, and highlight the circumscribed nature of this evidence. Fourth, I show the ways in which this agenda is not only continued, but expanded in *WBES 2020*. This is despite the causal role of neoliberalism in the current global economic crisis, the tenuous nature of the evidence that the private sector is more efficient, and the questionable investments of IFC. Finally, I reflect on neoliberalism as a political project, and the fact that, despite its manifest failings, for the moment at least, these failings appear to animate further rounds of neoliberal invention in the education sector.

## ENTER NEOLIBERALISM—CHICAGO-STYLE:
## EXIT STATE REGULATION—AND KEYNES

While most of us are familiar with the contours of neoliberalism as a hegemonic project, there are several points to make that are germane to this chapter. The first is that to understand the significance of opening up education to the private sector, we need to look back to the early 1970s, to the crisis of the post-war capitalist development project (a marriage between economic liberalism and social democracy) (Hobsbawm, 1994; Harvey, 2005), and the eventual introduction of free market economics as the dominant vision of how best to organize societies. Yet, realizing this vision was not inevitable, nor, therefore, is its eventual dislocation and demise. The second is that the 1970s crisis was not just a crisis of political ideas. Rather, it was also a structural crisis in the advanced economies of the West as a consequence of the exhaustion of the post-war Fordist development model (Harvey, 2005).

Ideas about a minimally regulated free market had circulated from the 1930s onward, but its advocates had not been able to secure a toehold in political and policy circles. Instead, Keynesianism, or a state-managed economy, dominated. Nor indeed were neoliberals in agreement with each other. As events unfolded, a clear divide emerged over the following decades between the eventually triumphant Chicago School, and the European-anchored ordoliberal position. These differences can be contrasted as a free economy/minimal state, on the one hand, and a socially embedded market order on the other. What held neoliberals together, however, was the shared embrace of market utopianism, and a visceral distaste for Keynesianism and socialism. And yet, as Peck (2010, p. 65) points out, neoliberalism's curse is that it can live neither with, nor without, the state. However, neoliberals differed sharply on where to draw the line with regard to the role of the state.

In any event, from the 1980s onwards, the ideas of the Chicago School, driven by the economists Friedrich von Hayek and Milton Friedman, were to eventually dominate. Picked up by the Thatcher and Reagan administrations in the U.K. and U.S. respectively, Chicago-style neoliberalism was to effect a "great moving right show" (Hall, 1979). As projects were rolled out in the 1980s, a cluster of key ideas featured: the unpicking of the state's protectionist policies to enable the freer movement of finance, trade, and labor across national boundaries (referred to as deregulation); the implementation of competition policies across the public and private sectors aimed at creating efficiencies; the privatization of a range of former state activity; and the rescaling of state activity (involving a dual process of decentralization and recentralization). The state went from being a handmaiden of economic growth to the principal obstacle blocking it, while "the international division of labor was transformed from a threat to a savior" (Rodrik, 2011, p. 163).

In policy and development circles, this cluster of ideas came to be referred to as "the Washington Consensus" (Williamson, 1993). Markets and competition, and the role of the private sector in new and old areas of service delivery, including education (Ball, 2007), were presented as "in the national interest," central to global economic competitiveness, as a means of arresting poverty and slowing economic growth, and the foundation for building knowledge-based economies. From the 1980s onward, key international agencies, such as the World Bank Group, the International Monetary Fund (IMF), and the Organization for Economic and Cooperative Development (OECD), played an increasingly instrumental role in promoting the Chicago School's free market ideas globally. In low-income countries, neoliberal political projects—often referred to as "policy in a suitcase"—were advanced through the World Bank/IMF's Structural Adjustment Policies (SAPs) (Samoff, 1994). However, this policy repertoire (decentralization, privatization, user fees, community financing) had devastating consequences, not only for the quality and capacity of these education systems but for their wider societies (Ilon, 1994; Klees, 2008; Bonal, 2002).

By the mid-1990s, the manifest failures of the Washington Consensus, in particular the considerably lower levels of economic growth it had presided over, left neoliberals with a conundrum. How to move forward without repudiating neoliberalism as a project? The Washington Consensus was rehabilitated by retaining its broad features while expanding it to include a range of additional reforms under the rubric of "good governance": extensive reforms in public administration, PPPs, the elimination of barriers to trade, and a new round of international trade agreements. The last of these, however, was to grind to a halt as the newly formed World Trade Organization (WTO) in 1995 was confronted with major difficulties in advancing negotiations that protected the interests of the developed economies at the expense of the developing economies. With regard to opening education to negotiations through the WTO as a global services sector, it too was faced with major organized protests around whether or not education was a commodity for sale.

These ongoing movements forward, collisions, and backflow of neoliberal restructuring lead to my third point: that because the utopian vision at the core of neoliberalism—a free market and free economy—is ultimately unrealizable, it inevitably faces failure. Yet, as Peck argues, this vision also drives a forward dynamic because:

> the pristine clarity of its ideological apparition, the *free market,* coupled with the endless frustrations borne of the inevitable failure to arrive at this elusive destination, nevertheless confer a significant degree of forward momentum on the neoliberal project. Ironically, neoliberalism possesses a progressive, forward-leaning dynamic by virtue of the very unattainability of its idealized destination. In practice, neoliberalism has never been about a once and for all liberalization, an evacuation of the state. Instead, it has been associated with rolling programs of market-oriented reform, a kind of permanent revolution. (Peck, 2010, p. 7)

In other words, including education, neoliberal projects tend to "fail forward" (Peck, 2010, p. 6). These rounds of neoliberal intervention, of de- and re-regulation, of flows, backflow, and undercurrents, create the actually existing worlds of neoliberalism. Furthermore, they are "not pristine spaces of market rationality and constitutional order; they are institutionally cluttered places marked by experimental but flawed systems of governance, cumulative problems of social fallout, and serial market failure" (Peck, 2010, p. 31). In the following sections, we will see these dynamics at work in the ongoing reinvention of the Bank's free-market project within the education sector, and in the accumulation of experiments regarding different privatization projects.

## LOCATING THE *EDUCATION SECTOR STRATEGY 1999* REPORT

It is against this backdrop, of a concerted effort to keep the failed Washington Consensus on the road through its revamping and repackaging, and the developed economies' attempt to advance a new economic model based on a globalizing services sector, that we can now locate the World Bank's *Education Sector Strategy 1999*. Sector strategy reports are forward-looking documents, playing a crucial role in guiding the Bank's investments in the education sector over a longer temporal horizon. In this case, the *Education Sector Strategy* is the fourth report in 30 years (the others were presented in 1970, 1975, and 1980) with 20 years between the third and the fourth reports. This temporal lag of 20 years suggests that the broad policy trajectory for the Bank's education sector over those years had, until the later 1990s, not changed in any significant way.

Despite difficulties the Bank was encountering with its hard-nosed, free-market policies, the 1999 Report confidently proclaimed that market economies now dominated the global economy, accounting for over 80 percent of the world's population (World Bank, 1999). Contrasting a "centrally planned economy of the past" (presented as having "more certainty but fewer opportunities") (World Bank, 1999, p. 11) with a dynamic market system, we are left in little doubt which was preferable. Yet, the Report encourages us to suspend judgment about the moral anchor of this market society that is driven by a relentless search for "wafer thin profit margins" and "do or die profit margins" (p. 11). Instead, education and educators are invited onto "center stage"—to be the means by which the future is either won, or lost, for "individuals, communities and nations" (p. 11). That there might be another more humane game in town is not countenanced. Instead, the Report offers full support for this revamped political project, asserting that now governments were becoming less the provider of goods and services, and more the facilitators and regulators of economic activity. The challenge for the education sector was also clear: how to create learners who were enterprising, agile and risk takers, on the one hand, and engage the private sector in a wider range of education activities (such as on-the-job training, publishing, technology initiatives, and education provision), on the other.

The 1999 Report, seemingly mindful that strong claims around privatization in education would likely be controversial, began by noting: "...education in most countries is both publicly financed and provided" but that "there is no *a priori* reason for all education to be publicly provided, funded and managed" (p. 34). It goes on: "There are arguments in favor of (1) selectively encouraging management and or ownership of institutions by NGOs, community of religious groups, and entrepreneurs, (2) allowing students and their parents to choose among different options, and (3) requiring some level of private financing at post-basic levels" (p. 34).

The 1999 Report then turns to legitimate its embrace of a greater role for the private sector, laying out a set of justifications in line with the Bank's pro-poor development mandate. For example: a greater private sector would extend educational opportunities to less well-off students; private financing would expand the number of places available—especially at the secondary and tertiary levels; public resources would then be freed up to be used by the poor, families would be provided with choices beyond the public sector, the private sector would be more efficient than the public sector while quality would be maintained at a lower unit cost, and the private sector would increase the potential for innovation (World Bank, 1999, pp. 28-29). These claims display a limited engagement with, or understanding of, the wider evidence that had been generated by national education systems that had moved to choice policies (Gewirtz et al., 1995), to new forms of financing—particularly of education infrastructures (Hatcher, 2006), and to nascent commercialization (Molnar, 2006). Instead the Bank drew on Bank-financed and supported projects, such as a primary education project in the Dominican Republic using Milton Friedman's famous voucher system, scholarships for girls to enable them to attend private schools, and private sector development of education in Mauritania and Burkina Faso.

Arguably the more ambitious project regarding the expansion of the Bank's new engagements with the private sector was the perceived potential for the IFC to expand its role in education. The IFC has the task, distinct from the other four branches of the World Bank Group, of supporting the private sector in what the IFC described as "emerging markets." The IFC was founded as a separate arm of the Bank in 1956, when member governments became concerned that private entrepreneurs were not being effectively supported by multilateral lending agencies. The IFC also grew out of a belief that economic development, and thereby poverty alleviation, was dependent on a robust private sector. According to the 1999 Report, the IFC's expertise in "understanding the actual and potential roles of private sector involvement in education" (World Bank, 1999, p. 28) meant that it could then be able to:

> ... play a role in the further development and nurturing of that private segment of the education market that expands educational opportunities for low-income students .... The more that better off families pay for education (as they do when they choose private education), the more the government can use its resource for the poor. (p. 28)

In other words, privatized services for the middle classes—the argument was—would in turn benefit the poor. To advance its efforts to open up education as an investment sector, the Report proposed continued support for EdInvest launched a year earlier (1998), a joint venture between the British-based not-for-profit education firm, the Centre for British Teachers (CfBT), and the IFC, as an information portal for global investments in the education sector.

How to advance such an agenda in the face of considerable hostility toward the Bank's privatization agenda that the Washington Consensus had engendered? The solution? The idea of partnerships, in particular PPPs, was canvassed in the Report. Arguing that "the job of strengthening education is too big for any single institution" (World Bank, 1999, p. 18), partnerships were a means of smoothing over the damage done by earlier forms of privatization while not abandoning them. Most importantly, partnerships enabled multiple framings, interests, and objectives to be realized (Newman, 2001). The idea of partnerships, therefore, was a useful portmanteau for the bank to continue to advance its privatization of education agenda. PPPs not only brought different actors together and therefore different constituencies and kinds of expertise, but they helped to broker in, rather than mitigate or mediate, privatization *in*, and *of*, education.

This Report therefore coincided with a wider set of strategies being advanced by the developed economies and the multilateral agencies aimed at creating competitive knowledge-based service economies that included an expanding education services sector. These included bringing private actors into the governance of education on the pretext that they generated greater efficiencies than the public sector, opening up the education sector to global trading rules, and the promotion of trade in education (rather than aid) as the basis for capacity-building and delivering on access and quality in education (Robertson et al., 2002).

Taken together, these priorities in the *Education Sector Strategy 1999* Report extend the Bank's activities in the private sector into new areas—beyond fees and private schools (Klees, 2002, p. 463). In offering an assessment of this Report, Klees (2002), argues that, despite the promissory vision (of "Quality Education for All"), closer scrutiny revealed not only very little substantive change, but that the Report is full of "...unexamined assumptions, questionable facts, and ideology substituting for knowledge" (2002, p. 451). Klees' assessment of the Report points to the clear continuities in the Bank's position on education with the earlier discredited Washington Consensus. Yet he underplays the extent to which the Bank's privatization agenda has been strategically advanced to include new actors with the Bank group and a remodeled packaging of free-market ideas for reforming education provision.

## BROKERING IN PRIVATIZATION THROUGH PPPs:
## THE GLOBAL EDUCATION POLICY ENTREPRENEURS

It is tempting to think of neoliberalism as a global regulatory architecture imposed from above. Yet like all political projects, neoliberalism requires continual work by socially-situated actors. These actors are the brokers of myths, the mediators of projects, and the makers of new spaces of neoliberalism. In this section I want now to focus on one privatization strategy—PPPs—referred to briefly in the *Education*

*Sector Strategy 1999* Report under Partnerships, but which is given life, direction and substance. This brokering work by the education policy entrepreneurs highlights the ways in which neoliberalism is not only lived, but is a constructed project by a network of actors located within and beyond the Bank.

The brokers of the Bank's privatization of projects through education PPPs are a small network of policy entrepreneurs and education experts located at the interstices of a select range of international organizations, transnational education consultancy firms, and global universities who have been responsible for promoting the idea of PPPs (Verger, forthcoming). In the 1990s, representatives of these organizations came together in the World Bank Economics of Education Thematic Group and opened a research and discussion line on private and alternative forms of education provision, initially with a focus on Sub-Saharan Africa. They started thinking about partnerships in education as an evolution of, and solution to, the hostility facing the privatization agenda. As Crouch remarks:

> A full blooded neoliberal approach to public services would have these moved fully into the market, with consumers paying for them themselves and government having no role at all. This has proved impossible, mainly for democratic reasons: the majority of voters will not support the abolition of the public services established during the heyday of universal suffrage. (2011, p. 95)

In 2001, the IFC launched a handbook on PPPs in education. The main authors of this collaboration were Normal LaRocque, then director of corporate finance at Anderson Consulting Company in New Zealand; James Tooley, professor of Education Policy in the U.K.; and Michael Latham, education advisor to CfBT Education Services, along with Harry Patrinos, senior education economist at the Bank. The network is narrow in scope but very cohesive, and can best be described as a small epistemic community that shares a common commitment to the ideas of the Chicago School, as well as being informed by a small group of largely U.S.-based economists of education. This group is central to advancing the PPP's agenda in education more globally; they are also behind the most well-known publications, policy-briefs, and toolkits on PPPs which have culminated in the widely disseminated World Bank report, *The Role and Impact of PPPs in Education*, released in 2009 (Patrinos et al., 2009). The network has organized a range of events where PPPs are discussed among policy-makers, donor agencies, with the staff of international organizations, and among select academics. Their members write and speak at each other's initiatives (publications, seminars, courses, and so on).

A central assumption made by this policy network is that "education is a consumer good, and that the student is the principal consumer through parents" (World Bank, 2001, p. 1). What follows from this assumption is that, in order for parents (and students) to choose, the education sector needs to be organized so that it operates according to the logic of a free market. This includes information on the nature of the provider's education offer including its quality; a set of incentives that ensure the right kind of performance behavior; regulatory guarantees to protect the interests of private investors; competition among providers; and an evaluation system that is able to feed back into the information system, creating a virtuous circle. A virtuous circle is also created between the Bank's objectives concerning what it is that PPPs should be able to realize (access, quality, cost, and overcoming inequalities), the ways in which different types of PPPs can affect educational outcomes, and the use of empirical evidence—much of which is funded by the Bank as part of its impact studies, or which comes from a select group of education economists.

PPPs are proving to be the perfect umbrella, for while the education provision operates according to free market principles (competition, efficiency, and so on), the state ensures the enabling policy environment, and most importantly, funding. As key Bank staffer, Harry Patrinos, observes:

> Government guides policy and provides financing while the private sector delivers education services to students. In particular, governments contract out private providers to supply a specified service of a defined quantity and quality at an agreed price for a specific period of time. These contracts contain rewards and sanctions in which the private sector shares the financial risk in the delivery of public services. (Patrinos et al., 2009, p. 1)

And, as Crouch notes, almost no one talks about the fact that universal public services, funded by government rather than by individual choice, provide wonderfully secure markets for those firms that specialize in contracting for public business. He points out: "neoliberalism departs astonishingly from the political and economic legacy of liberalism in not seeing any problem in a close relationship between firms and the state, provided the influence runs from firms to the state and not vice versa" (Crouch, 2011, p. 95). He is right. In countries such as the U.K. and the U.S., where education had been part of the state-citizen contract, reversals to the point that the market trumped the state have proven impossible. Instead, a new position has emerged that has suited the private sector: a publicly funded, privately provided education sector through PPPs. The question of how the state regulates private actors in the education sector, particularly when private actors hide behind "commercial sensitivity" laws, is an important issue with no evident solution. But an equally important question is how the state manages the deepening contradictions between education as a human right, public good, tradable commodity, and mechanism for social cohesion, and the crisis of regulation that now pervades the global political economy.

## CRISIS, MODERNIZING MULTILATERALISM, AND *WBES 2020*

While the global financial crisis began to emerge well before it attracted attention in 2007-2008, 2008 has become identified as its moment of rupture. Jessop argues that

> The global crisis is the product of the interaction of at least five processes: the global environmental, fuel, food and water crisis; the decline of U.S. hegemony, dominance and credibility in the post-Cold War geopolitical

order; the crisis of a global economy organized in the shadow of ongoing neoliberalisation; a range of structural or branch crises in important sectors (such as automobiles and agriculture); and the crisis of finance-dominated accumulation regimes. (Jessop, forthcoming, p. 17)

And while the crisis has passed through different stages and spread unevenly, our interest here is in whether, how, and in what ways, the crisis has destabilized the Bank's commitment to education development policy that has, as I have shown, been driven by market liberalism since the 1980s. In its opening remarks in its *New World, New World Bank Group (I) Post-Crisis Directions* published in April 2010, the Bank is confident that the worst of the crisis is behind it, but that new efforts are required in order move forward in this new world order. And while noting that "financial and supervisory failures lay at the heart of the financial failure" and that "effective government" (p. 4) is critical, its own role in advancing policies that have sought to limit state regulation is absent. Instead, the Report calls for an expanded role for the World Bank Group under what it refers to as "multilateral modernization" and a central role for the private sector in mechanisms such as PPPs, in order to meet the needs of the poor. Yet its own view of what is to be done continues to be shaped by an agenda that holds less regulation, rather than more, as the basis for competitiveness. It states:

Creating opportunities for private sector growth will be critical, particularly as stimulus packages wind down. A vibrant entrepreneurial private sector will be required to sustain growth. This will involve policy, technical and operational support for a broad competitiveness agenda to eliminate barriers and promote opportunities. (World Bank, 2010, p. 17)

It is this set of priorities that shape the Bank's Education Strategy 2020 report released in April 2011. Arguing that a "new" strategy is essential to help realize its goal for education—of ensuring "learning" in order to deliver a high quality knowledge base for economic development—the Bank sees both an important role for governments (p. 3) on the one hand, and an increased role for the IFC in education development (p. 31) on the other. In arguing that there are strong rationales for governments' promotion of education, including correcting for the failure of the market to invest sufficiently in education, and in ensuring access to those who cannot pay for education up front (p. 3), the Bank appears to recognize the limits of the market as a model for education development. Yet it also implicitly promotes a view that the state provides a safety net for those with insufficient resource to participate in the private sector.

A very significant innovation in the Report is the strong view around the reregulation of the education sector in what elsewhere I have referred to as the "resectoralization of education" (Robertson, 2011). In redefining the term "education system" to now include a wider range of actors—from "…national and local governments to private education providers, individuals and their families, communities, and non-profit and for-profit organizations" (World Bank, 2011), the door is effectively opened in a systemic way to the private sector.

The strengthening support for the privatizing of education is also evident in the expanded role for the IFC. It states:

> The main focus of IFC's education strategy is to provide financing for larger network providers who have the ability to invest across borders and go down-market to reach poorer populations; financing for education to small and medium enterprises which typically target poor populations and to students through partner banks; and advisory services to companies to support quality of education and to banks to ensure responsible lending to the sector. (World Bank, 2011, p. 16)

Despite these promises of pro-poor development, the IFC has been the target of considerable criticism because of its failure to meet the needs of the very poor. This then raises the question of what value it adds, particularly as many of the projects funded by the IFC do not have poverty or redistributional dimensions in their design. The Bretton Woods Project (2010, p. 3), a London-based watchdog organization that monitors Bank developments, argues that low income countries are concerned that IFC support goes mostly to a very few large projects and transnational investors, where the need for concessional financing is lower, and potential development benefits are smaller than in poorer countries and small and medium sized enterprises. They also point out that accountability and transparency are weak in the Bank's private sector work, and most of all for its expanding investments through financial intermediaries. The Independent Evaluation Group (IEG), the internal evaluation group within the Bank, has raised similar criticisms about the IFC and its failure to reach the very poor. Taken together, we can see that in the latest World Bank Education Strategy, far from reappraising neoliberal privatization, the crisis has created an opportune window for an expansion of this agenda. Like Colin Crouch (2011), we are encouraged to ask about the strange non-death of neoliberalism.

## THE STRANGE "NON-DEATH" OF PRIVATIZATION IN WORLD BANK EDUCATION POLICY

I have been arguing that neoliberalism as a political project, despite its manifest failings in the education development sector, for the moment at least, appears to animate further rounds of neoliberal invention over time (see Table 1).

Table 1. *The World Policies, Regimes, and the Privatization in/of Education*

| WB Education Policy | Report No. | Regime | Locating the "private" | Interpretation |
|---|---|---|---|---|
| *Education Policy Report 1970* | 1 | Rostovian/ Keynesian | Expansion of state-funded education | State-led manpower planning |
| *Education Policy Report 1975* | 2 | Rostovian/ Keynesian | Expansion of state-funded education | State-led manpower planning |
| *Education Sector Policy Paper 1980* | 3 | Washington Consensus | Fees, private schools, efficiency | Pockets of private within a distinct public private sector |
| *Education Sector 1999* | 4 | Post- Washington | "Public-Private Partnerships," competition/efficiency vouchers/nascent IFC | Blurring the boundary—using the private to discipline the public |
| *WB Group Education Strategy 2020* | 5 | New World Order/New World Bank | Redefining education *system* to include variety of actors/expanded role for IFC within WB group | Collapsing the boundary— redefining the education system to include the private "within" |

Understanding how this is the case and why, despite the current global crisis, neoliberalism is alive and well in World Bank education priorities is important for thinking through "what is to be done." As Peck argues, neoliberalism displays a certain level of "reproductive doggedness" (Peck, 2010, p. 28), in part because of its capacity to reinvent itself, and because of the relational spatialities of neoliberalism that continue to be embedded in a range of extra-local, transnational, and cross-scalar dynamics. In other words, and as I will elaborate shortly, neoliberal education projects have been advanced in national territorial and regional spaces which in turn reinforce the momentum and direction of the World Bank's privatizing of education policy. This is certainly the true regarding the Bank's persistence with neoliberalism as a paradigm. In addressing the question of "how," my analysis of the Bank's ongoing engagements with the privatization in/of education agenda highlights two broad dimensions: one strategic and the other structural.

*Strategically*, we can see how, over time, the Bank has used ongoing political and economic crises facing it to continue to reinvent its privatization of education agenda. We can see a number of different strategies and tactics being advanced, each triggered by crisis. To begin, we can see a shift from the Washington Consensus privileging of user-fees and private schools to the later advance of PPPs under a reinvented neoliberal post-Washington Consensus (though with free-market economics continuing to be the dominant logic guiding private provision and state funding), to the most recent iteration in *WBES 2020,* which redefines the meaning of an education system to now include, and enclose, the private sector (for profit/not for profit) as key actors *within*, as opposed to *outside* the education system. Each movement forward has expanded the ambit and agenda for the Bank, rather than closed it down.

Second, by pushing the privatization of education agenda out to a less familiar arm of the World Bank Group, the IFC, the Bank has deployed the tactic of "forum shifting" (Sell, 2009). Reflecting on the different ways in which the intellectual property agenda was tactically advanced through different UN agencies, including the WTO, Susan Sell notes:

> Forum-shifting can refer to several distinct dynamics, all of which are designed to yield preferred results by changing the game. Parties might move an agenda from one forum to another, exit a forum altogether (e.g. the US exiting UNESCO in the 1980s), or pursue agendas simultaneously in multiple forums. According to Peter Drahos, "forum shifting means that some negotiations are never really over." (2009, p. 1)

Similarly, for the Bank, "forum shifting" generates a new space and breathes new life into the controversial privatization of education agenda; it provides access to new resources, mobilizes new kinds of expertise, legitimizes its activity through viewing education as an "emerging market" in line with IFC objectives, and yet is able to remain less visible because of the fact that the IFC is not well known. Indeed most observers of Bank education policy tend to look at the activities of the International Bank of Reconstruction and Development (IBRD) as the space where education policy and programming is set rather than also the IFC.

The Bank manages knowledge in a very tactical way. First, it strategically deploys what I call "knowledge ventriloquism"—or what is an effort to create a virtuous circle between Bank "policy-research-evidence" and back again. In developing policy on the role of the private sector in education, the Bank tends to draw evidence from a very narrow menu of studies; either those commissioned and funded by the World Bank, or from work undertaken by its own small circle of education policy entrepreneurs and economists of education. By limiting what might count as evidence for policy, it in turn limits the potential challenges this evidence represents for ongoing policy-framing and policy-making and therefore for neoliberalism as an organizing paradigm. Second, it amplifies the evidence that supports the Bank's ideological position, on the one hand, and over-extends the particular pieces of evidence, on the other. For instance, the Bank's continued use of the education economist Ludger Wossmann's analysis of the OECD's PISA data (Patrinos et al., 2009) and the performance of students in private schools is repeatedly used to justify the expansion of private education. Yet there are many kinds of "private" education, some of it clearly not embedded in the same kinds of logics (competition/efficiency) that the Bank argues generates higher levels of student performance. The circle tightens even further when the Bank tends to over-generalize from limited pieces of evidence, take examples out of contest, or to smooth out differences in research findings. For example, in the chapter, "What Do We Know About Public-Private Partnerships in Education," from the Bank's report, *The Role and Impact of Public-Private Partnerships in Education* (Patrinos et al., 2009), the Bank displays a mixed picture of evidence; for instance, in many cases it is not possible to overcome problems of student and school selection, yet at the same time the Bank goes on to make strong claims about the efficiency and effectiveness of the private sector in education provision.

*Structurally*, not only has neoliberalism become embedded in a range of scales—from the local to the global—with the 2008 global crisis doing little to dislodge neoliberalism for the moment, but there is a deepening dependence by countries, such as the U.S. and U.K., on opening up services as the new value base for ongoing economic development. This is what Polanyi calls "economic institutedness" (Polanyi, 1992, p. 3) (in contrast to his concept of "embeddedness," meaning that markets are always in societies, not outside). What he means by this is that markets are instituted processes in that they are articulated through social institutions and legal and political strategies. Unpicking processes that have constituted, and constitutionalized, education as a market become particularly difficult, for it requires more than shifts in political ideas. Undoing whole ways of organizing an education economy, without significant disruptions to daily life, becomes more and more problematic.

For example, a specialist (increasingly corporate) industry has now sprung up around PPPs, particularly in those developed economies that have taken PPPs furthest (for instance, Australia, the U.K., U.S.). This industry, which increasingly exports its expertise globally, includes a rapidly growing number of private actors: specialist PPP firms, global consultancy firms, banks, local consultants, think-tanks, dedicated websites, rapid response teams, and specialist law firms, who increasingly act as market-oriented sources of authority that "establish rules, norms and institutions that guide the behavior of the participants, and affect the opportunities available to others" (Cutler et al., 1999, p. 4). This specialist PPP industry is then part of an emerging education services industry that includes an expanding number of education consultants operating globally and education management organizations, as well as education foundations and philanthropists engaged in shaping education policy and practice (Saltman, 2010). Similarly, a small cluster of large, powerful, global management firms also have large interests in PPPs. A small number of large companies (such as KMPG, PricewaterhouseCoopers, Deloitte and Touche, Grant Thornton, Ernst and Young, McKinsey, and the Hay Group) are engaged in PPPs; they also control almost half of the world's management consulting market (Saint-Martin, 1998; Hodge, 2006). All have major education portfolios. "For sheer expertise in the development of the legal frameworks concerning PPPs and the actual practice on the ground in leading countries, the global consultancy firms, given their superior knowledge of how PPPs are progressing, have few rivals" (Greve, 2010, p. 506). Saint-Martin argues it was not just the neoliberalism's good governance tools that account for this increase; it is also the openness of some governments to this kind of expertise (economic knowledge/accounting), and the permeability of the sector to outside experts: "There is a close relationship between the development of a given field of social knowledge—in our case management consultancy—and the openness of state institutions to the use of that knowledge" (Saint-Martin, 1998, p. 325). And it is here that governments, development agencies, such as the World Bank, IFC, the Asia Development Bank, along with the corporate consultants, have all played a critical role in shaping the conditions for the delivery of education by also constitutionalzing market liberalism in national territorial states' policies and regulatory frameworks. The term "consultocracy" is used to describe the power of consultants in advising government, and in shaping government policy. As Hodge (2006, p. 99) notes, the concern voiced through this label "is that the interests of profit-maximising management consultants may become the key determinants of managerialist policies." Given that these consultants are in some cases also the lawyers (Lovells & Lee, 2009) and auditors (Greve, 2010) of PPPs, these consulting relationships raise major concerns over conflicts of interest, transparency, and accountability.

There is also a vast and rapidly growing array of globalizing education companies, ranging from education consultants (such as Cambridge Education), education management organizations (for instance those operating charter schools in the U.S., or academies in the U.K.), and education corporations (like Laureate, Cisco Systems, deVry, Bridgewater, Edison Schools), to large conglomerate companies that have major holdings which include "education businesses," such as Apollo Global. All view the education sector as critical for offering a range of education services investment potentials, as long as the conditions are in place to realize profit-making (see, for example, Ball, 2007; Saltman, 2010; Hentschke et al., 2010).

How might we assess the rapid growth in private actors and their interests in a sector like education? Cutler's work on the legal implications of the blurring of the separation between private and public authority is compelling. Not only does she argue, like Gill (2003), that privileged rights of citizenship and representation are conferred on corporate capital, but that, as the state divests itself of activities we traditionally associate with the public sector and in the public interest, we can see an upward trend in the management of national, regional, and global affairs by economic—not state/political—actors (Cutler et al., 1999). Cutler calls this the rise of "private authority"; that is, when an individual or organization has decision-making power over a particular issue (p. 5). In the education sector, the state's ceding of the power to make decisions (as to how to frame the regulatory and operational basis of education activity) to economic actors (such as education corporations, consultant firms, and venture philanthropists), or those who do their bidding and bargaining (such as the World Bank and the IFC), represents a shift in authority from the public to the private realm, and from the national to the supra-national. This has significant implications for education, for societies, and for democracy (Crouch, 2011).

Yet there are contradictions in the Bank's privatization of education strategy. These include: the Bank's ventriloquism between policy and evidence, versus its insistence on robust evidence and knowledge-driven policy; the IFC's privatization projects, which it insists are pro-poor, yet the very poor have limited financial resources to spend on education as a commodity; that profits to education firms emerge from economies of scope and scale leading to standardization, but this undermines the basis for competitiveness which is dependent on innovation and creativity; the consolidation and expansion of firm activity across borders, which in turn undermines education's contribution to societal cohesion in national territorial states); pressures for the flexibility of teachers' labor, which in turn generates diminished professionalism and increased costs in teacher surveillance and accountability; the transformation of education into a commodity, which in turn generates debates around the political and social character of knowledge and education; and the governance of education through forms of private (unaccountable authority) versus the centrality of some form of democracy to ensure the ongoing rule and legitimacy of the state.

## ON WHAT IS TO BE DONE—BY WAY OF CONCLUSION

This chapter set out to explore, and explain, the strange non-death of neoliberalism in the World Bank Group's policy and programming in education. In viewing the Bank's engagements over time and as articulated in key reports, policies, and projects over the past decade, it is possible to trace out the ways in which the Bank has continued to strategically reinvent, and advance, this agenda in ways that contribute to the institutionalization of free market logics into the political, legal, and social structures within national and global regulatory architectures.

The question of what is to be done, then, is utmost in my mind and in this chapter. I believe that in many of our accounts of the privatization of education, we do not *sufficiently* develop an analytic approach that links the structural with the strategic; the local with multi-scalar articulations; actors and their agency; the maneuverings with failings and reinventions over time and space; or the "institutedness" of markets with the real work of constructing them. This is an intellectual project—but not one I see as the preserve of those within the academy. Rather, we must use our privileged space as organic intellectuals for the left to generate insights into the highly complex place of education in our societies and insist that education is political because it is about life chances and life changes. It is *more than* a human right, or just a system through which official knowledge is transmitted and acquired. It is also *more than* a public good. It is a highly contested space whose necessary "publicness" and "emancipatory" potential matters for our future, but whose very capacity to deliver on these are placed into question.

## REFERENCES

Ball, S. (2007). *Education plc: Private sector participation in public sector education*. London: Routledge.7

Bonal, X. (2002). Plus ça change .... The World Bank global education policy and the post-Washington consensus. *International Studies in Sociology of Education, 12*(1), 3-22.

Berger, M. & Beeson, M. (1998). Lineages of liberalism and miracles of modernisation: The World Bank, the East Asian trajectory and the international development debate. *Third World Quarterly, 19*(3), 487-504.

Bretton Woods Project (2010). *The World Bank and the International Finance Corporation: Bretton Woods project input into the DfID multilateral review*. London: Bretton Woods Project.

Crouch, C. (2011). *The strange non-death of neoliberalism*. Cambridge: Polity.

Cutler, A. C., Hauflter, V., & Porter, T. (1999). *Private authority and international affairs*. New York: State University of New York Press.

Gewirtz, S., Ball, S., & Bowe, R. (1995). *Markets, choice and equity in education*. Basingstoke: Open University Press.

Gill, S. (2003). *Power and resistance in the new world order*. London: Palgrave

Greve, C. (2010). The global public-private partnership industry. In G. Hodge, C. Greve, & A. Boardman (Eds.), *International handbook on public-private partnerships*. Cheltenham: Edward Elgar.

Hall, S. (1979, January). The Great Moving Right Show. *Marxism Today*.

Harrison, G. (2001). Administering market friendly growth? Liberal populism and the World Bank's involvement in administrative reform in sub-Saharan Africa. *Review of International Political Economy, 8*(3), 528-547

Harrison, G. (2005). Economic faith, social project and a misreading of African society: The travails of neoliberalism in Africa. *Third World Quarterly, 26*(8), 1303-1320.

Harvey, D. (2005). *A brief history of neoliberalism*. Oxford University Press: Oxford.

Hatcher, R. (2006). Privatization and sponsorship: The re-agenting of the school system in England. *Journal of Education Policy, 21*(5), 599-619.

Hentschke, G., Lechuga, V., & Tierney, W. (Eds.). (2010). *For-profit colleges and universities*. Virginia: Stylus.

Hobsbawm, E. (1994). *Age of extremes: The short twentieth century 1914-1991*. London: Abacus.

Hodge, G. (ed.) (2006). *Privatisation and market development: Global movements in public policy ideas*. Cheltenham, England: Edward Elgar.

Hodge, G., Greve, C., & Boarman, A. (2010). Conclusions: public private partnerships—International experiences and future challenges. In G. Hodge, C. Greve, & A. Boardman (Eds.), *International handbook on public-private partnerships*. Cheltenham: Edward Elgar.

Klees, S. (2002). World Bank Education policy: New rhetoric, old ideology. *International Journal of Educational Development, 22*, 451-74.

Klees, S. (2008). A quarter of a century of neoliberal thinking in education: Misleading analyses and failed policies. *Globalisation, Societies and Education, 6*(4), 311-348.

ILO. (2004). *A fair globalization: Creating opportunities for all, the World Commission on the social dimensions of globalization*. Geneva: ILO.

Ilon, L. (1994). Structural adjustment and education—Adapting to a growing global market. *International Journal of Education and Development, 14*(2), 95-108.

Molnar, A. (2006). The commercial transformation of public education. *Journal of Education Policy, 21*(5), 621-40.

Jones, P. (2007). *World Bank financing of education: Lending, learning and development*, 2nd ed. London: Routledge.

Jessop, B. (forthcoming). Imagined recoveries, recovered imaginaries: a cultural political economy perspective. *Economy and Society*.

Lovells, H. (2009). *PPP projects in the education sector—Key principles.*
http://www.hoganlovells.co.uk/files/Publication/bb9e9af9-213c-4568-87c0-
769e1c3e069a/Presentation/PublicationAttachment/94598918-0d93-4526-a06b-
86abc1d630fb/PPP_projects_in_the_education_sector_-_key_principles_-_Sept_11.pdf [last
accessed 9 Nov 2011]

Newman, J. (2001). *Modernising governance.* London: Sage.

Patrinos, H., Barrera Osorio, F., & Guáqueta, J. (2009). *The role and impact of public-private
partnerships in education,* Washington, D.C.: World Bank.

Peck, J. (2010). *Constructions of neoliberal reason.* Oxford: Oxford University Press.

Polanyi, K. (1992). The economy as an instituted process. In M. Granovetter & R. Swedburg (Eds.),
*The sociology of economic life.* Boulder: Westview Press.

Rodrik, D. (2011). *The globalization paradox: Why markets, states and democracy can't co-exist.*
Oxford: Oxford University Press.

Robertson, S., Bonal, X., & Dale, R. (2002). GATS and the education service industry. *Comparative
Education Review, 46*(4), 472-96.

Robertson, S. (2011). The new spatial politics of (re)bordering and (re)ordering the state-education-
citizen relation. *International Review of Education, 57*(3-4), 277-297.

Saint-Martin, D. (1998). The new managerialism and the policy influence of consultants in government:
An historical-institutionalist analysis of Britain, Canada and France. *Governance, International
Journal of Policy and Administration, 11*(3), 319-356.

Saltman, K. (2010). *The gift of education: Public education and venture philanthropy.* New York:
Palgrave.

Samoff, J. (1994). Coping with crisis: Austerity, adjustment and human resources. London/New York:
Cassell with UNESCO.

Sell, S. (2009). Cat and mouse: Forum shifting in the battle over intellectual property enforcement.
Paper presented at the American Political Science Association Meeting, September 3-6, 2009,
Toronto.

Verger, A. (forthcoming). Framing and selling global education policy: The promotion of public-private
partnerships for education in low-income contexts. *Journal of Education Policy.*

Wade, R. H. (2004). On the causes of increasing world poverty and inequality, or why the Matthew
effect prevails. *New Political Economy, 9*(2), 163-188.

Williamson, J. (1993). Democracy and the "Washington consensus." *World Development, 21,* 1329-
1336.

World Bank. (1999). *Education sector strategy.* Washington: The World Bank Group.

World Bank. (2001). *PPPs—A toolkit.* Washington: The World Bank Group.

World Bank. (2010). *New world, new world banking group: (I) Post crisis directions.* Washington: The
World Bank Group.

World Bank (2011). *Learning for all: Investing in people's knowledge and skills to promote
development.* World Bank Group Education Strategy 2020. Washington: The World Bank Group.

*Susan L. Robertson*
*Centre for Globalisation, Education and Societies*
*University of Bristol, U.K.*

# PART IV

# RESHAPING THE FUTURE

## CHAPTER 14

ANNE HICKLING-HUDSON AND
STEVEN J. KLEES

# ALTERNATIVES TO THE WORLD BANK'S STRATEGIES FOR EDUCATION AND DEVELOPMENT

## INTRODUCTION

Over the past several decades, policy has become increasingly global. In economics, for example, policy has followed the so-called Washington Consensus of privatization, liberalization, and deregulation. In education, global policy has included the proliferation of strategies including standardized testing, paraprofessional teachers, user fees, and privatization. There are many problems with these neoliberal policies. Foremost among them, is the havoc they wreak on the lives of so many children and adults. Poverty, inequality, and myriad associated problems have reached new heights in this neoliberal era. Moreover, these policies have been adopted uncritically and alternative policies have been ignored, which leads to our focus here.

The World Bank is the major architect in formulating a global education policy and has been so for decades (King, 2007; Klees, this volume). The World Bank likes to think that its policy recommendations are evidence-based, implying objectivity and impartiality. This is simply not true. The Bank does sometimes provide evidence to support its views but it is evidence from only one side of the political spectrum, mostly using research generated internally or by hired consultants. The World Bank's premises are ideologically-based as are its conclusions (Klees, this volume). Even its staff talk of the "thought police" inside the Bank that force conformity (Broad, 2006). For more than 30 years, this ideology has been neoliberalism and World Bank policy recommendations all followed from this. It is not a "knowledge bank" but a biased "opinion bank," and one with monopoly power.

Once a decade or so the Bank produces a statement about its education policy. The most recent, the World Bank's (2011) Education Strategy 2020 (*WBES 2020*, hereafter), builds on past neoliberal approaches. In this chapter, we pay some attention to *WBES 2020*, but look more broadly at some alternatives to Bank education and development strategy. We depart from the idea that the Bank is so ideologically compromised, in education and in general, that it should be shut down. We would argue instead that a new democratic and participatory international process needs to be initiated to devise a new global aid architecture, in general, and, specifically, a replacement for the World Bank. In education, we posit the development of a Global Fund for Education (GFE) that channels grant and loan money from the North to the South.[i]

This chapter does not discuss the organizational and operational structure of a new GFE. This would require a paper in itself and that would be only a starting point since such a structure must be the outcome of contestation and negotiation by the parties involved on a global scale. Nonetheless, some organizational features of a GFE might include: a Secretariat made up of tripartite representation by donor countries, recipient countries, and civil society; proposal review panels that recognize that "best practice" needs to be debated, and therefore the appointment of panel members who reflect a variety of positions; and country level committees composed of government and civil society representatives.[ii]

What this chapter does is suggest some alternative policy approaches, principles, premises, and conclusions that might substantively guide a new GFE. For decades, the Bank has provided one undebated set of policies shaped by its ideology. Alternatives to those policies are hardly ever considered by the Bank. Yet alternatives abound. We are by no means exhaustive here; our purpose is to suggest that other education and development policy directions are both feasible and sensible.

## THE RIGHT TO EDUCATION

A GFE would take as its central principle the right to education (Vally & Spreen, this volume). All grants and loans would be assessed, at least in part, on the extent to which they further the right to education. This is directly contrary to the stance of the Bank, which aside from a brief mention in some of its reports, ignores the implications of the right to education (e.g., World Bank, 2011). Indeed, its human capital approach, which evaluates education instrumentally in terms of achieving economic growth and other goals, contradicts a rights-based approach that sees education as an end in itself (Klees, this volume; Tomasevski, 2003).

Taking the right to education as a central principle would represent a major transformation in global education policy. Narrow and inherently distorted measures of cost-effectiveness and rates of return would be rejected (Klees, 2008b). While a focus on the right to education is relatively new, there has been considerable work done on what that right should mean in practice. UNESCO and UNICEF now base their design of education practice and policy on the right to education. ActionAid has helped develop the Right-to-Education Project (2011), a comprehensive look at a rights-based education, building on the pioneering work of the late Katarina Tomasevski while she was the U.N. High Commission for Human Rights' Special Rapporteur for the right to education (Klees &Thapliyal, 2007; Tomasevski, 2003, 2006).

Substantively, implementing the right to education would utilize Tomasevski's four As framework that moved the discussion beyond issues of access. Availability centers on the government's obligation to provide free and compulsory primary schooling. Accessibility must be provided, as it is often impeded by a variety of factors (even though schooling may be nominally available), including cost, gender, race, disability, and others. Acceptability focuses on the quality of education, which may include tackling diverse issues such as indigenous and minority rights, language of instruction, textbook censorship, unregulated privatization, inadequate spending, and teachers' rights (Tomasevski, 2006, pp. 69-99). Adaptability "requires schools to adapt to children following the yardstick of the best interests of each child in the Convention on the Rights of the Child" (Tomasevski, 2003, p. 52).

The Right-to-Education Project (2011) added a category Governance to the four As and has developed an inventory of over 200 indicators of the right to education. Its approach goes beyond primary school to include analysis of the implications of the right to education for secondary, tertiary, and nonformal education. As Tomasevski (2003, p. 53) pointed out, international agreements state that "post-compulsory education was to be made progressively available and accessible."

A rights-based approach would drastically change education policy. For example, instead of being satisfied with an average class size of 40 students—which masks many much larger classes—a class size maximum might be targeted. Instead of recommending untrained, inexperienced contract teachers, as the World Bank has been doing, the right to education implies that each student gets a qualified teacher. Instead of girls being subject to patriarchal schools, teachers, curriculum, and governance, schools would have to be "girl friendly." Of course, there are no instant solutions or clearly agreed upon criteria for the right to education. However, moving from the economics base of the Bank to a rights base changes the dialogue. It changes priorities, it changes what indicators are considered, and it changes how alternatives are evaluated.

## EDUCATION AND DEVELOPMENT

As part of the global debate, the new Global Fund for Education would be committed to exploring and supporting approaches to economics and education that are socially fairer and that contribute to environmental protection and sustainability (Daly, 1996; MacEwan, 1999; Yates, 2003). A GFE would reject the excesses of the neoliberal model of "development" that has been imposed on developing countries in order to drag them into the dominant "free-trade" arrangements that demand ever-greater privatization, the reduction or cutting of social welfare services, and the removal of protection for infant industries. The result has been that the industrial development of weaker countries in the world system has been thwarted or distorted while they have been flooded with the goods, industries and services of a few, dominant countries. While this approach has contributed to employment and economic improvement for some, it has more strongly contributed to perpetuating poverty, stagnation, or excessive pollution and exploitation in cases where multinational industry is seeking the cheapest labor force. Indeed, the gap between wealthy and poor, both within and between countries, is bigger than at any other time in history. Some scholars criticize the free trade model that now dominates, and advocate a certain amount of protectionism for infant industries in poor countries to give them a chance to develop (Reinert, 2007). Others advocate that countries should strive for a "post-development" model where consumerism is reduced so that the economy, while enabling people to live in reasonable comfort, ceases to devastate the planet (Esteva, 2010).

The Bank in past strategy reports has argued that "advances in literacy and other learning may well have done more to improve the human condition than any other public policy" (World Bank, 1999, p. 17). However, the GFE team members would explain the limitations of this argument. They would show how in many countries it may well be that economic development has stimulated widespread literacy and higher levels of education rather than vice versa. But when economic development is thwarted by the injustices of the global and national capitalism that maintains neo-colonial structures of exploitation and inequality, then educational modernization and expansion cannot be expected to be the main instrument for development (Hickling-Hudson, 2002).

In a crisis-ridden, decaying economy, improved education may only result in the twin problems of educated unemployment[iii] and a large migration of expensively educated people to the rich world. Only a strong economy and polity will be able to use surplus educated people, at home and overseas, as a source of strength. This is not to say that universal literacy and higher levels of education are not important goals. Rather, it is to stress that literacy and increased education cannot be seen as the panacea that will lead impoverished countries and societies into Western-style "progress." The fact is that neo-colonial economies are so deeply distorted and constrained by the injustices of international capitalism—deepened by the contradictions of globalization—as well as by internal inefficiencies, that it would take much more than higher levels of literacy and education to tackle economic problems. Improved education is only one component of a wider approach to change, and the GFE would support those who advocate that the structures of industry, production, finance, and commerce be altered to support a higher degree of international justice for recently independent countries with weak economies (Spring, 1998, 2004; Ng, 2006; Mundy, 2008).

## THE STRUCTURE OF EDUCATION

Another part of the debate has to be about the type of education system that the World Bank takes for granted and promotes. Challenging this, the GFE teams would promote analyses of the limitations of the Western-style education system that developing countries inherited from their colonial eras. They show that expanding this system and making it more "efficient" according to World Bank prescriptions is not necessarily the answer to economic and other problems (Hickling-Hudson, 2002).

Fundamentally problematic is the way in which the traditional curriculum and examination system stratifies school-based literacies and perpetuates social inequality. From this viewpoint, "literacies" refer to text-based skills, understandings, and ways of learning that are more specific than the generic term "knowledge". This combination of concepts helps us to visualize how inequity is structured and perpetuated through learning. Literacies are understood as discourses of knowledge into which people are initiated according to their socio-economic status, gender, and race (Hickling-Hudson, 2007). Education systems provide these discourses, which include domains that are epistemic (focusing on literary, artistic, mathematical, and scientific academic knowledge), humanist (cultural knowledge and confidence), and public (knowledge comprising social and political know-how). Since Western style schooling is deeply stratified by social class, gender, and ethnicity, it places people on different tracks or channels in the education hierarchy. This initiates some into dominant literacies in each domain, and this is used to justify their continuance in elite positions. Others are denied this initiation. Instead, they are shunted into the less adequate, often grossly under-resourced and neglected education channels that provide subordinate literacies, which are then penalized as being of inferior worth and status in the society.

When a political process is serious about putting in place change with equity, it has to learn how to change the stratified nature of these literacies (Hickling-Hudson, 2007). However, most countries that inherited from their colonizers the fundamentally inequitable model of stratified literacies have not decolonized sufficiently to change. Changing social class stratification is notoriously difficult. Most societies have entrenched the privilege of the best schooling for students whose families can afford to pay private school fees. This putative "private" schooling is usually highly subsidized by the government. The education system becomes a pyramid in which a minority elite at the apex enjoys the dominant and privileged literacies supported by a combination of private fees and public subsidies, while the majority at lower levels of the pyramid are provided with government schools or with low-status community education which operate on much lower levels of resources. This results in the perpetuation of a curriculum that inculcates subordinate and inferior literacies for those who cannot afford to pay for the best schooling. Some countries have improved government schooling, and have widened access to the best private schools through scholarships, but these improvements rarely result in conditions of equity between private and public schools.

Expanding the existing model of schooling, when so many problems are inherent in it, would obviously be counterproductive. Changing the stratified nature of the literacies taught through education is the nub of the problem. The GFE would argue that it would be far better to invest in making sweeping changes throughout the school system rather than in expanding the existing one it in all its manifest dysfunctionality.

The modernist, industrial model of the school needs to be changed. The age-graded structure of schooling and the lock-stepped curriculum constrains learning.

213

School experiments in some countries are challenging this rigidity by organizing students in multi-age groupings according to interest and competence in settings where teaching and learning are made more flexible through the use of the new media and information technology. Some schools in Australia, for example, are putting in place flexible and open learning spaces without walls, housing between 80 and 200 children and up to six teachers. There is a core national curriculum in each discipline area, which students must master. Using cutting-edge information and communication technology, they take a greater role than before in educating themselves and each other (Overington, 2011). At the same time, recognizing the need for structure in learning, teachers can inculcate students into the mastery of epistemic, humanist, and public literacies, including music and other areas of the creative arts in which discipline, challenge, and creativity are combined. It is possible to move schooling towards emulating examples of the world's best schools that nurture and develop the talents of all students (Caldwell, 2008) rather than miring them in curricula which they find boring, irrelevant, and even humiliating if they are of a cultural group maligned by Western ideological distortions (Willinsky, 1998). Educators involved in the development of ICTs would ensure that the content of programs developed for learning through ICTs included a range of perspectives rather than narrow views shaped by the pressures of the private corporations that make fortunes out of school texts. They would also need to monitor and counter the possible negative aspects of ICTs, including increased authoritarian control of ideology and data surveillance, the reduction of the role of teachers, and the danger of shallow digital learning (Spring, 2011).

Another deep problem hindering the building of a better society is the failure of the traditional modernist school curriculum to combine general and vocational studies in such a way as to prepare students for, and engage them in, the tasks of holistic and sustainable social and economic development. The curriculum in the model of schooling underlying the Bank's prescriptions is this modernist one, characterized by historical status divisions between the academic and the vocational. The problematic situation of teachers contributes to this unacceptable system, in that most governments have failed to provide a high level of qualification, recognition, and professional development that would help the bulk of the teachers utilize the best of epistemological, pedagogical, and technological possibilities to improve the educational experience. It is possible to change the curriculum so as to achieve a productive convergence of the academic and vocational strands, a curriculum that achieves genuine convergence between study and practical work in a seamless web of learning (Hickling-Hudson & Ferreira, 2004).

The new approach to learning would not be constrained by the Western industrial and hierarchical model of education that was established globally through European colonialism and perpetuated by global agencies like the World Bank. Changing ideas about educational goals and structures could be debated and experimented with through improving access to Internet infrastructure and e-learning. The new structures and forms of education would provide people with high-quality learning during childhood, adolescence, and adulthood, according to their interests and talents. This new structure would involve collaborative pedagogical networks for subject teaching as well as interdisciplinary learning, a variety of apprenticeships for practical learning, an immersion in the creative arts and additional languages, and a facility with media and information technology. Preparing educators would be a priority, so countries would be assisted to improve teachers' qualifications, attend to their regular in-service development, encourage their professional associations, and give priority to a reasonable level of pay and conditions.

With education now seen as a human right, some of the additional resources would be spent on areas such as higher education and adult education that have been neglected by the Bank's imposition of narrowly conceived priorities. Each country would put in place the necessary infrastructure to support and develop the various stages of education. The goal of lifelong learning would not primarily be to support economic growth, but would intertwine the goals of enabling people to earn a living, enjoy and benefit from "the best that has been thought and said" globally, and develop a sharp ability to critique information and ideologies. This more reflective education would facilitate people in making an informed contribution to developing sustainable and harmonious societies.

## GLOBALIZATION AND CONSUMERISM

The World Bank supports a global economy based on open markets where people and companies compete to maximize their economic returns. Its educational goals envisage a world in which people gain skills that enable them to thrive in this competitive global economy, and are socialized into flexibility and an adaptability to change in a world "where tradition is replaced by the instability of market economies and the migration of businesses and people" (Spring, 2004, p. 49). The industrial and consumerist paradigm stressed by the World Bank and many nation states results in events being evaluated according to their effect on economic growth and the opportunity to consume. In this model, "the hidden curriculum of schools is the imparting to students an industrial and consumerist paradigm" (Spring, 2004, p. 165).

It seems obvious that this paradigm "will not and cannot provide the best life for all the world's peoples" (Spring, 2004, p. 167), given differences in military power, the limits on natural resources, the inability of the Earth to handle industrial wastes, and the uneven outcomes of the globalization of the market economy including ever larger gaps between the wealthy and the poor, increased exploitation of labor, and growing ecological devastation. Environmental destruction threatens the basic human right to life and, therefore, students should have the right to choose opportunities for biosphere education and active global citizenship which would help them to safeguard the planet (Spring, 2004, pp. 139-163).Helping indigenous peoples and guaranteeing them the right to preserve, develop, and teach their holistic knowledge of nature would be a necessary antidote to a history that has forced them into a Eurocentric education that ignores or distorts non-European perspectives (Madjidi & Restoule, 2008; Nakata, 2004).

The right to maintain chosen elements of traditional culture would, at the same time, need to be balanced by the recognition of universal human rights and decisions about how to secure these rights, particularly for women and children.

An educational alternative to the consumerist market paradigm is arguably necessary to give people the opportunity to choose to be educated in global citizenship of a kind that challenges and eschews unsustainable consumption. Our Global Fund for Education would see it as only fair to require that teachers and students be taught these alternative educational ideologies and their implications. "Human rights educators tend to emphasize the protection of local cultures and languages. Human rights doctrines include the right to one's own culture and language. Environmental educators consider traditional knowledge as a source for understanding sustainable patterns of living and community organization" (Spring, 2004, p. 166). In an alternative vision for education, there would be many teachers and schools that would promote multicultural and global perspectives, postcolonial understandings (Hickling-Hudson, 2010, 2011), planetist ideas (Ellyard, 1999), and futures studies (Hicks & Slaughter, 1998; Slaughter, 2004).

## CURRICULUM AND ASSESSMENT

The World Bank Education Strategy calls for a "learning for all" strategy but it is really about "testing for all" (Klees, this volume). The GFE would recognize that testing carried out in the currently dominant, narrow, standardized way perpetuates social stratification and abstract learning. Approaches to authentic assessment would include applied project learning that is assessed not through standardized testing, but through a variety of methods including the appraisal of individual and collective portfolios (Barton & Collins, 1997). An interesting model experimented with by an Australian state in the first decade of the 21$^{st}$ century was that of "productive pedagogies" in which innovative teams of local teachers in selected schools restructured the curriculum around four new interdisciplinary areas of learning:

- Life pathways and social futures
- Multiliteracies, numeracies, and communications media
- Active citizenship
- Environments and technologies

Students were asked to do a series of "rich tasks," about seven each year, to demonstrate what they had learned by studying these areas. These tasks challenged students to work and study with intense intellectual engagement to tackle life-world issues and problems, and were assessed at both individual and collective levels. Examples of "rich tasks" involved such activities as the following:

- preparing a plan and taking some action to assist in the survival of an endangered animal or plant or to help reduce pollution
- designing or improving, making, and developing a marketing plan for a product that added to the quality of healthy lives

– discussing and critiquing issues of product design, service delivery, and marketing techniques.

The "Productive Pedagogies" experiment was successful in the pilot schools (Lingard et al., 2003), yet it was not widely adopted. By 2010, the state directed schools to return to much narrower modes of testing driven by the introduction of a centralized national curriculum.

It will indeed be difficult to change the centuries-old subject-divided curriculum traditions in favor of a more flexible, interdisciplinary model. The categories analyzed by Hickling-Hudson (2010) in considering curriculum in postcolonial contexts draw our attention to trends of change that tackle colonial inheritances of systemic inequity, assessment, representations of cultural identity, race and gender issues, the interlinking of knowledge with European languages of instruction, and historically distorted interpretations of the curriculum. Our proposed Global Fund for Education would assist the process of experimenting with curriculum change by widespread communication about the achievements of innovative schools, and by encouraging learning designed to promote excellence along the lines of the multiple intelligences, multiliteracies, and biosphere education emphasized by various scholars (Gardner, 1983; Bowers, 2001; Spring, 2004; Healy, 2008). More varied and dynamic assessment to develop creativity would be an integral part of redesigning learning—for example assessment by portfolio, media productions, performances, quiz shows, problem-solving initiatives, workplace innovation, inventions, and sustainable product design. The problems inherent in the old style of exam-bound competitiveness would be highlighted. As Meadmore points out (2004, p. 34), "Rather than enhancing learning, external examinations can inhibit it by delimiting the curriculum and reducing pedagogy to fit examination requirements." Assessment would be redesigned to build in creativity, collaboration, and teamwork in solving local and global problems.

The recognition and exploration of these problems would be more likely if we organized education for "conscientization" along lines developed by Paulo Freire in the last third of the 20th century (Freire, 1970; Bickmore, 2008). Freire and his colleagues organized adult learners into dialogical culture circles in which they left behind the passivity and rhetoric of the traditional classroom. Instead, they discussed the interaction between individual, societal and global problems and sought ways of tackling problems through praxis, a process of reflection through dialogue, putting theories into practice, and engaging in further collaborative reflection until acceptable solutions were arrived at (Hickling-Hudson, 1988). It is surely this kind of "education as communication praxis" that holds some hope of helping all involved in education to tackle the urgent global problems of vast wealth juxtaposed with grinding poverty, environmental devastation caused by the cancer of overconsumption, and the continual escalation of political conflict, violence, and war.

The valuing of gender fairness would also be built into the new-style curriculum, so that boys and girls would not be constrained by the gender inequity inherent in the old model of schooling. This would necessitate a collaborative consideration of what aspects of culture need to change in order to sustain agreed norms of equity for women, ethnic groups, and groups suffering various forms of social disadvantage. After all, new norms for education can seriously destabilize traditional culture. To tackle these issues, new forms of family and community organization might have to be experimented with and agreed upon in order to modify traditional patriarchal ideologies, household customs, and child rearing.

## QUALITY AND EQUITY

A GFE will need to struggle with the complex interrelationships between educational quality and educational equity. *WBES 2020* mentions educational quality numerous times but considers it separately from equity and offers a narrow and instrumental view: "[I]nvestments in quality education lead to more rapid and sustainable economic growth and development .... Quality needs to be the focus of education, with learning gains as a key metric of quality" (pp. v, 4). The World Bank's previous strategy paper offered a little more: a slightly broader definition of improving quality ("detectable gains in the knowledge, skills and values acquired by students," 1999, p. 7). But its assumptions about what would lead to educational quality (1999, pp. 29-35) were inadequate because the question of equity was not addressed. The 1999 document singled out the following areas as being likely to have a big impact on the quality of teaching and learning: expanding early childhood education, decentralizing school governance, using new technologies, and upgrading the school curriculum, especially for girls and for the poorest. But, other than through narrow testing regimes, it spelt out no way of determining what would show that the upgraded and decentralized product and its delivery through new technologies was as good as the education being received by students in a country's traditionally best, elite schools. Not to specify what quality means in the recommended strategies empties the word "quality" of meaning. The 1999 document implied neither quality in the sense of equity, nor quality in the sense of equality (Farrell, 2008, pp. 158-159). It implied, instead, a restricted idea of quality as the "improvement" of the existing system, an expansion of education for the poor, especially for girls, making it somewhat "better" than previously.

Current strategies, even if they improve education compared to what has gone before, will not lead to educational quality, and do not establish anything like educational equity. Improving education in the way the World Bank advocates is token, in the sense that even if it improves narrow measures of learning outcomes, it will not address the inequality that distorts so many education systems. It will almost certainly not bring about the amazing outcomes of "greater economic competitiveness, lower poverty and inequality, stronger democratic institutions, and greater social stability" (World Bank, 1999, pp. 33-34) so often flagged in World Bank documents.

How might it look to experiment with working towards educational equity? Cuba attracts a high level of international controversy over its political system, but the commitment of that system to working for the common good has made it one of the few low-income countries in which a government has made significant progress on this path. The result is that it has built one of the most successful education systems in the global South (Spring 2004; Carnoy et al., 2007). The Cuban strategies that differ from those used by most wealthy Western countries are its abolition of private schooling and of single-sex schooling, and the provision of free vocational and tertiary education for its citizens as well as for thousands of foreign students who are given full scholarships to study in Cuba (Hickling-Hudson, 2009). Other strategies may be more familiar: the expansion of educational infrastructure, the utilization of a core national curriculum and examination system, the requirement that all teachers have a five-year degree which includes training in pedagogical research, the provision of regular periods of in-service professional development for teachers, and free school meals and equipment (Martin-Sabina et al., 2012). The combination of strategies that pushed for equity and excellence resulted in pivotal and deep-rooted change in Cuba. Some of these strategies would not currently be considered feasible in many societies, and if considered and accepted, implementation would be highly contested. However, the GFE, in order to encourage the building of an education model to promote social justice, would need to help nations work out strategies that could more effectively bring about conditions necessary for equity.

Our proposed new Global Fund for Education will decide on criteria to determine the extent to which the educational strategies that it funds are pushing forward quality with equity in the education system. We posit that in global debates promoted by the GFE, agreement could be reached that the following sets of criteria are important indicators of quality:

1) Equity must be demonstrated by showing that the "literacies" being provided at whatever level and in whatever aspect of the system are *not of a subordinate type,* but as valuable, as dominant, and as powerful as the literacies being taught to elites.

2) Schools will demonstrate quality by providing programs for all students to develop their "multiple intelligences" along lines advocated by Howard Gardner (1983), their "multiliteracies" (Healy, 2008), and their "planetism" (Ellyard, 1999) to suit new conditions of learning in the global age. These programs would be assessed in broad and creative ways, as discussed above.

3) The third criterion is about comprehensive, problem-solving education. Schools would have to show that they were combining general, technological, and vocational studies for all students rather than selecting out some for academic-only and some for vocational-only pathways.

4) Education systems would demonstrate their implementation of strategies towards quality by equivalent resourcing of schools and equivalent training of teachers.

All of this would, of course, necessitate a complete restructuring of the curricula and of teacher education. It would mean talking about education of high quality not only in terms of strategies and institutions but, additionally, in terms of values, culture, and substance. Quality would integrally involve equity in its definition.

Assessment would evaluate not only student work, but also the extent to which countries are improving education by pursuing the criteria characterizing a system that combines quality with equity.

## PRIVATE VS. PUBLIC INTEREST

A principle that would govern the GFE educational policy is to act in the public interest. This is meant to counteract over three decades of a push toward privatization in education led by the World Bank. User fees, charters, vouchers, and other efforts to finance and/or rely on private interests would be minimized. This position rejects the twisted, abstract logic that the "invisible hand" governing the private sector operates in the public interest. To the contrary, we argue that private provision of education leads society to ignore the many externalities, inequalities, and public goods that public schooling can respond to. There is no evidence that private schools perform significantly better than public schools for similar students (Klees, 2008a). Principal-agent theory, used to argue that public sector workers do not have the public interest at heart, is narrowly ideological. It ignores the reality that teachers, school administrators, and most public sector workers enter their jobs with a commitment to public service. We need mechanisms that take this broad commitment to public service and translate it into a participatory policymaking structure rather than follow past efforts to find narrow and mechanical ways to control teachers, administrators, and students.

What this principle means in practice must be worked out on the ground with broad democratic participation. It probably does not mean prohibiting private schooling, although some countries, like Finland and Cuba, follow this route in order to equalize educational opportunities. If not prohibited, private schooling for the wealthy will continue to exist as they search for ways to pass on their advantages to their children. A goal of public education would be to make the quality sufficient to attract most people to public schooling. So-called "low-cost private schools for the poor" would quickly disappear if free, high quality public schooling were available. Strategies could include a large increase in the material resources to public, non fee-paying schools, and the promotion and support of excellent programs and highly qualified teachers who could be attracted with extra incentives to teach in the schools that need most help. Since it is unlikely to be politically acceptable for current elites in most countries to agree to end the system of private schooling, perhaps governments could at least insist, in return for the subsidies that they routinely give to private schools, that the most successful ones be made the hub of a cluster of public schools that would share their resources and programs.

For primary and secondary education, a GFE should generally not subsidize private schooling. However, the efforts of and joint ventures with civil society organizations (CSOs) might be subsidized. Most CSOs have a strong public service orientation and many have been very innovative at the local level in education and other areas (Hoff & Hickling-Hudson, 2010). We are not endorsing the talk of a "third way"; that is, giving CSOs a position of prominence between public and private in building a new, more just society. Our position is that governments are key; CSOs can innovate and help make a dialog more participatory, but it falls to the public sector to bring innovations to scale and to develop legitimate decision-making processes. Nonetheless, CSOs can be very important to education policy development and, as such, should be integrally included in a GFE mandate.

The situation with post-secondary education is particularly complex. During the neoliberal era, privatization has resulted in an increase in post-secondary education. Private training institutions, colleges, and universities have proliferated, expanding access, but often to the detriment of quality (Klees, 2008a). Given this context, a GFE should address the need to strengthen public post-secondary education, which has been weakened over the past three decades.

## EVIDENCE, DEBATE, AND DECISION-MAKING

A GFE would reject simplistic calls for "research- or evidence-based policy." The way the World Bank and many others use this phrase is false. They are not calling for "evidence," they are calling for their evidence. Such calls are simplistic because they have a simplistic view of what such calls mean and what evidence means, tied to a belief in a straightforward process through which evidence tells you what to do, We are not saying that a GFE rejects calls for evidence but that it rejects such simplistic ones. What these calls have gotten us is not a reliance on research but a reliance on neoliberal ideology and handpicked "evidence" to support that ideology. The Bank turns that ideology into educational policy decisions for literally billions of people. Instead, to the contrary, a principle that would govern a GFE would be to rely on debate and participation in research and decision-making. Bank reports have long been criticized for overwhelming reliance on research done at the Bank or by its consultants (Broad, 2006; Stromquist, this volume). Research has been almost exclusively quantitative, ignoring quantitative research that disagrees with Bank conclusions and ignoring research based on other traditions such as qualitative and transformative (Mertens, 2010). The result has been to ignore controversy and debate. This is unjust, unscholarly, and undemocratic.

This problem goes far beyond the Bank. In the post-World War II era, there was growing belief in the power of positivist research methods and their embodiment in the policy "sciences." Over time, there has been an increasingly strong critique of positivist assumptions. This is based on the understanding that there is not a single objective truth out there that gives firm guidance about policy choices. Instead, even positivist, quantitative research gives multiple and contradictory answers to policy questions. Adding research from other traditions increases the debate. There is significant disagreement about the impact of any public policy—whether it is privatization of schooling on student test scores or fiscal policy on economic growth and employment (Klees, 2008b; Klees, this volume).

Thus, for a true democracy to function, widespread debate about public policy is essential. The World Bank is the complete antithesis. It is a biased, ideological

221

institution with monopoly power in education that relies on its own research and brooks no debate. A GFE must be organized around widespread debate. On a broader, society-wide level, this means a transformation to more participatory forms of democracy (Barber, 2003; Crocker, 2009; Edwards & Klees, forthcoming), including the sharing of best-practice and other forms of collaboration between countries of the global South (Martin-Sabina et al., 2012).

## CONCLUSIONS

For over 30 years, the World Bank and other neoliberal-dominated institutions have treated people around the globe as their guinea pigs, subjects for a far-reaching experiment in education and development policy. Without any valid basis, the social responsibility of government was disparaged, privatization was required, narrow versions of accountability were implemented, and one model of education was promoted. This model works to prepare some people to be competitive modern workers in a global market-driven, consumerist economy. The result has been, among other things, inadequate, inefficient, and inequitable education systems.

The World Bank has ignored contrary views and alternative perspectives. This should simply be considered unacceptable. Such behavior might be expected from right-wing private think tanks like the Cato Institute or the Heritage Foundation. But the Bank is publicly funded, pretends to be non-partisan, and has a global influence. It should be incumbent on the Bank to offer a fair and balanced view, but it does not and probably cannot. Hence, as we have argued, we need to replace the Bank with an institution, like a GFE, that operates more along the principles, premises, and approaches discussed in this chapter.

The alternatives that we have discussed and supported in this chapter include education for:

– challenging and undermining the old imperial world order in which a few nations impose inequitable socio-economic conditions on the majority;
– promoting global ecological sanity as a primary responsibility;
– considering what aspects of traditional cultures need to change in order to sustain agreed norms of equity for women, ethnic groups, etc.;
– protecting the best that has been thought, said, and created in a pluriverse of cultures whether traditional, indigenous, or modern; and
– using the power of today's communication systems towards these ends.

As we said at the outset, the alternatives put forth in this chapter are not meant to be complete or immutable. It is through developing new mechanisms of widespread stakeholder participation and debate that alternative directions and policies need to be established. We need to develop new forms of democracy, from the local to the global. And we need to channel considerably greater resources to education and other development priorities. A growing belief in the right to education and other development necessities legitimates the need for additional resources. As a global society, we need to face up to the illegitimacy of life chances being so determined by an accident of birth. A fair and sane society must recognize that, at the very least, all children should be given the opportunity to succeed. We believe that, despite the regressive nature of the politics and economics of the past 30 years, around the world there is a growing ethos and movements that see the need for alternatives and the possibilities for achieving them.

## NOTES

[i] There have been calls for a GFE (Oxfam, 2010; Sperling, 2009). Part of the impetus was dissatisfaction with the Education for All—Fast Track Initiative (FTI). As a result of a variety of political struggles, FTI has recently been revamped, making more space for developing country and civil society participation, and re-naming itself the Global Partnership for Education (GPE). While this represents some progress, the existing GPE is quite far from the GFE we posit here.

[ii] Money to support the GFE would have to come mostly from government donors, as it does for the GPE and the Global Fund to Fight Aids, Tuberculosis and Malaria (GFATM). While GPE and GFATM have some of the organizational features above they do not have all and they do not operate according to the type of substantive principles outlined in this chapter.

[iii] Educated unemployment is a problem at all educational levels. For example, for decades there have been promises made of attaining universal primary education (UPE), now enshrined in EFA and the MDGs. However, by the time this promise is fulfilled, it is likely that, in most countries, there will no longer be employment opportunities for those with just a primary education. Secondary and higher education can follow and, in some countries, have followed similar trajectories. It is the dysfunctionality and inefficiency of our economic system that is at the root of this problem, not the lack of education. Promising societal well-being only through education reform is convenient, taking attention away from all the other areas where reform is desperately needed, as discussed above.

## REFERENCES

Barber, B. (2003). *Strong democracy: Participatory politics for a new age.* Los Angeles: University of California Press.

Barton, J. & Collins, A. (Eds.). (1997). *Portfolio assessment: A handbook for educators.* Menlo Park, CA: Innovative Learning Publications.

Broad, R. (2006, August). Research, knowledge, and the art of "paradigm maintenance": The World Bank's development economics vice-presidency. *Review of International Political Economy, 13*(3), 387-419.

Bickmore, K. (2008). Education for conflict resolution and peacebuilding in plural societies: Approaches from around the world. In K. Mundy, K. Bickmore, R. Hayhoe, M. Madden, & K. Madjidi (Eds.), *Comparative and international education. Issues for teachers* (pp. 249-272). Toronto: Canadian Scholars Press, and New York: Teachers College Press.

Bowers, C. A. (2001). *Education for eco-justice and community.* Athens: University of Georgia Press.

Caldwell, Brian. (2008). *Why not the best schools? What we have learned from outstanding schools around the world.* Camberwell: Australian Council for Educational Research.

Carnoy, M., Gove, A., & Marshall, J. (2007). *Cuba's academic advantage. Why students in Cuba do better in school.* Stanford: Stanford University Press.

Crocker, D. (2009). *Ethics of global development: Agency, capability, and deliberative democracy.* Cambridge: Cambridge University Press.

Daly, H. E. (1996). *Beyond growth: The economics of sustainable development.* Boston: Beacon Press.

Edwards Jr., D. Brent & Klees, S. (forthcoming). Participation in international development and education governance. In A. Verger, M. Novelli, & H. Kosar-Altinyelken (Eds.), *Global education policy and international development: New agendas, issues and programmes*. New York: Continuum.

Ellyard, P. (1999). *Ideas for the new millennium*. Victoria, Australia: Melbourne University Press.

Esteva, G. (2010). Development. In W. Sachs (Ed.), *The development dictionary*. London and New York: Zed Books, pp. 1-3.

Farrell, J. (2008). Teaching and learning to teach: successful radical alternatives from the developing world. In K. Mundy, K. Bickmore, R. Hayhoe, M. Madden, & K. Madjidi (Eds.), *Comparative and international education. Issues for teachers* (pp. 107-132). Toronto: Canadian Scholars Press, and New York: Teachers College Press.

Freire, P. (1970). *Pedagogy of the oppressed*. New York: Continuum.

Gardner, H. (1983). *Frames of mind. The theory of multiple intelligences*. London: Heinemann.

Healy, A. (Ed.). (2008). *Multiliteracies and diversity in education: New pedagogies for expanding landscapes*. Oxford University Press

Hickling-Hudson, A. (1988). Towards communication praxis: Reflections on the pedagogy of Paulo Freire and educational change in Grenada. *Journal of Education* (Boston University), *170*(2), 9-38.

Hickling-Hudson, A. (2002). Re-visioning from the inside: Getting under the skin of the World Bank's education sector strategy. *International Journal of Educational Development, 22*(6), 565-577.

Hickling-Hudson, A. & Ferreira, J-A. (2004). Changing schools for a changing world? Curriculum trends for a "planetist" future. In B. Burnett, D. Meadmore, & G. Tait (Eds.), *New questions for contemporary teachers: Taking a socio-cultural approach to education* (pp. 153-168). French's Forest, NSW: Pearson.

Hickling-Hudson, A. (2007). Beyond schooling: The role of adult and community education in postcolonial change. In R. F. Arnove and C. A. Torres (Eds.), *Comparative education: The dialectic of the global and the local*, 3rd ed. (pp. 197-216). Boulder: Rowman and Littlefield.

Hickling-Hudson, A. (2009). Cuba's policy of internationalism in education: a social justice approach to educational aid and collaboration. *Norrag News, 42*, 53-57.

Hickling-Hudson, A. (2010). Curriculum in postcolonial contexts. In P. D. Pearson & A. Luke (Eds.), *International encyclopedia of education*, 3rd ed. Amsterdam: Elsevier.

Hickling-Hudson, A. (2011). Disrupting preconceptions: Education for social justice in the imperial aftermath. *Compare, 41*(4),453-465.

Hicks, D. & Slaughter, R. (Eds.). (1998). *Futures education*. London: Kogan Paul.

Hoff, L. & Hickling-Hudson, A. (2010). The role of international non-governmental organisations in promoting adult education for social change: A research agenda. *International Journal of Educational Development, 31*(2), 187-195.

Lingard, B., Hayes, D., Mills, M., & Christie, P. (2003). *Leading learning. Making hope practical in schools*. London: Open University Press.

King, K. (2007). Multilateral agencies in the construction of the global agenda on education. *Comparative Education, 43*(3), 377-391.

Klees, S. (2008a). A quarter century of neoliberal thinking in education: Misleading analyses and failed policies. *Globalisation, Societies and Education, 6*(4), 311-348.

Klees, S. (2008b). Reflections on theory, method, and practice in comparative and international education. *Comparative Education Review, 52*(3), 301-328.

Klees, S. & Thapliyal, N. (2007). The right to education: The work of Katarina Tomasevski. *Comparative Education Review, 51*(4), 497-510.

MacEwan, A. (1999). *Neo-liberalism or democracy? Economic strategy, markets, and alternatives for the 21st century*. New York: Zed.

Madjidi, K. & Restoule, J-P. (2008). Comparative Indigenous ways of knowing. In K. Mundy, K. Bickmore, R. Hayhoe, M. Madden, & K. Madjidi (Eds.), *Comparative and international education. Issues for teachers* (pp. 77-106). Toronto: Canadian Scholars Press, and New York: Teachers College Press.

Martin-Sabina, E., Corona Gonzalez, J. & Hickling-Hudson, A. (2012). Cuba's education system: A material foundation for the capacity to share. In A. Hickling-Hudson, J. Corona Gonzalez, & R. Preston (Eds.), *The capacity to share: A study of Cuba's international cooperation in education.* New York: Palgrave Macmillan.

Meadmore, D. (2004). The rise and rise of testing: how does this shape identity? In B. Burnett, D. Meadmore, & G. Tait (Eds.), *New questions for contemporary teachers. Taking a socio-cultural approach to education* (pp. 25-37). French's Forest, NSW: Pearson.

Mertens, D. (2010). *Research methods in education and psychology: Integrating diversity with quantitative and qualitative Approaches,* 3rd ed. Thousand Oaks, CA: Sage.

Mundy, K. (2008). "Education for All," Africa, and the comparative sociology of schooling. In K. Mundy, K. Bickmore, R. Hayhoe, M. Madden, & K. Madjidi (Eds.), *Comparative and international education. Issues for teachers* (pp. 49-75). Toronto: Canadian Scholars Press, and NY: Teachers College Press.

Nakata, M. (2004). Indigenous knowledge and the cultural interface: Underlying issues at the intersection of knowledge and information systems. In A. Hickling-Hudson, J. Matthews, & A. Woods (Eds.), *Disrupting preconceptions: Postcolonialism and education* (pp. 19-38). Flaxton, Australia: Post Pressed.

Ng, E. (2006). Doing development differently. In P. Darby (Ed.), *Postcolonizing the international. Working to change the way we are.* Honolulu: University of Hawaii Press, pp. 125-143.

Overington, C. (2011, September 10-11). Funky school. *The Weekend Australian Magazine,* 12-17.

Oxfam International. (2010). *Rescuing education for all: How reform of the fast track initiative should lead to a global fund for education.* Washington, D.C.: Oxfam International.

Reinert, E. (2007). *How rich countries got rich and why poor countries stay poor.* London: Constable.

Right to Education Project. (2011). http://www.right-to-education.org/

Slaughter, R. (2004). *Futures beyond dystopia. Creating social foresight.* London and New York: RoutledgeFalmer.

Sperling G. (2009). *A global education fund: Towards a true global compact on universal education.* Washington, D.C.: Center for Universal Education.

Spring, J. (1998). *Education and the rise of the global economy.* New Jersey: Lawrence Erlbaum Associates.

Spring, J. (2004). *How educational ideologies are shaping global society. Intergovernmental organization, NGOs, and the decline of the nation-state.* New Jersey, London: Lawrence Erlbaum Associates.

Spring, J. (2011). Education networks: power, wealth, cyberspace and the digital mind. Public lecture at the Queensland University of Technology, Australia, 29 November.

Tomasevski, K. (2003). *Education denied: Costs and remedies.* London and New York: Zed Books.

Tomasevski, K. (2006), *The state of the right to education worldwide. Free or fee: 2006 report.* Copenhagen: Right to Education Project.
http://www.katarinatomasevski.com/images/Global_Report.pdf

Willinsky, J. (1998). *Learning to divide the world: Education at empire's end.* Minneapolis, MN: University of Minnesota Press.

World Bank. (1999). *Education sector strategy.* Washington D.C.: The International Bank for Reconstruction and Development/The World Bank.

World Bank. (2011). *Learning for all: Investing in people's knowledge and skills to promote development. World Bank Group Education Sector Strategy 2020.* Washington, D.C.: World Bank

Yates, Michael D. (2003). *Naming the system: Inequality and work in the global economy*. New York: Monthly Review Press.

*Anne Hickling-Hudson*
*Faculty of Education*
*Queensland University of Technology, Australia*

*Steven J. Klees*
*College of Education*
*University of Maryland, U.S.A.*

# CONCLUSIONS

Throughout this book we have been concerned with the World Bank's role in shaping global education policy. Seven core themes stand out.

## On Neoliberal Ideology

One cannot understand World Bank education policy without understanding the nature of the Washington Consensus as well as the feeble efforts to develop a post-Washington Consensus. From the perspective of scholars and practitioners, the neoliberal model—of delegitimizing and cutting government, privatizing, deregulating, and liberalizing—intensified in the 1990s and brought with it the displacement of the production and distribution of social rights and the handing over of the common good to market forces (Jamarillo, 2011).

World Bank education policy is based on neoliberal ideology, not evidence, as almost every chapter has argued. One cannot understand World Bank education policy without understanding its context in over three decades of neoliberal reforms of capitalism. The World Bank has been captured by neoliberal ideology. Despite a pretense of non-partisanship, the World Bank has become, in part, a right-wing think tank. It looks almost exclusively at "evidence" that is supplied by itself or its allies (as argued in most chapters). Yet it is so much more than a think tank in that, as Steiner-Khamsi argues, it takes public money to review the education sector throughout the developing world, identify reform packages, lend money, and evaluate effectiveness. Imagine the uproar, as Klees suggests, if such power were given to right-wing think tanks like the Cato Institute or the Heritage Foundation in the U.S. Yet the World Bank has been able to maintain an undeserved aura of legitimacy (not completely, of course).

Neoliberalism has been a three-decade-plus experiment on the disadvantaged of the world. What we have seen is that global elites are much better off as a result while those in the most difficult circumstances have generally seen little change or even a worsening of their situation. While there has been some improvement in educational access, there is still a long way to go to meet EFA targets and MDGs. Moreover, improved access has come with a deterioration of quality due to neoliberal constraints on government. Clearly, these circumstances go beyond the World Bank and thus many arguments in this book reflect a much broader critique of neoliberal education reforms that have been implemented throughout the world, in developed and developing countries alike. For example, Steiner-Khamsi shows how World Bank education policies are quite similar to U.S. and U.K. aid to education policies (embodied in USAID and DFID). She also points out that such policies are not uncontested, even by other aid agencies, such as in Canada and Denmark. Relatedly, Klees points out that the current "Learning for All" strategy in practice is really a "Testing for All" strategy, based on the No Child Left Behind reform of the U.S. What neoliberalism has given us in education, and elsewhere, is a one-size-fits-all global strategy of reform, based purely on a political ideology without regard to alternative views and evidence.

While, as pointed out above, the issues raised in this book go far beyond the World Bank, this organization needs to remain a focal point of contestation. The World Bank has been the global architect for educational policy reform in developing countries, in the forefront of aid agencies and country policies alike. The World Bank has closed itself to alternative perspectives. Despite much fanfare, the consultation process for *WBES 2020* may have heard alternative perspectives, but the strategy report remained neoliberal. Moreover, whom the World Bank hires and how report arguments are vetted continue to result in thoroughly neoliberal views dominating. The internal "thought police" continue to do their work (Broad, 2006). There is no "knowledge bank," only an "opinion bank" and it only offers one opinion at that.

Nordtveit points out that the use of the year 2020 in the *WBES* title gives it almost a science fiction flavor, certainly evoking a view to the future. Yet there is nothing really new being offered and there is certainly no imagination brought to thinking a decade ahead. Most chapter authors stress the continuity between previous World Bank strategies and the current one. The two authors who note some change (Kamat and Robertson) saw only an unfortunate deepening of neoliberal ideology and strategy.

*On Evidence-Based Policy*

Empirical validation for the recommendations made by the World Bank is selectively chosen. It has several characteristics: (1) It derives only from research conducted by the World Bank itself or carried out under its auspices. (2) It is ideologically driven. (3) It is devoid of any contradictory findings carried out by academic scholars and researchers in various parts of the world. (4) It is highly decontextualized and thus it seeks to be universally applicable across time and space.

As Verger and Bonal observe, the education agenda of the World Bank has broadened over time, presenting stronger prescriptions of what needs to be done to improve educational systems. This is captured by its shift from "years of schooling" to "learning achievement." In principle, while what is learned matters more than the amount of time spent inside a classroom, there is a perverse twist to the learning concern: The World Bank now proceeds to rely on international standardized testing as exclusive evidence that learning has taken place, discarding all products of learning other than math and reading, and ignoring the very important fact that many countries—for various economic, social, historical, and political reasons—create different contexts in which educational systems function and in which students learn (or fail to learn). The chapters by Verger and Bonal, Soudien, Siqueira, and Klees vigorously assert that learning is a highly contextualized human activity and that there is solid empirical evidence showing that learning processes—and the evaluation of such processes—need to be responsive to local contexts. Neither the reliance on universal measurements such as those embodied in PISA and TIMMS nor the measurements themselves are subject to systematic critical review, either by the World Bank or by its close associate, OECD (Mahon & McBride, 2009).

Linked to the reliance on international standardized tests is the stubborn exclusive use of quantitative methods to determine the impact of educational systems. Cross-country regressions, cloned and applied universally, assume similar processes throughout the world and imply similar results attached to whatever educational interventions are put in place. Given that educational systems are both blindly endorsed by some and opposed by others, more qualitative investigations must take place—investigations able to capture perspectives and experiences of social actors in different locations of the educational system. Likewise, qualitative and participatory investigations capable of articulating and reflecting the voices of those affected (whether positively or negatively) should be an integral part of research and evaluation.

Methodologically, it is well known that the use of questionnaires (indispensable to quantitative studies) gather data from the perspective of those who design such instruments. Respondents are confronted with predetermined questions and then a narrow range of possible answers. Questions that they would like to consider are often not part of the questionnaire, except for an occasional section where "other" may appear as a possible response and one or two lines provided for explanation. Qualitative and critical methodologies are not part of the World Bank's approach to education research, which is an enormous weakness in its knowledge production. In this regard, we reiterate that the social sciences address human beings and that efforts that have failed to recognize their aspirations, expectations, experiences, and fears and hopes for the future simply missed recognizing them as active agents in organizing their communities and determining their future.

## On Education and Learning

We have noted repeatedly in this book that the World Bank holds a restricted view of education. The chapters by Verger and Bonal, Crain, Ginsburg, Siqueira, Stromquist, Samoff, and Klees make this clear. In this regard, we see with apprehension that the World Bank, through SABER (System Assessment and Benchmarking for Education Results), seeks to establish itself as the main authority on education policy. SABER's 13 policy domains cover key aspects of educational system functioning and thus decision-making. SABER seeks to become a "global education benchmarking tool." To this effect, as Siqueira remarks, it will develop a conceptual framework for each domain, together with diagnostic tools, project concept notes, and results to date—all of this to become part of the World Bank's growing "knowledge-based website."

While the SABER development does not represent a change in perspective or approach to education, it does signal a tighter manipulation of policy and its concomitant processes and procedures. It is most likely that low-income countries

229

will be overwhelmed by the wide array of multiple tools prescribed by the World Bank and strong-armed by the tie-in between SABER and World Bank loans, and thus become unable to resist adoption of its many proposals across the 13 policy domains. Armed with the argument that it is based on scientific research and supported by a "system approach," World Bank advice is likely to increase in influence and control. Informed and critical voices in governments of developing countries do exist but they find it extremely difficult to neutralize or even contest World Bank influences.

The World Bank looks at education in the very narrow terms of test performance, particularly math and reading, while it shows a lack of attention to teachers, adult education, transformative learning, and the many other things that are expected of education throughout the world. The World Bank's incursion into learning through SABER is worrisome, as it will further reinforce a transnational, one-size-fits-all dimension to many educational processes and instruments. Many of the chapters, notably those by Siqueira, Soudien, and Ginsburg, alert us to this.

*On Social Equity*

Several of the chapters in this book note that *WBES 2020* makes explicit reference to equity. Stromquist, for instance, finds the term used 12 times throughout the document. Yet, it is not developed and, as Samoff notes, it is used as synonymous with equality. Verger and Bonal expand on its use, showing that equity becomes an empty discourse because it does not deal with *why* inequality exists. Knowledge we have gained through previous research—external to the World Bank—such as the role of education systems regulations, school segregation, and the increasing differences in school quality are brushed aside. Instead, what receives attention in the effort to reduce inequalities is the World Bank's strategy of targeting. Educational policies should certainly consider the relevance of focused policies, i.e., those that target specific groups for particular benefits. But reducing equity to targeting is seriously shortsighted as it runs the risk of dealing with the superficial manifestations of inequality, not its root causes. Addressing a particular group by itself—whether indigenous people, women, or ethnic or "racial" minorities—will not dismantle the complex architecture underlying the disadvantage of those groups, and will thus be inattentive to who benefits—whether consciously or unconsciously—from the existing disadvantage, and how. Targeting does not address issues of scale and complexity, but provides only limited coverage and a narrow, immediate solution.

It must be noted that although SABER is going to be the main strategy for implementing the World Bank's policy recommendations, the policy domain entitled "Equity and Inclusion" is not yet developed. It is unclear whether this has occurred because the issue is overly complex, or because the World Bank staff lacks agreement on what is needed to operationalize it, or because it is simply not one of its priorities.

Achieving educational equity will require considerable additional government funding, not less. In this context, it is sobering to consider one of the arguments endorsed by the World Bank in its SABER strategy on testing, as noted by Siqueira: "Testing is the least expensive innovation, costing far less than increasing teachers' salaries and reducing class size."

Verger and Bonal make an observation we should keep in mind at all times: We should consider how development policies and contexts such as conditions of inequality affect the education of children, not just focus on how education affects development. This point is extremely valuable because it highlights the fact that education is itself affected by many strong forces, a fact the World Bank usually underplays. Education is far from being merely an independent variable. On the contrary, it is affected by multiple political, cultural, and economic factors, and by not recognizing this, the World Bank offers a very incomplete view of education.

*On Privatization*

It is evident that, while not given prominent discussion in *WBES 2020*, the principle of privatization continues to be a central element in World Bank educational policies since it is a pillar of any market-oriented effort in education.

Vally and Spreen argue that *WBES 2020* is linked to a global agenda that is highly dependent on international competition, the market, and standardized assessment of skills and learning outcomes and that ignores important historical and contextual factors that influence educational outcomes. This global agenda has been fundamental in a push towards privatization of education, a reshaping of the private sector's involvement in public education, and a significant narrowing of public responsibility and accountability.

Privatization is extolled by the World Bank as a proven means both to expand education and to improve its quality. But, as Verger and Bonal argue, the World Bank engages in a misrepresentation of the research literature regarding the effects of markets by providing a categorically positive view of markets and ignoring contradictory evidence (see also Robertson). Indeed, the (external) research literature does not provide grounds for such a categorical position. It must be asked, then, if it has not been proven that effective why does the World Bank endorse privatization so strongly? One explanation can be offered: The role of the market is a fundamental tenet of neoliberal capitalist ideology—opening education to the market instantly opens a previously untapped social area for profit. The idea of competition leading to better products is taken as a religious dogma and therefore any question of what the evidence really shows in the area of education is not an issue.

World Bank schemes to privatize education are periodically modified. As the chapters by Verger and Bonal and Robertson show, privatization of education now considers not only the creation of for-profit institutions in the provision of education, but also privatization of "public" education, that is, constantly dreaming up new ways for users of the public educational system to pay for its services— through direct subsidies to private schools, user fees at the public secondary and tertiary levels, and voucher programs. None of these is explicitly identified in *WBES 2020* but they have all become indispensable elements in World Bank loans.

To pursue its privatization agenda, the World Bank actively works through its private arm, the International Finance Corporation (IFC). Although not nearly at the level of the World Bank, IFC functions as a major source of funds for education entrepreneurs, particularly those working on a small scale. According to its own assertions, IFC is the world's largest multilateral investor in the private education sector in emerging markets (IFC, n.d.). Education at the IFC has been growing fast in recent years; data for 1991-2004 indicate that it grew 5 percent per year during that period. By 2010, IFC was involved in 62 education projects in 30 countries, with 35 percent of those projects located in the world's poorest countries (Nuthall, 2011). In all, IFC funding covers the schooling of about 1.2 million students annually, and is now undertaking a major initiative to support the establishment of low-cost community schools in many cities of sub-Saharan Africa. Though the fund is only about $50 million, that volume of funding can be a significant contributor to privatizing education in African countries. Independent research on the expanding work of IFC is needed.

Public-private partnerships are likely to be strengthened through the expansion of the IFC. A number of observers believe that privatization of schooling should be recognized as unavoidable given the increased demand of children and youth for schooling. They also consider that many private schools, even though they operate for profit, are able to deliver a good quality education (at least one that many parents find satisfactory), compensate for the insufficient government supply, have low costs, and show greater efficiency than public schools. The evidence is mixed. There are private schools of both good and poor quality. If they cost less than public schools, these come at the expense of low teacher salaries and the decline of teachers as professionals. Even at low cost, private schools require tuition fees. In part discouraged by those fees, poor parents, who need their children's labor, either do not send them to school or withdraw them before completion. So-called "low cost private schools for the poor" exist only because three decades of neoliberalism have so decimated many public schools that poor people have been left with little choice. Klees' chapter asks how we can legitimately promote a public policy that is based on charging fees for the most disadvantaged people in the world to attend school.

Lack of adequate funding by the state can only worsen access to schooling. Private schools of low quality are numerous and many condemn children to terminal schooling, with little possibility of advancing to higher levels of education. The negative effects of low quality private schooling are severe and cannot be glossed over. Research comparing social effects of private schools in developing countries, especially those in rural areas, does not provide an optimistic forecast. Such research, it must be admitted, is not abundant. Yet, we cannot ignore its findings. The connection between privatization and equity—or, to be more precise, the unfavorable balance of greater privatization and less equity—is invisible in *WBES 2020*.

The issue of privatization raises another major question: What are the long-term implications of non-state provision for equity, national identity, and social cohesion? Can the fragmented forces of the market manage to maintain them?

Both its logic and historical and contemporary evidence render unpersuasive the claim that a system that functions on the basis of profit can assure the common good. And, finally, how does privatization fit with the notion of education as a human right, as endorsed by all nations and highlighted by Vally and Spreen in this book?

## On Gender

One of the most severe inequalities in society is that of gender, which is greatly compounded by other social factors such as wealth, income, rural residence, and ethnic/racial minority status. Gender inequality is clearly supported by a deeply ingrained and pervasive patriarchal ideology that has substantial economic and political consequences, a fact aptly captured by Nancy Fraser's identification of symbolic and material dimensions shaping gender in many contemporary societies (1995). Despite advances in theory and empirical studies in mapping the core attributes and causes of gender asymmetries, for the World Bank—and other international development agencies—gender continues to be framed primarily as a "disadvantage." In other words, being a woman is a "disadvantage." Expanding this characterization to education, the problems affecting gender are seen as problems of access and discrimination toward girls, a process that other disadvantaged sectors—the poor, ethnic and "racial" minorities, and individuals with physical and mental disabilities—also face. But what creates such discrimination? It is certainly not an independent condition, operating entirely on its own, but rather derives from prevailing ideologies regarding the "proper" role, identity, and social space women and men should have. The World Bank places great importance on girls' access to education, and this is most welcome. At the same time, research conducted in many industrialized and developing countries indicates that it is possible for girls and women to attain high levels of education while at the same time endorsing the traditional ideas of their predominant role as future wives and mothers. In other words, higher levels of education are not necessarily associated with the questioning of social norms and practices that create marked divisions between femininity and masculinity and between the private and the public worlds. *WBES 2020*, like previous education sector strategies, refuses to acknowledge that schools are gendered settings and that education systems are gendered institutions.

A consideration of the content of learning and the nature of the experience of girls and women in educational systems is essential to deconstruct and challenge the myth of schools as neutral institutions committed to the dissemination of neutral knowledge. But World Bank policies do not address issues of content, invoking the position that curricular issues are national issues. However, the same World Bank hesitates little when intervening in the curricula that pertains to the acquisition of reading, math, and science. Why is this? Gender is perceived as controversial; because it involves human rights, gender equity is addressed by most donor agencies, but they look almost exclusively at its superficial manifestations not its root causes. This approach has the virtue of "addressing" a problem while not shaking the system.

*WBES 2020* contains a number of contradictions in its approach to gender issues. For instance, the World Bank's endorsement of faith-based education, noted in the chapters by Kamat and Stromquist, implies a greater presence of educational authorities and teachers who may not be sensitive to gender issues. This applies to the expanded use of madrasas in Pakistan. Although these schools have become "secularized" and now accept both girls and boys in co-educational settings, most of the teachers continue to be not only men but also those who tend to uphold very traditional views about the role of women in society. This being the case, the expansion of schooling can hardly be expected to introduce new values and perspectives among girls and boys; consequently, the gender reproductive role of schooling will intensify.

Two other important contradictions emerge from the administrative reforms proposed by the World Bank: decentralization and privatization. There are no assurances that local bodies will be more enlightened than national authorities, who if not more progressive are at least more visible and thus accountable. If girls have a high opportunity cost, as is the case of those in low-income families, there are no assurances that parents will not set a low ceiling on the years of education they are willing to invest in, particularly as costs go up for secondary levels of education. Tensions naturally emerge in proposed policies and policies frequently produce unintended effects. This is to be expected. But what becomes indispensable is to explore the consequences of these policies when they are put into practice, to identify their negative effects, and to move toward correcting them. A blanket endorsement of access to school, decentralization, and privatization does little to counter negative outcomes linked to ostensibly positive remedies.

To the extent that gender is a deep social phenomenon, it requires an effort that involves multiple actors—some in power and some outside. It will need a comprehensive effort to deal with parents, communities, and women-led groups in civil society. On this point *WBES 2020* is silent. Addressing gender will also call for efforts to engage multiple governmental institutions and ministries. This implies work beyond that which could be conducted by a ministry of education and its regional/district offices. The new education strategy by the World Bank refers to the need to have a system approach to education. A careful reading of this concept reveals that the approach is very inward-looking, considering education as a self-enclosed activity. The concept refers to multiple stakeholders, none of which includes women-led organizations. The World Bank excludes women-led groups and women's movements generally because it wishes to pretend that such reforms are apolitical and not in conflict with neoliberal ideology.

A final point regarding gender touches on quality. As the chapters by Verger and Bonal, Soudien, and Vally and Spreen reveal, quality has been narrowly construed to mean performance in reading and math, occasionally science, and seldom civic education. We need to stop here and reflect on what "quality education" should mean. One definition is that an education of high quality should prepare students to deal with future demands upon them and to prepare them to deal with their sociocultural and economic environment so that it does not oppress or marginalize them. Under such a definition, a "quality" education goes beyond math and reading to include both social knowledge and skills to modify negative features of one's society. From a gender perspective, quality education would include substantial consideration of civics, human rights, and gender-sensitive knowledge such as domestic violence, rape, and abortion in the curriculum. The narrow definition of knowledge by the World Bank preempts the treatment of such issues.

We need to be clear about equity and equality. Although the WB uses the term equity, it really means equality, as it pays attention to enrollment parity and school completion. Equity means providing special support to some groups so that this differential treatment may enable them to reach new levels and forms of development. Equality means a numerical representation that is balanced between two or more groups—thus, for instance, equal enrollments and completion rates between girls and boys. The World Bank does consider instruments that would help girls fight the oppressive consequences of poverty. Conditional cash transfers (CCTs) would enable families to be compensated for the loss of their children's labor, especially daughters. CCTs are definitely equity instruments. Yet, *WBES 2020* does not argue for their expansion nor does it locate them in a set of wider interventions to modify gender relations.

## On Alternatives

Of the many problems with World Bank education policy discussed here, perhaps the one that is most harmful, most detrimental to children around the world, is that the World Bank uses its ideology to select a very narrow set of recommended policies. It pretends that these policies are common sense or that they are the only ones supported by evidence. To the contrary, there is a wide range of alternative education policies that are theoretically sound, empirically supported, and eminently reasonable and sensible in practice. Many chapters considered alternatives, one chapter (Hickling-Hudson and Klees) focused on them. Among the alternative policies that warrant consideration and action are:

- build alternative education policies based on a commitment to the right to education;
- restructure education from a model that focuses on exclusion, emphasizes failure and hierarchy, and serves elites to a mass model of education that emphasizes inclusion, success, and democracy;
- replace the focus on standardized testing in a few subjects with attention to a broader array of education outcomes using multiple assessment tools;
- develop curriculum alternatives that are more interdisciplinary, more ecologically sane, and more progressive (e.g., drawing on Freire);
- instead of making teachers into villains and deprofessionalizing them, partner with teachers and teacher unions;

- re-fashion schools as learning communities and teachers as learners;
- center discussions of alternative forms of governance and management around deep, democratic participation of students, teachers, and communities;
- instead of using narrow ideas about accountability to blame students, teachers, parents, and countries for failure, develop and rely on broader conceptions of commitment, responsibility, and success;
- reduce subsidies to private education and assign high priority to improving public schools;
- increase the resources committed to achieving EFA and MDGs and other necessary education reforms;
- require that the use of evidence in policy reflect widespread, democratic, and participatory debate among different perspectives and methods;
- re-configure the approach to research to build local capacities, go beyond quantitative methods, draw on practitioners and, again, make debate central; and
- recognize that the transformation of education must be linked to the transformation of the neoliberal model of development and of society more broadly.

This is not meant to be a blueprint for educational reform, only to suggest some of the many possibilities before us. That most of these alternatives are not addressed in *WBES 2020* should be considered outrageous and an embarrassment. Outrageous that the self-proclaimed architect of global education policy can simply do as it pleases and embarrassing to the non-partisan stance that the World Bank pretends to take. Hickling-Hudson and Klees argue that the World Bank is simply too compromised to be reformed and posit an alternative Global Fund for Education. Perhaps replacing the World Bank is the only way we will have serious consideration of alternative education policies.

*Final Thoughts*

In two path-breaking articles in the *Comparative Education Review*, Simon Marginson and Marcela Mollis (2001) and Stephen Carney (2009) make us aware of the impact of global policies that cut across nation-states and are decontextualized and deterritorialized. Carney admonishes us to look into "policyscapes" or policies that can no longer be understood only in the context of national decision-making. The concept of "policyscapes" is useful to understand the transnationalization of educational policies. We argue that a major actor in this process is the World Bank through its combined use of education strategy, policies, and conditionalities in the loans it provides to developing countries. The immense leverage of the World Bank is undeniable and, as we have shown, dangerous.

The World Bank has developed an unshakeable commitment to neoliberal ideology. This shows in its constant reference to privatization, to an equation of education with economic productivity, to its narrow view of accountabilty, and to empty rhetoric about equity.

The multiple meetings that the World Bank organized in preparation for *WBES 2020*, documented in detail by Steiner-Khamsi, give evidence that the Bank hears but does not listen to others. The failure to listen results in failure to learn. The self-referential character of World Bank research makes it even more resistant to change, as underscored in all of the chapters in this book. While the Bank declares itself determined to increase "learning" among the world's population, its own unwillingness to learn from a wide range of research evidence—research that challenges many of its recommendations—undermines the legitimacy and validity of the World Bank as an authority in education.

It is well recognized that the market is not a moral agent. The state therefore must play that role, despite its difficulties. A deep issue then concerns the function and responsibility of the state in the provision, content, and structure of education. The World Bank's continued commitment to privatization, now relabeled as public-private partnerships, raises enormous questions linked to the role of the state and the role of education in modern society. Is education merely another service? Should schooling be open to entrepreneurs of all kinds? Is the expansion of fee-paying primary school congruent with the UN Universal Declaration of Human Rights (Article 26), which calls for free education? And, given the lack of financial and pedagogical support for public schools, why the insistence on standardized testing as an indicator of learning?

Often, the stronger the power wielded by a country, institution, or individual, the less it is acknowledged. On this, the World Bank is strikingly un-self-reflective and un-self-critical. The formidable leverage of the World Bank through the nature of and conditionality clauses in its loans and grants is totally absent in *WBES 2020*. One of the conditionalities is the data-gathering requirement for any funded project, a mechanism that ensures that the World Bank will have always access to data for their quantitative studies. In addition, the World Bank has a very large research budget, far beyond the funds available to education institutions and research institutes in poor countries. Since the World Bank conducts research for subjects in which it is interested, it is not surprising to see subsequently that its research findings are invoked to support its policy recommendations. The dissemination of the World Bank's policies and their subsequent adoption by developing countries are not simply the products of irrefutable evidence backing these policies. Rather, they reflect the power of a particular institution and its specific intentions. In our view, this is a clear manifestation of the complex but real relation between power and knowledge.

We would like to end the book with a positive and yet realistic note. Rebuilding a social order is arduous but not impossible. We can learn much from social movements, from ecology to the recapturing of democratic life, as well as from ideas originating in the academy and elsewhere. The World Bank has proclaimed its commitment to learning for all. Laudable. Yet as we have shown, its assumptions, methods, approach, models, self-referential use of research, un-self-critical orientation, and its own lack of learning render it an obstacle, not an ally to those pursuing a learning-for-all agenda. Its funds and its unique position, not its history of incisive insights or effective practical recommendations, secure its influence. Pursuing learning for all requires shifting the center of attention in global education policy and practice to institutions that reflect and are more responsive to the needs, voices, and preferences of those for whom education remains a distant dream. Learning for all is possible. We should accept no less.

## REFERENCES

Broad, R. (2006, August). Research, knowledge, and the art of "paradigm maintenance:" the World Bank's development economics vice-presidency." *Review of International Political Economy, 13*(3), 387-419.

Carney, S. (2009). Negotiating policy in an age of globalization: Exploring educational "policyscapes" in Denmark, Nepal, and China. *Comparative Education Review, 53*(1), 63-88.

Fraser, N. (1995). From distribution to recognition? Dilemmas of justice in a "post socialist" Age, *New Left Review, 218*, 68-93.

IFC. (n.d.). Creating opportunity. *IFC in education—Key facts*. Washington, D.C.: International Finance Corporation.

Jamarillo, P. (2011). We need to be more human and democracy needs humanities and social sciences. Working Group on Education. Virtual Exchange "Education in a World in crisis: Limitations and Possibilities with a view to Rio+20." http://dialogos2012.org

Mahon, R. & McBride, S. (Eds.). (2009). *The OECD and transnational governance*. Vancouver: UBC Press.

Marginson, S. & Mollis, M. (2001). Theories and reflexivities of comparative education. *Comparative Education Review*, 45(4): 581-715.

Nuthall, K. (2011, May 9). GLOBAL: Massive growth in private tertiary sector. *University World News*.

# INDEX

CPSIA information can be obtained at www.ICGtesting.com
Printed in the USA
LVOW10s2054130714

394127LV00008B/666/P